Indians

OF SOUTH AMERICA

A Modern Cuzco Native

Indians

OF SOUTH AMERICA

Paul Radin

Professor of Anthropology, Black Mountain College

THE AMERICAN MUSEUM

OF NATURAL HISTORY

Science Series

1942

Doubleday, Doran & Company, Inc.

GARDEN CITY, NEW YORK

PRINTED AT THE *Country Life Press,* GARDEN CITY, N. Y., U. S. A.

To
FREDERICK THOMPSON
In gratitude and affection

I then sailed northwards till I came to a very high mountain. . . . I believe it is impossible to ascend thither, because I am convinced that it is the spot of the earthly Paradise, whither no one can go but by God's permission.

Columbus to Ferdinand of Spain, announcing the
discovery of South America

Acknowledgment

The author wishes to thank these individuals and institutions for their kindness in permitting him to use the following plates and photographs: the Grace Line for the frontispiece: "A Modern Cuzco Native"; *Natural History Magazine* for "A Carib Village along the Coast" and "A Typical Carib Dugout Canoe" (photographs by H. M. and E. L. Ayers); *Natural History Magazine* and Mr. Junius Bird for "The Remains of the Aboriginal Fuegian Horse"; *Natural History Magazine* and Dr. Harold E. Anthony for "A Native Spinner from Ecuador"; the Field Museum of Natural History of Chicago, Dr. J. A. Mason, and *Natural History Magazine* for "A Native Priest with His Wife and Child," "A Young Boy Neophyte Training for the Priesthood," and "The House of a Native Priest's Wife," Colombia; Dr. A. Metraux and American Museum of Natural History for "A Mataco Indian from the Gran Chaco"; for "Wooden Cups from Cuzco" from the story of the American Indian by Dr. Paul Raden, published by Liveright.

Preface

UNTIL THE END OF THE NINETEENTH AND THE
beginning of the twentieth centuries South America, anthro-
pologically speaking, was far more unknown than the interior
of Africa or New Guinea. This despite the fact that from 1498
on it had been penetrated in all directions, its numerous rivers
ascended, and its forests and jungles repeatedly traversed. But
the adventurers, travelers, scientists, and missionaries—Spaniards,
Portuguese, French, Dutch, Germans, English, and Scandi-
navians—to whom its exploration was due were interested only
incidentally in the native populations as such. The missionaries,
it is true, were interested in saving their souls, but this activity
implied little concern with their aboriginal way of life.

This is not to say that these various visitors, temporary and
permanent, did not at times note down many of the strange and
interesting customs and beliefs they encountered. They did
indeed, particularly in the sixteenth and seventeenth centuries,
and their accounts are frequently excellent and on a par with
the best of those we possess for North America. But even the
best of them were fragmentary, vague, and incomplete. The
picture of the native populations thus obtained was not even
remotely accurate and well-rounded.

But if our knowledge of native South America—the great
Andean civilizations always excepted—was thus regrettably poor
and wholly inadequate until the end of the nineteenth century,
we must not ascribe this exclusively to indifference or to a lack
of scientific interest. South America is an enormous continent.

Jungles, forests, marshes, arid deserts, and torrential rains, combined with other natural obstacles and unfriendly aborigines, made for difficulties utterly unknown in North America. And when we add to these the political turmoils and the backward economic conditions that prevailed in South America throughout the nineteenth century, there is some excuse for the persistence of our ignorance.

Beginning with the great expedition of Karl von den Steinen to the interior of Brazil in 1884 the situation changed materially. Nevertheless, since this and all the subsequent work done there has had to be in the nature of explorations and preliminary surveys rather than intensive studies in the sense in which this could be done in most of the other regions of the world, our knowledge of South American anthropology, even today, is only in its preliminary stage.

To essay, under these conditions, to give a connected picture of the cultures and civilizations of the South American native populations is confessedly dangerous. If, despite this, the author has had the temerity to attempt it, it is not to be interpreted as mere recklessness on his part or as due to some uncontrollable urge for rushing in where wise men fear to tread. On the contrary, it is due to the keen realization that the time for a preliminary synthesis has arrived and that enough is known today to make such a synthesis both possible and profitable.

Bearing this in mind we can then proceed to state the purpose of the present book. It is intended as a general, nontechnical survey of the main aboriginal cultures of the great South American continent, in order to show: first, what are their distinctive and specific traits; second, what relationships, if any, these cultures bear to one another; and, third, what are their connections with the cultures of Central America and North America. In describing these cultures, naturally only the high points of each one have been stressed. This is somewhat unfortunate but obviously inevitable in a book of this kind. Likewise, only one or two representative tribes of each culture have been dealt with. Whatever defects inhere in such a presentation—and the author is fully conscious of them—the reader can be assured that it has not been allowed to interfere in any way with the proper portrayal of the individual cultures and that it has not led to inaccuracy or distortion.

In discussing the various relationships of the cultures to one another and the even more fundamental problem of the relationship of these cultures to those of North America, difficulties of an entirely different nature have entered. Many specialists would probably contend that the time for such a determination has not yet arrived. The author, however, is more sanguine and feels that the thorough and suggestive work that has been done in the last two or three decades by innumerable anthropologists from all parts of the world is more than adequate to permit the drawing of reasonably correct conclusions. The conclusions and inferences which the author has drawn are naturally somewhat tentative. But they are tentative, he must insist, only in so far as the details are concerned and not as concerns their broad outlines. Many of them have been put forward by other students; hesitatingly, it must be admitted. All that the author has done is to make some of these inferences and generalizations more concrete and specific.

In only one respect does he claim any originality at all; namely, for his contention that the more complex cultures east of the Andes are relatively young, not older than 1000 to 1100 A.D., and that they have resulted not through the spread of culture from the great civilizations of Bolivia and Peru but through the spread of the complex cultures of Mexico across the Gulf of Mexico, mainly along its northern shores.

To what extent the interpretations and conclusions advanced are correct, time alone will tell. The author is quite convinced of their essential truth. He has made no attempt to fit the facts into his theory nor has he, for that matter, been primarily concerned with theories or interpretations. His desire has been, first and foremost, to give a living and meaningful presentation of the facts so that North American readers, in particular, can obtain a well-rounded picture of the achievements of the aboriginal populations to the south of them. As we all know, such knowledge has been long ridiculously neglected. And this neglect, be it remembered, is not a matter of regret simply for the antiquarian and the archeologist and the anthropologist. It

means much more than that. Although the aboriginal cultures
of South America are, in their primary sense, dead or on the
verge of extinction, so many of their traits have been incorporated in, and integrated with, the Spanish civilization that it
is not a mere figure of speech to say that for many parts of
South America they are as important as are the Spanish-European
elements. In fact they can be said to constitute, after a fashion,
a continuation, on a new level, of the old aboriginal civilizations.

It is from this angle then—from the realization that the aboriginal cultures of South America are not dead in the sense in
which this holds true for North America—that we must approach
their study. After all, approximately more than 12 per cent of
the population of South America is Indian in blood. But far
more significant is the fact that it is Indian in feeling too; that
is, that these people regard themselves as definitely set off from
the whites and from much of the culture which they have
introduced.

The description of South American native cultures here presented makes no attempt to give an adequate account of the
great civilizations of Bolivia and Peru. This has been done so
frequently and adequately of late that it can be presumed that
most readers are fairly well acquainted with them. In so far as
the author has concerned himself at all with these civilizations,
and naturally some account of them had to be given, he has
limited himself to specific problems and to a description of their
modern descendants.

In conclusion, the author wishes to express his great indebted-
ness to all those scholars on whose works he has so heavily and
obviously leaned. Without them this book would have been
completely impossible. In particular he wishes to thank his old
friend, Professor Robert H. Lowie, of the University of California, who so generously placed at his disposal not only his
excellent library of books and pamphlets on South America but
also his notes, and thus made the task immeasurably simpler and
more pleasant.

PAUL RADIN

Black Mountain College, N. C.
January 1942

Contents

xvi   Contents

PART III

The Great Civilizations

Illustrations

PART I

Wanderers and Disseminators

CHAPTER I

The Discovery of South America

ACCORDING TO THE GENERALLY ACCEPTED BE-
lief, South America was discovered by Columbus in 1498. He
himself announced this discovery to the Spanish sovereigns in
a famous letter.[1] The great admiral seems, however, to have had
little interest in the tropical coast line that greeted his eyes as
he entered the Gulf of Paria or in what lay beyond the mountain
so clearly visible from the deck of his ship. He did not even
bother to set foot on the new land. What impressed him most,
apparently, was the "roar as of thunder" made by the waters of
the great Orinoco as it met the sea, and the height of the waves.
All the strange and erroneous notions concerning the new lands
he had discovered seemed here to find their full corroboration.
He argued, quite rightly, that so mighty a stream could hardly
have its source in an island and that, consequently, territories of
considerable extent must lie to the south. That, however, it was
a continent, he was not convinced. Only in Paradise could so
great a volume of water have its origin; only in the resplendent
Garden of Eden from which our primal parents had been driven.
His letter is full of such musings. Small wonder then that he
convinced himself that he had been given a mission by God and
that the successful conclusion of that mission was now at hand.

[1] See Bibliography, p. 307-313.

3

It is a strange meandering document, this third letter of Columbus, and the strangest part of it is the incidental and seemingly offhand manner in which he treats the new continent he had found. Was the aging admiral really so unaware of what he had discovered, or did he have some reason for minimizing the results of his voyage? This would have seemed a meaningless question fifty years ago. The recent rediscovery of a manuscript, describing a voyage apparently made by caravels sent out by Columbus to what is clearly the coast of Venezuela in 1494, has given this question, however, a new and added significance. The description is in the form of a letter written by a certain Angelo Trevisan to the king and queen of Spain, and it was published in 1502 or 1504. While some details still await confirmation, there seems little reason for questioning the fundamental point—namely that South America was discovered not by Columbus in 1498 but by sailors he had sent out four years earlier. The Trevisan letter thus contains the earliest description of the natives of South America and merits full quotation:[2]

By an oversight it was omitted, in the story about Columbus, how he sent five caravels from the Island of Hispaniola to that neighboring country which they call Cuba, with orders to skirt the coast toward the south and southeast to a certain place where he had information that pearls were found.

Well, setting out and keeping close to land, they went through some intense and awful heat that they could hardly endure, and the water ran low in the barrels, and the hoops burst, so they decided to drop down more to the south and southwest. The farther they got away from the southeast, the more moderate they found the weather.

Just as they caught sight of land, a tremendous rain poured down on them. And the islanders from Hispaniola, who were with them, began to beat and bemoan themselves, declaring that they were lost and drowned. For where they were driving in toward land, all the banks were very steep and high, so that no one could escape. The crew of the caravels asked where these banks and cliffs ended. [The islanders] pointed out a cape where, they said, was the place in which they fished and got pearls. [The sailors] set their course sideways to the wind, or by the bowline, according to our fashion, so that they put that cape to leeward. And those islanders, where they had just been moaning, now began to cheer and show great joy and sing and cheer with their hands and with joyful faces.

Passing that cape, they came to a very good harbor, where two canoes came toward them with six men inside, fishermen, who came out to those caravels with pleasure, as if they had been there before, and they gave [the sailors] some of the fish they had caught. They saw on the beach men signaling that they wanted to come out to the ships. One of the ships' boats was launched in the sea. And when it put shore, many persons came out to the ships, among whom there was one young man with a string of pearls on his neck and on his arms, and from the waist downward he had a covering of colored cotton cloth. And [the natives] gave [the sailors pearls] for little bells and certain other trinkets.

Then, through the interpreters from the Island of Hispaniola, who it seems understood a few words of that language, they said that not very far away there was a very populous village, and that this young man was one of the honored chiefs of that land. There the captain of those caravels decided to send some of his men, who went off with those people. And they went about three leagues and found a very fine village of about 150 to 200 houses. It was made in this manner: all the houses were joined all the way around, with an open square in the middle, and some trees in the middle of the square, where they made abundant shade. The houses were tall, made of timbers, covered around and up to a point, tent-fashion, with palms and with other leaves of trees. There they were led to a house formed in this manner: it was [not] made round, [but] with beams and two rooms; it was remarkably constructed.

And entering, they found an old man of advanced age (who, it was judged, was the father of that young man who came to the caravels) sitting on a chair wrought out of black wood, highly polished; and he had many others brought in, some black and some of various colors. I believe that the black was ebony, and that the red ones were brazilwood. And when they were seated, he had twenty young men bring in plates wrought out of wood, and in them many sorts of fruits unknown to me, but sweet, good, and smooth; also bowls or cups wrought of wood, full of wine—not, however, from grapes, but from various sorts of very pleasing juices of fruits, and they banqueted sumptuously. And they talked a great deal but could not understand each other or give answers.

Afterward they went into a room and saw many women sitting on the floor, their shameful parts covered; they were beautiful with blue covering; their heads were combed, with their hair neatly parted. When they saw the old man and us, they all got to their feet and made a gesture of reverence. They took one another by the hand and began to make merry, to dance and sing, beating with their hands, all shouting. From the body downward they were covered with cottons of various colors, and their ears, arms and neck with pearls and certain objects—of wood, [the sailors] judged—in squares, in bits and long pieces, strung on their neck and arms. These were shining and well polished, said to look like glass and stones, yet they were nothing but wood, as I have said.

The houses were of timbers, but artfully fashioned with beams of various colors; and likewise the rooms were of boards that were certainly beautiful for a person to see who has had no experience of such things. There were in that square many men who seemed to be from different countries.

Pearls they obtained there in very great quantity. They have certain baskets with which they go down with cords of palm on to the bottom in the water, and with a weight inside, and they go fishing for the oysters just as we do, and they catch a great many, and eat them, and in them find pearls. But because they do not have any means of piercing them, they scatter and ruin them. Yet they are very beautiful "oriental" pearls, of which [the sailors] bought some for little bells and other trinkets and especially for pieces of mirror and bits of copper.

In that place we did not see any metal of any sort. We saw vessels baked from earth, of various sorts, of which [the sailors] took some for their own use. They did not see there any four-footed animal. They [the natives] live on roots made by the trees of the place that was mentioned above. [The visitors] saw millet larger and finer than ours, and panic grass. They saw many fruits and herbs, very good, but unknown to those who saw them.

They live, as I have said above, for the most part on fish and on the containers of the pearls and on flying birds, that is, geese, ducks, and other large birds like peacocks, very handsome, white, and with red necks, handsome beak, feet like the goose, the beak being sharp, pointed; [also] numberless parrots of every sort. They saw forests of the most beautiful trees, unknown to them, except locust trees and wild pines; meadows, very beautiful, which were all green and flower-

Typical Carib Dugout Canoe

ing, and it was the month of October, which seemed to be spring for them; the finest sweet water, and very large rivers. They saw much cotton, which [the natives] took to make themselves caps and to clothe themselves from the waist down.

The men, of light color, with long hair and beards, are of fine stature, gentle, and show a desire for new things, and this was indicated by signs. And they indicated with the hand that the interior of the country was very populous and had various peoples; for when we asked them about both the chair and the utensils, they managed to indicate by signs with the hand that people came from inside the country and took shells of the pearls—or rather, of the containers [i. e., oysters] and pearls—for their garments. [Those natives] had also some clothes of cotton.

They received perfect hospitality. The day when they returned to the ships, they decided to depart and go back to the captain Columbus, whom they had left on the island of Hispaniola. They sailed along that coast, where in many places they found the woods so thick that, even if they had wanted to go ashore, there was no way that they could enter. Still from the ships they could see smoke inside the forest, so that they believed there were habitations inside this forest. In certain other places where they wanted to go ashore, [the natives] suddenly fled, so that they had no speech with them or any sign of a word.

They said, moreover, that they sailed along that coast toward the west for 35 days, found beaches, bays, many ports and numerous islands, but did not go onto these because they were worried about shelves and insufficient depth; and they hesitated to approach the shore of the land because of such doubts, except where they saw, in their judgment, that they were safe in approaching the shore at a given place. And with fair weather they returned to Hispaniola, satisfied with what they had found, and especially with the pearls.

This voyage is connected with the third voyage, because the Admiral had sent them on various routes that he might have knowledge of such unknown and unheard of land and people. From their departure to their return was 45 days. In this time they had every sort of weather, rainstorms, winds, and much sea, and also periods of calm with pleasant mildness of air, since it was the beginning, according to them, of their summer season, and [yet] it was in the month of October. They returned to the Island of Hispaniola on the 14th day of November. They said that they had sailed along that coast toward the west for approximately 2500 miles, from the first glimpse of land that they had. They went to the south-southeast for 12 days, and 35 days to the west. They started from the Island of Hispaniola on the 28th day of September.

To what group the Indians here described belong we can safely infer. They are the *Arawak*, and they once extended from Florida and the West Indies to the Guianas, then southward, in scattered groups, throughout the Amazon Basin to Bolivia, to Matto Grosso in southeastern Brazil and the Gran Chaco in northern Argentine. It was an Arawak tribe Columbus encountered, the *Lucayan*, when he first discovered America, and Arawak tribes greeted him in Cuba and Haiti (Hispaniola), and, 400 years later, it was an Arawak tribe, the *Mehinaku*, that the famous German ethnologist, Karl von den Steinen, encountered in the interior of Brazil when he first opened up to scholars that mysterious region in 1884.

Thus they have persisted, and with their customs and beliefs only slightly impaired, for more than 400 years, and we may well begin our journey through the great South American continent with them. That journey will reveal to us scenes of the most varied and contrasting type. It will take us from the semi-temperate coasts of Florida, Cuba, and Haiti, across the hurricane-infested Caribbean, to the mouth of that great river which the medievally obsessed mind of Columbus felt could have its origin only in the Garden of Eden. Here along the shores of the Orinoco many of the geographic traits of the great continent first reveal themselves—the impenetrable jungle, the unexpected and dangerous rapids and cataracts, and the easy portages from one stream to another.

Let us keep these portages in mind, for by their means the vast regions from Venezuela and the Guianas to southeastern Brazil, as well as the tremendous area that lies between Bahia and Rio de Janeiro to the extreme east and the Bolivian and Peruvian highlands to the extreme west, all these can be easily traversed by dugout and canoe. So can the dangers and obstructions of the jungle be neutralized. Only their existence enabled the

Arawak to spread over so vast a territory. Thus it was their simple predecessors must have come too.

Yet it is not only the luxuriant and animal-infested jungle and stream that we shall have to traverse. An Arawak tribe, the *Mojo*, will carry us close to the mountains of Bolivia, where life is not so easy. Another, the *Guana*, will take us to the monotonous and not very hospitable headwaters of the Paraguay River, and still another, the *Paressi*, to the wholly unfriendly and difficult terrain of the Brazilian Matto Grosso. We will cross the path of tribes of the most varied type. We shall meet members of the extremely simple *Ge* group, who possibly represent approximations to the peoples who first populated the continent, then the inhabitants of the Bolivian and Argentinian Chaco, whose culture is almost as crude, if no cruder, alternating with others who have been in contact with the invigorating influence of the great and sophisticated civilizations of Ecuador, Bolivia, and Peru.

Our journey will not be merely one of antiquarian interest or significance. These Indians have meant much to us. Some of the commonly used words in English have come from the native languages of South America: hammock, hurricane, cannibal. In the word *hurricane* there survives the memory of an Arawakan *Taino* god; in *cannibal* the name of a marauding West Indian and South American Indian tribe, the *Carib*, as well as the memory of a practice which, in its cruder and more naïve forms, has always been highly repugnant to the sensibilities of Europeans.

But not only has the English language become enriched from the stores of native culture. Our whole economic life would be unthinkable without the potato, maize, and tobacco, and these have all come to us from South America. How helpless would the modern physician appear without quinine and curare? These too, however, represent a gift from the natives of the southern continent. Nor must we think that their cultural contributions have necessarily stopped for all time. On the contrary. All indications point to a new resurgence of Indian influence upon the cultures that are now taking form in Brazil, Argentine, and Chile and, far more significantly, in Bolivia, Peru, and Ecuador.

This then and more we must always bear in mind as the changing human panorama passes in kaleidoscopic procession before our eyes, from the Caribbean to the Straits of Magellan and from the Atlantic to the Pacific oceans.

CHAPTER II

The Link between the Two Continents

THE WEST INDIAN ARAWAK

AMERICAN ANTHROPOLOGY BEGINS PROPERLY with the work of an unknown priest, Ramon Pane. The Spanish chronicler, Peter Martyr,[3] refers to him as "One Ramon, a hermit whom Colon had left with certain kings of the island to instruct them in the Christian faith. And tarrying there a long time he composed a small book in the Spanish tongue on the rites of the islands." The Indians he described were the Arawak of Haiti, and the study of their culture takes us at one step into a whole maze of problems. Where did they come from? What are their affiliations, cultural and linguistic? How much of their culture is the result of a fusion with elements from still older occupants of the island?

It has generally been assumed that most of their customs and beliefs came from the mainland of South America. The justification for that assumption lies in the fact that there are no Arawak-speaking peoples anywhere else, none in North America, with the exception of the tip of Florida, and none in Central America. Yet we find that they have trait after trait in common with the Indians of the southeastern part of the United States. Only a few need be noted: human sacrifice, rectangular dwellings, burial mounds, palisaded villages, urn burials, dugout canoes, cane splint basketry, pottery, blowgun, maize, clans and the reckoning of descent in the mother's line, fish poisons, labrets, fronto-occipital head deformation, belief in plural souls. Such similarities can be accounted for in only one of two ways. Either there has been a long and fairly intimate contact between these two areas, or they are survivals from an older and common heritage. The second alternative seems by far the most likely hypothesis, although later contact between the two areas must have continued uninterrupted.

Clearly, to reach the Antilles and South America the Indians must have first traversed North America. How did the ancestors of the Arawak make this journey?

To. judge from certain of the traits that they share with the Southeast and of which not a few are to be found as far north as the upper Mississippi and the Missouri, that trek must have largely followed the well-known path from the northwest coast of Canada across the Rockies into the great northern plains of the United States. This older culture assuredly had neither agriculture nor clans. But it must have possessed boats, either the bark canoe or the dugout. Maize, we know, came to the peoples of southeastern United States long after, certainly not earlier than the twelfth century A.D., if not later. It came from Mexico, and it must have reached the West Indies not long following its first arrival in the Southeast. We need not assume that this proto-Arawak invasion preceded the spread of agriculture by more than half a millenium. That the Arawak found an earlier and simple culture in the islands when they arrived there, archaeological investigations have amply demonstrated. Considerable fusion, culturally and linguistically, must have taken place between the two peoples.

Thus, influences came to the island Arawak from Central America and even Mexico proper certainly from the fourteenth century on. That seems to admit of little doubt. And if we add to all these invasions and contacts the fact that an alert, nomadic, and nonagricultural tribe from South America, the Carib, raided the Arawak continually, possibly from their earliest arrival onward, and that, in many instances, these Carib effectively conquered them, then it should not surprise us to find that the resulting Arawak culture was a highly specialized one, although exhibiting its conglomerate origin again and again.

But let us pause for a moment and see what the first official anthropologist, Ramon Pane, wrote, that Ramon Pane whom Columbus ordered "to collect all their [Indian] ceremonies and their antiquities although so much of it is fable that one cannot extract anything fruitful from it beyond the fact that each one of them has a certain natural regard for the future and believes in the immortality of the soul."

What the good friar and hermit, Pane, of the Order of St. Jerome, discovered was much more than a regard for the future and a belief in the immortality of the soul. He found each individual worshiping idols which they called *cemi*, these idols symbolizing and representing deities residing in heaven, immortal beings who cannot be seen, beings who have no beginning and who were born of women, so he writes.

In answer to a question as to whence they had come, the friar received an origin myth, the first one recorded at any length from the New World. Let us see what it was like:[4]

Española has a province called Caanau in which there is a mountain which is called Canta where there are two caves, the one named Cacibagiagua and the other Amaiuua. From Cacibagiagua came forth the larger part of the people who settled in the island. When people were in these caves watch was kept by night and the care of this was given to one whose name was Marocael; and him, because one day he delayed to come back to the door, the sun carried him off. And when it was seen that the sun had carried him off they closed the door; and so he was changed into stone near the door. Next they say that others going off to fish were taken by the sun and they became trees, called by them *iobi*, and otherwise they are called *mirabolans*. The reason why Marocael kept watch and stood guard was to watch in what direction he wished to send or to divide the people, and it seems that he delayed to his own greater hurt.

It came to pass that one man whose name was Guahagiona said to another whose name was Giadruuaua, that he should go to gather an herb called *digo* with which they cleanse the body when they go to wash themselves. He went before day, [but] the sun seized him on the way and he became a bird which sings in the morning like the nightingale and is called *giahuba bagiael*. Guahagiona seeing that he whom he had sent to gather the digo did not return resolved to go out of the cave Cacibagiagua.

That [then] Guahagiona resolved to go away in anger, seeing that those whom he had sent to gather the digo for washing themselves did not return; and he said to the women "Leave your husbands and let us go into other lands and we will carry off enough jewels. Leave your sons and we will carry only the plants with us and then we will return for them."

Guahagiona set forth with all the women and went off in search of other lands, and came to Matinino where he left the women; and he went away into another region called Guanin· and they had left the little children near a brook. Then when hunger began to trouble them, it is related, that they wailed and called upon their mothers who had gone off; and the fathers were not able to give help to the children calling in hunger for their mothers, saying "mama" as if to speak, but really asking for the breast. And wailing in this fashion and asking for the breast, saying *"too, too,"* as one who asks for something with great longing, and very urgently, they were changed into little animals, after the fashion of dwarfs [frogs] which are called *tona* because of their asking for the breast, and that in this way all the men were left without women.

And later on another occasion women went there from the said Island Española, which formerly was called Aiti, and is so called by its inhabitants; and these and other islands they called *bouhi*. And because they have no writing nor letters they cannot give a good account of what they have learned from their forbears; and therefore they do not agree in what they say, nor can what they relate be recorded in an orderly fashion.

When Guahagiona went away, he that carried away all the women, he likewise took with him the women of his *Cacique* whose name was Anacacugia, deceiving him as he deceived the others; and, moreover, a brother-in-law of Guahagiona Anacacugia, who went off with him went on the sea; and Guahagiona said to his brother-in-law, being in the canoe, see what a fine *cobo* is there in the water and this cobo is the sea snail, and him peering into the water to see the cobo Guahagiona his brother-in-law seized by the feet and cast into the sea; and so he took all the women for himself, and he left those of Matinino [i. e., at Matinino] where it is reported there are no people but women today. And he went off to another island which is called

Guanin and it received this name on account of what he took away from it when he went away.

That then Guahagiona returned to Canta [Cauta], mentioned above, whence he had taken the women. They say that being in the land whence he had gone Guahagiona saw that he had left in the sea one woman, and that he was greatly pleased with her and straightway sought out many washes [or washing places] to wash himself being full of those sores which we call the French disease. She then put him in a *guanara* which means a place apart; and so he was healed of these sores. Then she asked permission of him to go on her way and he gave it to her. This woman was named Guabonito; and Guahagiona changed his name and thenceforward he was called Biberoci Guahagiona. And the woman Guabonito gave Biberoci Guahagiona many *guanins* and many *cibe* to wear tied on his arms. Because in those countries *colecibi* are of stones like marble and they wear them tied on the arms and on the neck and the guanins they wear in the ears making holes when they are children; and they are of metal as it were of a florin. And the beginnings [the originators] of these guanins they say were Guabonito, Albeborael, Guahagiona, and the father of Albeborael. Guahagiona remained in the land with his father whose name was Hiauna. His grandson on his father's side [i. e., Guahagiona's son] was named Hia Guaili Guanin which means grandson of Hiauna; and thence thereafter he was called Guanin and is so called today. And since they have no letters nor writings they cannot relate well such fables nor can I write them well. Wherefore I believe I shall put down first what should be last and last what should be first. But all that I write is related by them as I write it and so I set it forth as I have understood it from the people of the country.

They say that one day the men went off to bathe and being in the water, it rained heavily, and that they were very desirous of having women, and that oftentimes when it rained, they had gone to search for the traces of their women nor had been able to find any news of them, but that on that day while bathing, they say, they saw fall down from some trees and hiding in the branches a certain kind of persons that were not men nor women nor had the natural parts of the male or female. They went to take them but they fled away as if they had been eels, wherefore they called two or three men by the order of their cacique, since they were not able to take them for him, in order that they might watch to see how many there were and that they might seek out for each one a man who was *Caracaracol* because they have their hands rough, and that so they could hold them tightly. They told the cacique that there were four, and so they brought four men who were *Caracaracoli*. This Caracaracol is a disease like scab which makes the body very rough. After they had caught them they took counsel together over them what they could do to make them women since they did not have the natural parts of male or female.

They sought a bird which is called inriri, in ancient times inrire cahuuaial, which bores trees and in our language is called woodpecker [pico]. And likewise they took these women without male or female organs and bound their feet and hands and took this bird just mentioned and bound him to the body and he thinking that they were logs began to do his accustomed task pecking and boring in the place where the natural parts of women are wont to be. In this fashion, then, the Indians say that they had women according to what the oldest men relate. Since I wrote in haste and did not have paper enough I could not put down in its place that which by mistake I transferred to another place, but notwithstanding that I have in reality made no mistake since they believe it all as has been written.

Let us turn now to that which we should have recorded first, i. e., their belief as to the origin and beginning of the sea. . . .

Now this marked concern with women and the great role assigned to them was not merely an expression of sexual interest, as the simple friar must have thought. These people were not women-obsessed, nor was the eternal feminine leading them on either in the sense of Goethe or Anatole France. Our story reflects something essentially different. It reflects the social position of woman, her high and special status, the fact that descent was reckoned in the female line, that a man upon marriage went to live with his wife's relatives. This was at least true for the major part of the population. For the hereditary chiefs there seems to have developed a tendency for descent to be reckoned in the father's line, and it is possibly a reflection of this change that permitted the custom of burying the chief's wives upon his death. Where motherright prevailed, this is inconceivable and would unquestionably not have been sanctioned.

The account of Ramon continues with an interesting myth of how the sea came into existence:[5]

There was a man called Giaia whose name they do not know and his son called Giaiael which means son of Giaia. This Giaiael wishing to slay his father, he sent him into exile where he remained banished four months, and then his father slew him and put his bones in a gourd and fastened it on the roof of his cabin where it remained fastened some time. And it came to pass that one day Giaia, longing to see his son, said to his wife, "I want to see our son Giaiael; and she was pleased at that; and he took down the gourd and turned it over to see the bones of his son, and from it came forth many fishes large and small. Wherefore, seeing that the bones were changed into fishes they resolved to eat them. One day, therefore, they say that Giaia having gone to his *conichi*, which means his lands that were his inheritance, there came four sons of a woman whose name was Itiba Tahuuaua, all from one womb and twins; and this woman having died in travail they opened her and drew out these four sons, and the first that they drew out was Caracaracol which means scabby. This Caracaracol had a name. . . . The others had no name.

Then the four sons, all born together, of Itiba Tahuuaua who died in travail with them, went to lay hold of the gourd of Giaia where his son Giaiael was who was changed into a fish; and none of them ventured to lay hands on it except Dimiuan Caracaracol who took it from its place and all satisfied themselves with fish; and while they were eating they perceived that Giaia was coming from his farms, and wishing, in this haste to fasten the gourd to its place again they did not fasten it well and so it fell to the ground and broke. They say that so great was the mass of water that came out of the gourd that it filled the whole earth, and with it issued many fish, and from this according to their account the sea had its beginning. These then departed from thence and found a man whose name was Conel and he was dumb.

Now these [brothers] as soon as they came to the door of Bassamanaco and perceived that he carried Cazzabi, said, "Ahiacauo Guarocoel" which means "let us know this our grandfather." In like manner, Dimiuan Caracaracol seeing his brothers before him went within to see if he could have some *cazzabi*. And this cazzabi is the bread that is eaten in the country. Caracaracol having entered the house of Aiamauaco asked him for cazzabi which is the bread above mentioned; and he put his hand on his own nose and threw at him a *guanguaio* hitting him in the back. This guanguaio was full of *cogioba* [tobacco] which he had made that day; the cogioba is a certain powder which they take sometimes to purge themselves, and for other effects which you will hear later. They take it with a cane about a foot long and put one end in the nose and the other in the powder, and in this manner they draw it into themselves through the nose and this purges them thoroughly. And thus he gave him that guanguaio for bread, . . . and went off much enraged because they asked him for it.

Caracaracol after this returned to his brothers and told them what had happened to him with Baiamanicoel and of the blow that he hit him with the guanguaio on one shoulder and that it pained him very much. Then his brothers looked at his shoulder and saw that it was much swollen. And this swelling increased so much that he was like to die of it. Wherefore they tried to cut it and could not; and taking a stone axe they opened it and there came out a live turtle, a female; and so they built their cabin and cared for the turtle. Of this I have not heard [or understood] anything else, and what we have written was of little profit. And further they say that the sun and the moon came out of a cave which is situated in the country of a cacique named Maucia Tunuel and the name of the cave is Giououaua and they hold it in high regard, and it is all painted in their fashion without any figure, with many leaves and other things of that sort, and in this cave there are two cemis, of stone, small about a foot high with their hands tied, and they looked as if they were seated. These cemis they hold in great regard, and when it did not rain they say they went there to visit them and suddenly it rained. And one of these cemis is called by them Boinaiel and the other Maroio.

There are numerous reminiscences here of themes and motifs from the mythologies of North and South America, easily as many from the northern as from the southern continent. Thus again do these island Arawak function definitely as the link between the two.

However, when we come to Ramon's description of the beliefs concerning the dead, of the observances of the priests and the *shaman* and of the details of their religious practices, the affiliations with South America begin to increase markedly and significantly and we begin to discern the vague outline of connections with still another area: Central America and Mexico.

"They believe," so Ramon Pane goes on to say, "that there is a place whither the dead go which is called Coaibai. . . . The first man that was in Coaibai was named Machetaurie-Guaiaua and he was lord of this Coaibai. . . ."

In this home of the dead the spirits are permitted to go out to walk only at night. It is then that they eat the *guannaba*, a fruit with something of the taste of a quince. But perhaps it is better to let Peter Martyr continue the narrative as we have it in the quaint English translation of Richard Eden:[6]

[They affirm] also that they the dead are conversant with living people even in their beds, and to deceive women in taking upon them the shape of men, shewing themselves as though they would have to do with them: but when the matter cometh to actual deed, suddenly they vanish away. If any do suspect that a dead body lieth by him, when he feeleth any strange thing in the bed, they say he shall be out of doubt by feeling of the belly thereof; affirming that the spirits of dead men may take upon them all the members of man's body, saving the navel. If therefore by the lack of the navel he do perceive that a dead man lieth by him, the feeling [contact] is immediately resolved [relaxed]. They believe verily, that in the night, and oftentimes in their journeys and especially in common and high ways, dead men do meet with the living: against whom, if any man be stout and out of fear, the fantasy vanisheth incontinently: but if any fear, the fantasy or vision doeth so assault him and strike him with further fear, that many are thereby astonished and have the limbs of their bodies taken.

The inhabitants being demanded of whom they had those vain superstitions they answered, that they were left them of their forefathers, as by descent of inheritance, and that they have had the same before the memory of man, composed in certain rhymes and songs which it was lawful for none to learn but only the king's sons, who committed the same to memory because they had never any knowledge of letters. These they sing before the people on certain solemn and festival days as most religious ceremonies: while in the meantime they play on a certain instrument made of one whole piece of wood somewhat hollow like a timbrel.

Their priests and divines whom they call *boitii* instruct them in these superstitions. These priests are also physicians devising a thousand crafts and subtleties how to deceive the simple people which have them in great reverence for they persuade them that the cemis used to speak with them familiarly, and tell them of things to come. And if any have been sick and are recovered they make and believe that they obtained their health of the cemis.

These boitii bind themselves to much fasting and outward cleanliness and purgings, especially when they take upon them the cure of any prince, for then they drink the powder of a certain herb by whose quality they are driven into a fury, at which time (as they say) they learn many things by revelation of the cemis. Then putting secretly in their mouths either, a stone or a bone or a piece of flesh, they come to the sick person commanding all to depart out of that place except one or two whom it shall please the sick man to appoint. This done, they go about him three or four times, greatly deforming their faces, lips and nostrils with sundry filthy gestures, blowing, breathing, and sucking the forehead, temples and neck of the patient, whereby (they say) they draw the evil air from him and suck the disease out of the veins. Then rubbing him about the shoulders, thighs and legs and drawing down their hands close by his feet, holding them yet fast together, they run to the door being open, where they unclose and shake their hands, affirming that they have driven away the disease and that the patient shall shortly be perfectly restored to health. . . .

Divers of the inhabitants honor cemis of divers fashions: some make them of wood, as they were admonished by certain visions appearing unto them in the woods: others, which have received answer of them among the rocks, make them of stone and marble. Some they make of roots, to the similitude of such as appear to them when they are gathering the roots called *ages*, whereof they make their bread. These cemis they believe to send plenty and fruitfulness of those roots. . . .

The inhabitants of this island attribute a cemi to everything, supposing the same to give ear to their invocations. Whereof, as often as the kings ask counsel of their cemis as concerning their wars, increase of fruits or scarceness, or health and sickness, they enter into the house dedicate to their cemis, where, snuffing up into their nostrils the powder of the herb called *cohobba* [tobacco] they say that immediately they see the houses turned topsy turvy, and men to walk with their heels upward. . . . As soon as this madness ceaseth, he embraceth his knees with his arms holding down his head. And when he hath remained thus awhile astonished, he lifteth up his head, as one that came new out of sleep: and thus looking up toward heaven, first he fumbleth certain confounded words with himself, then certain of the nobility or chief gentlemen that are about him (for none of the common people are admitted to these mysteries) with loud voices give tokens of rejoicing that he is returned to them from the speech of the cemis, demanding of him what he hath seen. Then he opening his mouth, doteth that the cemis spake to him during the time of his trance, declaring that he had revelations either concerning victory or destruction, famine or plenty, health or sickness or whatsoever happeneth first on his tongue.

But now whereas I have declared thus much of the cemis in general, I thought it not good to let pass what is said of them in particular. They say therefore that a certain king called Guamaretus, had a cemi whose name was Corochutus, who (they say) was oftentimes wont to descend from the highest place of the house where Guamaretus kept him close bound. They affirm that the cause of his breaking his bands and departure, was either to hide himself or go seek for meat: and that sometimes being offended that the king had been negligent and slack in honoring him, he was wont to lie hid for certain days. They say also, that in the king's village there are sometime children born having two crowns, which they suppose to be the children of Corochutus the cemi. . . .

He hath also another cemi called Epileguanita, made of wood, in shape like a four-footed beast: who also is said oftentimes to have gone from the palace where he is honored, into the woods. As soon as they perceive him to be gone, a great multitude of them gather together to seek him with devout prayers and when they have found him, bring him home religiously on their shoulders to the chapel dedicated to him. . . .

They honored another cemi in the likeness of a woman, on whom waited two other like men, as they were ministers to her. One of these, executed the office of a mediator to the other cemi, which are under the power and commandment of this woman, to raise winds, clouds and rain. The other is also at her commandment a messenger to the other cemis, which are joined to her in governance, to gather together the waters which fall from the high hills to the valleys, that being loosed, they may with force burst out into great floods and overflow the country, if the people do not give due honor to her image.

There remaineth yet one thing worthy to be noted wherewith

we will make an end of this book. It is a thing well-known, and yet
fresh in memory among the inhabitants of the island, that there was
sometime two kings which were wont to abstain five days together
continually from meat and drink, to know somewhat of their cemis
of things to come, and that for this fasting being acceptable to their
cemis, they received answer of them, that within few years there
should come to the island [Hayti] a nation of men covered with
apparel, which should destroy all the customs and ceremonies of the
island, and either slay all their children or bring them into servitude.
The common sort of the people understood this oracle to be meant
of the Canibales [Carib], and therefore when they had knowledge
of their coming, they ever fled, and were fully determined never
more to adventure the battle with them. But when they saw that the
Spaniards had entered into the island, consulting among themselves
of the matter, they concluded that this was the nation which was
meant by the oracle. *Wherein their opinion deceived them not, for
they are now all subject to the Christians, all such being slain as
stubbornly resisted.* . . .

All these customs and beliefs relating to the dead are specifically South American and we shall meet them again, first
throughout the Guianas, Venezuela, and Brazil. In that region
likewise we shall find priests functioning as do these Arawak
boitii. Idols like the cemis, however, a highly organized hereditary chieftainship, a clear-cut division of the population into
nobles and commoners, for that we shall seek in vain in South
America east of the Andes. Some type of division of the population into nobles and commoners we do indeed find among a few
of the far-flung Arawak tribes of Brazil. However, to find a
truly analogous type of idols and a truly analogous type of social
structure it is to Central America and Mexico that we shall have
to go. That both—the idols and the stratified structure of the
society—were not very old constituents of Arawak culture seems
clear. Innumerable indications point in that direction. The same
can be said of maize.

It is useless perhaps to speculate from what part of Central
America or Mexico, and when, these elements were brought to
the Antilles. Yet the attempt is worth while. The suggestions

that have been made, and with some show of reason, emphasize in particular two areas, that of the Huaxteca, near Tampico, and that of the Guetar, of Costa Rica. The case for the Huaxteca is much stronger than that for the Guetar. To determine when this took place is another question. To assume that it occurred before the introduction of maize into the Southeast of the United States from Mexico somewhere around 1100 A.D. would be quite unwarranted. Either these new elements came in the wake of the surge that brought so much of Mexican culture to the southeastern United States, around 1100 A.D., or later. The absence in the Antilles of the pyramidal mounds that form so fundamental a feature of the twelfth century cultural invasion from Mexico would seem to indicate that it was actually later. Indeed, we may well have to date this invasion two centuries later and have it contemporaneous, in a general way, with the second of the Mexican invasions that archaeologists now predicate as sweeping up along the Gulf of Mexico and which introduced into eastern United States the constituent elements of the last phase of the so-called Mound-Builder culture.

The island Arawak civilization in short was the result of many different influences, was based upon elements that probably belong to the oldest cultural possessions to reach the New World. To these were successively added traits that had been secondarily developed from the great source of so many of the higher aspects of American aboriginal civilizations, Mexico and Central America. And at all times, let us remember, it was subject to raids. Early and late, the Carib, a people who had only recently progressed much beyond the simplest of cultures, attacked and threatened to disrupt all their attempts at integration. To these Carib we must ascribe the introduction of many of the specifically South American traits into the West Indies. In what terror they were held by the more cultured Arawak, Ramon Pane has told us. They must indeed have felt very much as did those other islanders, the English of the ninth century, when they were raided by the Norsemen, and their prayer might have been much the same: "From destruction and sudden death and from the wrath of the Carib, good gods deliver us!"

But in spite of sudden death and destruction, in spite of occasional resolve no longer to do battle with their foes, not only did the island Arawak hold fast to their own achievements but they ventured out to sea themselves, again and again, bent on adventure and in search of new homes, until they finally came to the mouth of that river whose churning waves had so frightened and overwhelmed Columbus. In his letter the aging admiral told the king that, "There are great indications of this being (in the neighborhood of the) terrestrial paradise. . . . I have never either read or heard of fresh water coming in so large a quantity, in close conjunction with the water of the sea. . . . If the water of which I speak does not proceed from the earthly paradise, it seems to be a still greater wonder, for I do not believe that there is any river in the world so large and so deep."

Let us then proceed to investigate this gateway to the terrestrial paradise and see what lay beyond the mountain covered with monkeys which the sailors discerned so clearly from their caravels.

CHAPTER III

Pioneers and Culture Bearers

THE CONTINENTAL ARAWAK

THE FIRST ARAWAK TO COME TO THE ORINOCO must have been just as perturbed and puzzled as was the Italian Columbus. They were clearly more intrepid. What they brought to cope with the unknown and formidable difficulties awaiting them was a variegated assortment of possessions: at best the dugout, the bow and arrow, and the war club; an agricultural mode of life, with maize and manioc as staples; and, finally, a closely knit social structure with matrilineal clans, stratified classes, and a highly centralized chieftainship. If they arrived with all this cultural equipment at one time, we must date their incursion into South America very late, possibly not before 1300 A.D. That would barely leave two hundred years for their amazing dissemination over almost a third of the southern continent. Certainly maize could not have been in their possession before 1000–1100 A.D. when, as we saw, the first of the two major waves of Mexican influences swept around the Gulf of Mexico to southeastern United States and thence to the Antilles.

To be able to penetrate the tropical jungle successfully and either to overwhelm or enslave the natives, who must have opposed their progress step by step, a number of things were necessary, something more important than mere military prowess. They had to possess effective means of transportation, adequate methods for obtaining their food and safeguarding it, and sufficient adaptability to adjust themselves to a natural environment utterly different from the one to which they had been accustomed in their island homeland.

No one can make a frontal attack on the tropical jungle. It has to be circumvented in some fashion or another. Otherwise progress is slow and hazardous if possible at all. Fortunately the geography of northern South America came to the aid of the Arawak invaders as it must have come to the aid of the Tupi invaders who preceded them. The land is so rich in streams and watercourses of all kinds, there are so many and such short portages, that it is a comparatively easy matter to float down the Orinoco and then down its southeastern tributaries until you reach the region where a portage to the Rio Negro is feasible and possible. The large number of Arawak-speaking tribes along the Rio Negro until the latter strikes the Amazon at Manaus is the best corroboration that this route was both feasible and possible and that it actually had been taken. From the Rio Negro and the Amazon both western and south-central Brazil were open to them. Now, to successfully traverse this immense area they needed boats that could adequately cope with streams of all descriptions, with rapids and with cataracts; boats that could withstand the torrential rains of the tropical forest and resist the attacks of all the forces so destructive of the materials from which the boats have necessarily to be made. With a description of their boat, let us then begin.

The Arawak had two types of boats: a narrow dugout made of the single trunk of a tree and a kind of canoe made of a single piece of the tough bark of the purpleheart tree. This tree attains a very large size. There is a difference only in unimportant details between those boats used by the Arawak and their great enemies, the Carib. The rafts or *balsas* are likewise practically identical. In spite of their insecurity, these balsas were very generally employed, for they are so easily constructed. They consist of pieces of timber, bamboo, or bundles of reeds lashed together and none too securely.

The dugout was pointed at the stem and markedly rounded

at the stern. The larger craft, however, were made without pointed head or pointed or rounded stern, the gaps filled with triangular timbers, the outer sides being painted with various fantastic devices. The bow and stern were frequently decorated with patterns such as diamonds, the sun, or the moon. In windy seasons a washboard, running from stem to stern, was fixed up to prevent the waves from breaking over the vessel.

Its manufacture, as known today—and there is no reason for believing that much has changed in the last four hundred years except the use of modern implements—is a fairly tedious process. Fire was first applied to the tree, and then it was felled with stone axes. Considerable time and labor was required until it had been lopped to a convenient size. A fire is now started along the top, leaving a thickness of approximately three fingers' breadth on either side. The wood is thus gradually burnt out until an equal thickness is attained at the bottom. This done, the concave hollow trunk is filled with water, and a gentle fire started on the outside with dry palm leaves. In this fashion, by the presence of water within the hollow trunk and the application of fire from without, the hollow is widened and the sides are opened. To further widen the dugout, strong sticks and beams are inserted in the hollow, which help to prevent the sides from closing after they have once been forced open. After all this has been attended to, the fire is scattered and the flames extinguished on as much of the outer surface as has caught on fire.

An extremely arduous and tedious operation now follows, that of scraping the charcoal, both outside and in, until the boat acquires a lusterlike jet. This is not done for esthetic reasons but for very practical ones. The great danger to a boat is the damaging or rotting of the timber from the action of the water. The charcoal on the outer side effectively prevents this.

When long journeys had to be undertaken, a sort of tent was added, to protect the goods being transported. Such a tent is constructed by bending a number of sticks into semicircles, the two ends fastened, one against each side of the dugout, so as to make a framework. The sticks are held in place by cross-sticks tied at right angles. On a framework thus constructed is laid a thatch of palm leaves.

What has always excited the wonder of white observers in the construction of the dugout is the complete absence of nails, even today, after four centuries of contact with Europeans. Everything is made of wood, even the gougings and the screw pins with which the steering paddle is turned from side to side. Nor did they, in the ancient days, use either oakum or pitch or tar in the calking of the hatches or the washboards. Boats were calked in the following manner. The bark of a tree growing like the mangrove either in or near the water on river banks was secured. After being well-pounded, a sticky mass was produced, which was held together by the many fibers contained in it. This pulpy substance was used in lieu of pitch or tar to close tightly all the openings and seams of the dugout.

For the smaller streams and for passage through rapids the dugout was cumbersome and frequently quite useless, and the bark canoe replaced it, despite the fact that such a canoe is unsteady and can easily be upset.

The canoe proper, or wood-skin, as it is called in the Guianas, is made of the tough bark of the purpleheart tree, as mentioned above. An incision is made in the tree to the extent required, and the bark removed by driving in wedges. After the bark has been loosened from the wood, it is kept open by cross-sticks. A wedge-shaped piece, the base of which corresponds with the free edge of the bark, extending on both sides approximately two or three feet from either end, is cut away from the outer layer of the bark in such fashion as to leave intact the corresponding inner layer. This is subsequently folded up on itself, and thus all entry of water is prevented. W. E. Roth, from whom the foregoing descriptions of both the dugout and the wood-skin have been taken, continues his description of the final process in the making of the wood-skin in the following words: [7]

The two ends of the whole strip of bark—that is to say, the short piece between each end and the nearest wedge-shaped incisions—are

[now] raised until the edges of the wedge-shaped slits meet; and these edges are then overlapped and sewn together with bush rope. This, therefore, raises the bow and stern at an angle from the water, while the body of the craft floats parallel to the water line. It remains for several days, supported at the extremities by two beams, exposed to the weather before it is fit to use. The boat now finished, they cut a few pieces of the *ite* palm and force them in as seats.

The great advantage the canoe has over the dugout is that being flat, it can float where even the smallest dugout is completely useless, and that one man can, without great effort, carry his boat on his head in crossing the cataracts.

In size, the dugouts varied far less than the canoes. The average for the former was, in the old days, probably 30 to 35 feet in length; 1 foot, 9 inches in width, and 1 foot, 2 inches in depth, whereas the latter is known to have varied from 30 to 14 feet in length.

The boats have other difficulties to face besides the problem of seaworthiness. The small streams, for instance, are often obstructed by debris of various kinds and by logs lying across their surfaces. Often it is impossible to remove such a log, and it has to be crossed, and to permit this the Arawak and other tribes resort to a very simple and ingenious method. Pieces of bark are stripped from a tree called the kara-kara. The inner surface of this bark happens to contain a kind of viscous slime. This bark with the slimy side up is then placed upon the log, and the boat is drawn over it much in the same way as a sled glides over the snow.

But logs in a stream do not constitute the only problem. Another one encountered again and again in a country where rapids and falls are frequent is that of safely ascending them. One example of how these difficulties are surmounted must suffice. The rapids do not, in many instances, fall in one sheet over a level edge. Instead they force themselves through a number of fissures, the different shoots of the fall being divided by large intermediate blocks of granite. An eddy is formed at the base of these blocks, and the canoe forced into it. Thus it becomes stationary, for there is no current either way. The crew of the boat now spring upon the rock and wade up as far as they can find footing. By the use of a long and strong rope the canoe is then hauled into one of the shoots of the fall where there is enough water to float it. After it has been pulled up the ascent it is taken out of the current and its stern laid against the top of the rock from whose bottom the men have just mounted, the head of the boat right up the stream. This is the point where the greatest danger of failure exists. The men must all jump into the boat together and pull with all the strength they possess, so as to cross the different currents diagonally until they get into another eddy.

Still other problems arise when the weather is stormy, particularly on such large rivers as the Orinoco. To navigate the great river on such occasions, two dugouts are used, placed a short distance apart but joined by strong timbers fixed across stem, center and stern. The Arawak, like good boatsmen, were apparently prepared for every emergency. "There is no such thing as shipwreck on the coast ever heard of," states an older writer. "If swamped, the occupants jump overboard, where with one hand, they hang on to the canoe, and with the other, and a calabash, they bail out the water."[8]

Yet excellent as was their seamanship, quick and ingenious as they showed themselves in coping with new situations on river and stream, they would soon have been swallowed up by the inimical jungle and forest and have lost most of their identity had they not possessed one great asset: agriculture and a settled mode of life. How important they must have felt this to be in the struggle to maintain their cultural integrity one fact alone demonstrates. Never, in their far-flung travels, did they give it up. Much of what was specifically theirs they had at times perforce to surrender. Even so vital a factor in their culture as the boat was lost in the more remote corners of this new world, and much of their language itself. But never maize. This always remains the specific trait that informs us that we are still in the area of Arawak culture when all the other outlines of their ancient island tradition are blurred and when they have become otherwise indistinguishable from their neighbors.

This retention of maize as a main food staple is all the more significant when the richness of the available food supply from other sources is remembered. Manioc, both the bitter and sweet variety, was unquestionably known in the Orinoco area before the Arawak reached it. With the bitter variety they had, in fact, been well-acquainted in the Antilles. Nor were the conditions for maize-growing self-imposed by nature. The land had to be cleared and the ground prepared for planting; the crops had to be protected against enemies, animal as well as human; some provision had to be made for storing the maize. Then there were the accessories and accompaniments of such an economy—the division of labor and the discipline involved therein, the settled mode of life, the type of house, and the nature of the household.

Assuredly this was the hard way to begin the penetration of a new country. To have attempted it and to have achieved the success the Arawak manifestly did meant that they must have arrived fully equipped and prepared for conquest. Possibly they may have, at first, entered with other intent, but only by imposing their control over others could they have maintained so much of their own specific culture intact. This did not necessarily signify that it was always imposed by force. Yet this seems generally to have been the case, to judge by the fact that, in so many instances, non-Arawak-speaking people were often found in definite subjection to an Arawak-speaking caste of apparent overlords. It is, of course, true that the tribes encountered had a much simpler culture than the Arawak invaders, although some of them must have known the cultivation of the bitter manioc, and it is true that the conquest was not so difficult as might have been supposed. Nor did it require a great length of time.

The Arawak thus appear in a new role in South America. From being harassed, displaced, and even reduced to slavery by the Carib, as they were rapidly becoming in the Antilles, they became in their turn the harassers, the conquerors, the enslavers. Instead of an Arawak dialect being confined to Carib women and Carib slaves, the wheel of fate had made a complete revolution. Now the languages of other people were to play that role in relation to Arawak. Here in South America the

Arawak were to meet their ancient foes and terrorizers, the Carib, again, but this time the Carib were to succumb. Culturally the latter were to become almost entirely dependent upon the former. In some cases, indeed, they were to be completely absorbed.

To be the pioneers of a new type of civilization implies, however, more than the simple giving and imposition of a culture. It also signifies a willingness to take from those whom you conquer, whether forcibly or peaceably, as well as the experience and ability to integrate what has been so taken with an old cultural core. At this the Island Arawak were past masters for, as we saw, their culture was a most eclectic, although, at the same time, a remarkably unified, one.

The older aspects of Arawak civilization we have already dwelt upon. Let us now turn to the new ones, those that are specifically South American—their type of house, the blowgun, the use of narcotics and poisons, the cultivation of the manioc, and certain special customs and beliefs.

Although the Arawak admittedly brought with them both rectangular houses and the custom of constructing palisades around them, both customs were apparently abandoned within a short period of time and the typical South American house types adopted. The number of types was quite considerable, some used as temporary, others as permanent, shelters. We shall concern ourselves only with the permanent structures, for they represent a specific achievement of the aboriginal populations of the southern continent.

There are two main types, one circular, the other elliptical. The second is clearly a development of the first, and only the first need be described. This will be done in terms of the Indians of north-central British Guiana, a land inhabited at the time of the discovery of South America prevailingly by Arawak and Carib tribes and a few remnants of the older inhabitants whom they had displaced. But let us turn to the house types.

A typical circular house is constructed in the following manner: First, a post is inserted in the center of the prepared ground. This is the basic element of the structure to be erected, for from it are measured the exact distances to spots where the side framing posts are to be placed. These must be fixed at equal distances from the center post and from one another. A circular plate, made of vine rope, wattle, or other such material, is then raised to the tops of the side framing posts, which have been notched to receive it. This plate is now tied on with vine rope. It is next supported by other and thinner posts, except in front and in back, where a pair each is attached to form the framework of the doors. A crosstree is then lashed on at the top. The crosstree is made up of four logs running from the outer circle of the framing posts, at an angle of forty-five degrees, to a higher point on the center post. Later when the thatching is applied, this portion of the main post above the crosstree will remain exposed. Four pairs of rafters are now placed in position with their thicker ends tied to the plate below. As a result, the thinner, tapering extremities can be conveniently tied to the outsides of each corresponding pair of crosslogs. These tied joints are further strengthened with purlins. A second set of purlins is then attached to the rafters about halfway between crosstree and plate. The tie beams and the collar ties of wattle are now put in place. The walls and doors are tied on subsequently.

Such houses often had very large dimensions. The well-known English ethnologist, Roth, saw one that measured fifty feet in circumference and was between sixty-five and seventy feet high.

More specifically South American than even these elaborate houses, however, is the famous blowgun. Although found among the tribes of southeastern United States, it is clearly an intrusion there. It seems to have been known in the Antilles but apparently was not very common. Everything we know points to its being primarily a possession of the Indians living in the area of the Orinoco and the western affluents of the Amazon. To what particular tribes its invention is to be ascribed will, however, always remain uncertain. The Arawak and Carib may have perfected it, but they did not invent it.

So peculiar a weapon naturally excites interest and curiosity as to its ultimate origin, especially when there are few other places in the world where its analogue exists. Many theories have consequently been developed concerning it. According to one school of ethnologists the similarity of the South American to the Malayan blowgun is so marked that its independent invention in America is unthinkable; according to another school the differences in the construction of the two are so great and the conditions for its independent origin in South America so propitious that no justification exists for connecting the two historically.

Far more is involved here than a mere quarrel of specialists over what might appear to the laymen to be unimportant details. The same question will arise again in connection with other South American culture traits—the panpipe, the signal drums, the bull-roarer, the men's house, certain initiation rites and masked dances, and even certain specific traits of social organization, not to mention a significant number of mythical themes and motifs. However, we must postpone that discussion to Chapter VI, where it properly belongs.

Let us return to the blowgun. Three principal types are found: those built up of two complete tubes, one within the other; those with an inner tube encased in another made of two split halves; and those consisting of a single tube composed of two split halves. A vast variety of reeds is used.

An old traveler quoted by Roth gives a fairly detailed description of how the first type was made, which runs as follows: A reed called the *ourah* is selected because it grows hollow and has no knot or joint along its whole length. Since by itself it is too slender to serve as a blowgun, a species of palma, larger and stronger than the ourah is used as a case. Into this the ourah is inserted. The palma reed just mentioned has joints five to six inches from each other and the pulp inside is easily extracted by steeping it in water for a few days. The end which is applied to the mouth is tied around with a small silk-grass cord to prevent it from splitting. The other end, which is apt to strike against the ground, is firmly secured by means of a fruit called *acuero*. This fruit is first cut horizontally through the middle and a hole is made in the end. Through this the extremity of the blowgun is forced. About two feet from the end through which the native blows, two teeth of the *acouri* are fastened, and these serve him as a sight.

The third type of blowgun is used in the upper Amazon and is far more difficult to make. It is generally nine or ten feet long and consists of two separate lengths of wood, each scooped out so as to form half of the tube. An enormous amount of patient labor and considerable mechanical ability is required to do this with the necessary accuracy, especially when it is recalled that the only tools the Indian possesses are the incisor teeth of animals. When finished, the two half tubes are firmly secured by means of a very close and tight spirally wound strapping, consisting of long, flat strips of the wood of the climbing palm tree. The whole is then smeared with black wax obtained from a Meligona bee. The blowgun tapers toward the muzzle, and at the broad end a cup-shaped mouthpiece is fitted in. The blowgun used by a mature man is heavy and requires great practice for its effective use. Young boys employ smaller and lighter ones.

Generally the blowgun arrow is nine to ten inches long and is made from the leaf of a species of hard and brittle palm called in British Guiana *coucourite*. It is pointed as sharp as a needle, about an inch of the pointed end being poisoned. The other end is burned to make it still harder, and wild cotton placed around it for about an inch and a half. Considerable practice is necessary to put this cotton on well, for it must be just large enough to fit the hollow of the tube and it must taper off to nothing.

The poison employed differs among the various tribes, but that called *curare* is perhaps the best known. Two famous names are connected with its history, Sir Walter Raleigh and Alexander von Humboldt. Many fantastic tales were associated at first with its manufacture. It was, for instance, described as being derived from the fangs of the most dangerous snakes and ants, and there were stories that only old women were employed in making it and that they regularly died from the effects of the vapor arising out of the pots. Actually, however, its preparation is attended with no danger whatsoever. The Dutch traveler, Schomburgk, who witnessed its manufacture, relates a whole series of customs that must be observed. A new house must be constructed, new pots must be used, a special fire made, and no assistance of any kind permitted. The man preparing it must fast before and after. No woman, especially no pregnant woman, must come near the house while it is being cooked, nor must anyone watching the process eat sugar in any form.

To apply the poison, the end of the arrow or dart is dipped into it a number of times, depending upon the strength desired, and this, in turn, will depend upon the objective in view. Where, for instance, the Indians wish merely to stupefy an animal temporarily, as in. the case of the toucan, whose feathers the Guiana Indians use for cloaks, a weak concoction will be used. The animal, it. is hoped, will then recover. Its feathers can then be plucked again.

The blowgun is used specifically for shooting animals, mainly birds. When the user is about to blow into it to expel the poisoned dart, a small piece of cotton is lightly inserted in one end of the tube. The arrow or dart is then dropped in at the other end and falls down to the cotton.

Curare is, of course, only one of many poisons employed by these very ingenious hunters and. fishermen. The number seems to be legion. In fact the whole region of the upper Amazon was already known in early times as the "River of Poisons." An early source reported a poison bamboo for killing alligators. Tapirs, likewise, were killed by arrows made from a bamboo possessing particularly virulent qualities. The poison rubbed on arrows used in warfare among the Carib seems primarily to have been obtained from the juice of a tree called *manceniller* or the milk of *ficus venenata.*

The next of the definitely South American constituents in Arawak culture was the manioc, from the roots of which cassava is made. We know it in the form of tapioca. The Arawak had, of course, already known it in the Antilles, but there it was more specifically a crop cultivated by the Carib invaders, who must have brought it from the mainland.

In its preparation the women take a conspicuous part, in definite contrast to their role in the cultivation of maize, where the men do all the work.

To plant the cassava stem, the soil is first loosened and then heaped up in the form of a small mound, long pointed sticks being used for the digging. It is customary to insert two slips of approximately twenty inches in length in the ground, to allow for the failure of one of them to take root and mature. Nine months to two years are required for the crop to ripen. The same field can at times be replanted, but this depends entirely upon two factors: the nature of the soil, and the depredations of certain ants. There were certain regions where the cassava was propagated by seed, but this practice was not.followed in the Orinoco drainage.

Of the two varieties—the sweet and the bitter—which the Arawak cultivates, it is only from the latter that they make the meal for their bread. To extract the poisonous juice, a very ingenious method has been perfected. After the root has been peeled—the old method was to use the teeth—it is grated and placed in a squeezer, which presses out the poisonous substance. The residuum is then removed and dried. There are tribes, however, that do not even make use of the squeezer but force out the juice by hand pressure through a circular sifter supported on a triangular frame. This is then collected in a receptacle below. As we shall see, the extracted poisonous juice as well as the residuum is used.

The residuum, as soon as it has dried, is pounded up in a mortar, passed through a sifter, and placed in a circular clay grid where, over a hot fire, it is made either into thin cakes or into what is called in Portuguese *farinha*. This latter is made by constantly stirring it up so that it cannot form into an entire cake but assumes the form of an accumulation of small dry crumbs of wheaten bread.

Out of the extracted poisonous juice a sauce is prepared by allowing its starch sediment to settle. The water is then carefully poured off. Peppers are then added and the whole allowed to boil for approximately three hours, by which time it has become thickened and is ready for use.

Yet not only material things did the island Arawak add or secondarily elaborate in their new home. Social customs too

were adopted. And of these new social customs, assuredly none
is more strange and unusual than the well-known couvade, the
"lying-in" of the father which takes place upon the birth of
a child. Perhaps the laymen will be astonished to know that a
similar custom prevailed among the Basques as late as the eighteenth century, that it is mentioned and described in a famous
medieval French romance *Aucassin and Nicolette,* and that it is
still practiced among the Albanians. There not only does the
husband lie in bed like a woman in confinement when his wife
has been delivered of a child, but a special term is used to desig-
nate such a person.

As in the case of the blowgun and the cultivation of the cassava plant, all the facts at our disposal indicate that here too the
Carib were probably the intermediaries of this custom to the
Arawak and that the latter themselves obtained it from the more
primitive tribes of northwestern and central Brazil. The custom
itself is among the oldest possessions of the American Indians
and seems to crop out everywhere. It is known to the *Wappo*
Indians near San Francisco, California, and is found in Tierra del
Fuego among the *Yahgan* and *Ona.*

Among the Arawak of British Guiana, then, it is not the wife
but the husband who is really isolated at the birth of a child.
Of the many descriptions of the couvade given, one of the best
is that by the Dutch traveler Pinard. Although it refers to the
Surinam Carib specifically, it holds with few changes for the
Arawak. His account follows:[9]

On the return of the mother and baby from the forest where she
has just been confined, back to the house to resume her household
duties, the father takes to his hammock to be pampered. This takes
place on the supposition that the infant's body proceeds from the
mother, but the spirit, on the contrary, from the father, and that a
mysterious connection binds the child's spirit to the father's for
some weeks after birth. With newly born children the middle of
the skull is very soft and pulsates with the respiration of the heart.
In prematurely born children the attachments are even open, which
perhaps has given cause for the supposition that the child before
birth is nourished not through the navel-string but through the skull,

and that its spirit penetrates through a little hole in the skull into its brains. As long as this spot is not hardened, it is believed that the little spirit is not yet entirely freed from that of the father.

Thus it was supposed the life of the child depended entirely upon that of the father.

He was also forbidden to undertake any heavy work or to hunt, because his arrow might strike the little infant. If he climbed over a tree-trunk he always placed two little sticks as a sort of bridge for the child's little spirit that always followed him. If he crossed a river or creek, a calabash or fruit shell then served to facilitate the passage across of the child. He everywhere trod cautiously and carefully around, avoiding thorny places. And if he by chance met a jaguar he did not speed away, but courageously advanced on the beast. Verily his child's life depended on it.

The little spirit nevertheless could get a fright and lose its way in the forest. Even at night the father had to take care to save his child pain. However badly something bit him, he must scratch very carefully, because his nails could harm the infant. And woe to him if he forgot himself and attempted, in too rough a fashion, to get rid of a louse that was worrying him, because the bare head of his little darling suffered for it.

There were likewise various foods that the father was forbidden to eat out of fear of hurting the child. . . . If the child, in spite of all the father's care, took sick, the latter then visited the *piai* (medicine man), who by calling upon the spirits in the usual fashion, speedily recognized the cause (generally a stranger) of the trouble. If the cause was not due to the snake spirit, the father was advised to make certain incisions on his breast and arms. Mixed with water, the infant was then given the blood to drink; or the evil spirit was, with the help of certain ants, bidden out of the child's body, or charmed away with *tu la la* . . .

The actual "lying-in" of the husband lasts as long as that of the mother, about a week. Among the island Carib it lasted ten to twelve days and the man had to subsist on a little cassava and water. He was permitted only to eat the insides of the cassava cakes. What was even more onerous, however, was the fact that he had often, for a period as long as a year, to abstain from such meats as manatee, turtle, hog, and fish. Such extreme abstention, however, only took place after the birth of the first male child. Finally, when the fasting period was to terminate, the father had to submit to a scarification upon his shoulders. Under no circumstances must he emit the slightest sound while this operation was taking place. The more stolidly he bore his pain, the more valiant would his son prove. The blood that flowed from the wounds was not allowed to fall on the ground but was caught and smeared on the infant's face to make it courageous.

The last of the new culture elements the Arawak were destined to absorb and make their own in their South American home was the belief in the bush spirits so widespread throughout the southern continent and many of whose characteristics are quite foreign to the tribes of North America. In this particular case the invaders paid heavily. So completely did these new animistic and religious beliefs take possession of them that little remained of the cemis, little indeed of the higher aspects of the role of the medicine men. In fact it is impossible to distinguish between the beliefs of the Arawak and the other tribes with whom they are associated. This holds particularly of the Carib and the numerous tribes linguistically independent of either of these two major groups. For that reason it seems best to postpone their description to the chapter on the Carib, to whom they more properly belong. A few examples from the Arawak will, however, be given, to illustrate the role these bush spirits play.

According to the generally accepted belief of all the Indians of the Orinoco, the Rio Negro, the western Amazon, and adjacent areas, these bush spirits emanate from the human corpse and find their ultimate resting place in forest and bush, particularly in trees. The ideas held as to the form, shape, and peculiarities of these spirits naturally vary from tribe to tribe. Among the Arawak of British Guiana most of them are supposed to have so much hair that their faces cannot be seen. Their dwellings are underground in the forest. They may be men or women and can be encountered at any time without warning, although they are often accustomed to give a premonitory sign of their approach. The following three short stories give some idea of the nature of their association with human beings.[10]

1

THE MAN WHO ALWAYS HUNTED SCRUB-TURKEY

There was a man celebrated for his skill in hunting *maam;* he would regularly bring home four or five of these scrub-turkeys, and people warned him that if he continued in this way he would get into trouble with the maam's "mother" (i.e., Spirit), for killing so many of her brood. But he did not care, and went on destroying the birds in the same wasteful manner. On one occasion he stayed out later than usual, waiting to see on which particular trees the maams were going to roost. He could hear their peculiar call in all directions around; indeed, the birds were so plentiful about, that he was somewhat at a loss to know which particular one to follow. However, he proceeded to track one, but the farther he went, the farther off sounded the note, until at last he found himself deep in the forest. As night was beginning to fall, he had to hurry home, not daring to remain out in the dark for fear of the *Yawahu* (Spirit of the Bush) catching him.

The same thing happened next day; he heard many birds calling, and, following one, again found himself deep in the forest, but this time he succeeded finally in coming up with the quarry. Locating the tree, he peered in among the branches to see where the bird was "hollo"-ing, but could see only a woman's leg. Recognizing this to be the Arch Spirit of the maams, he took careful aim, and shot an arrow right into the center of the foot. The leg fell down, and directly it touched ground, changed into an extraordinarily big scrub-turkey, which he immediately killed and carried home. There his friends knew it at once to be the maam's "mother" (Spirit), and advised him to cook and eat the whole of it himself, and not give away even the smallest particle of it. He did what was advised, and in subsequently hunting for maam he was invariably even more successful than before. And now that he had destroyed the maam-Spirit, he was not afraid of killing as many birds as he liked.

2

THE SPIRIT'S BRAIN AND THE GOAT-SUCKER

A man went out hunting for land crab, and was waiting for the rain to fall, because it is only under this condition that the animal creeps out of its hole into the swamps. Now, when the rain fell, it wet his hair. To protect himself, the huntsman, using his calabash, like a cap, pressed it firmly down upon his head, so that but a little of the hair projected from beneath its circumference. Just then a *Konoko-kuyuha* put in an appearance, and seeing the man in this guise, and not knowing what it was, could not help exclaiming, "What a fine smooth head you have! How did you manage to get it?" The man told him that he had just taken a knife and cut his head all the way round, and that if he wished he would gladly do the same for him. The Spirit was delighted, and allowed the skin all round his head to be cut, and peppers to be rubbed over the raw surface to make it heal the quicker. The latter process, however, caused him to groan in pain, but by this time the huntsman had quietly slipped out of sight.

A long time afterward, many years in fact, the same man, going out into the bush close to the neighborhood where the above event had occurred, met the same Konoko-kuyuha, whom he recognized by the peppers on his head, which had grown into big bushes. The recognition was mutual, and the Spirit reproached him after this manner: "You are the man who peeled off my head. I will kill you." But the man replied: "No. You are mistaken. The person who really did it has been dead a long time. Come with me and I will show you his bones." And he led him to a place where there was a stack of deer bones. These the Spirit took up and threw one by one into his *waiyarri*. He then said to the man, "Let us dance, and make his bones rattle." Whereupon they both started dancing, and while dancing they sang. The song of the Spirit was "*Bassana! Bassana!* It was you that peeled my head. It was you that punished me. How do you like to hear your own bones rattling for music?"

After a time, the man remarked, "This is not a good place to dance. Come over there where I can see a fine flat baking-stone that will suit better." So they shifted their quarters, and the Spirit recommenced dancing on the flat stone. "Bend your head lower," said the man, "you are not doing the figure properly." So the Spirit bent his head lower, but his companion told him that even this was not low enough; so he tried again, and directly he had bent his head quite close to the stone upon which he was dancing, the man suddenly crushed it thereon.

The Spirit's brains thus were scattered, and from each piece there "grew" a *wokorai-yu* (goat-sucker). This is why we Indians always dread these birds, and leave them severely alone; they come from the Spirits of the Bush, and give us warning of evil—a token that we may expect trouble of various sorts.

3
THE KILLING OF THE BUSH SPIRIT AND HIS WIFE

This is another story about a man who went out hunting one day and took his wife with him. But when he left her as usual one morning at the *banab*, he did not know anything about a Bush Spirit in the neighborhood and hence could give her no warning as to how she should behave herself. At any rate, it was not long after her husband had taken his departure that a Konoko-kuyuha came to the house and asked her how she fared and where her man had gone. She told him that he had gone out hunting and that she did not expect him until late in the afternoon. The Spirit went away but not before mentioning that she might see him again in the course of the evening. You see, he was greedy and thought it would be less trouble to kill and eat them both at one and the same time.

Now, when the husband did return, she told him that a Something had been to see her, and that It intended coming again that very night. "You are not speaking the truth," was all the thanks she got for the warning which she gave him and after eating his meal, he turned into his hammock where he soon fell asleep and snored heavily. By and by the Konoko-kuyuha came along, giving warning of his approach in the usual way we Indians always signal when we approach a dwelling, that is, by striking a few times on the buttresses of the trees. The wife heard the noise, and recognizing what it was, tried to wake her husband, but was unsuccessful. He slept too soundly. She quickly hid herself. Once in the banab, the Bush Spirit approached the sleeping man's hammock, and tried to wake him. Failing in this, he broke his neck, drank his blood, and left him dead. The Spirit then wandered all over the place looking for his wife, but could not find her. She, however, could hear him saying, "If I had known that she intended giving me the slip, I would have finished her off this morning." She saw him leave the banab and go back into the bush, but she remained in her hiding-place until the dawn when, after burying the body, she ran back home and told her brother all that had taken place, and that she was now a widow. The brother was exceedingly angry, and determined upon killing the Spirit.

Next day, he went with his sister to the same banab where the late tragedy had taken place, and the following morning left her by herself there, just as his poor brother-in-law had done, but instructed her to fool the Konoko-kuyuha, should he come, by telling him that her husband was still alive and that he would be glad to see him in the evening. The Spirit did appear again, and was certainly surprised to see her there. He asked her as before, how she fared, and where her man had gone. She told him that he had gone out hunting, that she did not expect him until late in the afternoon, and, if he liked to pay them a visit in the evening, that her husband would be very pleased indeed to see him. The Spirit was only too glad to have the opportunity and promised to come. In his mind, he said that if he broke the man's neck-bone this time, he would make sure of killing him, and then deal with the wife. As had been previously arranged, the brother returned to the banab soon after midday, and made a special arrow while his sister did the cooking.

After partaking of the food, he instructed her how to tempt the Spirit into having a dance with her, and at the same time showed her how to hold his hands, and not to embrace him too closely, so that when he let fly this special arrow it might not, by any chance, strike her. He then went and hid himself.

By and by, just as the darkness began to fall, the Konoko-kuyuha walked up, and asked her where her husband was. After telling him that he had not yet returned, she obtruded the glory of all her charms and asked him to dance with her. The Spirit, yielding to her temptations, only too readily agreed. They began to caper, and holding him as she had been warned, she circled him round and round, closer and closer to where her brother lay ambushed. It was not long before the latter was able to take good aim, and, letting fly the special arrow, sent it right through the wicked Spirit who fell mortally wounded. Before dying, however, Konoko-kuyuha looked reproachfully at the woman and said, "I did nothing to you, to make you wish to kill me." But when her reply came, "No, indeed, but you wanted to," he closed his eyes. How glad the brother and sister were! And the brother said, "We had better tarry awhile, because Konoko-kuyuha's wife will come and look for him." Sure enough, they soon heard the moaning of the Spirit's wife as she came along crying, and saying, "I must get payment for my husband" (i.e., her husband's death must be avenged). So they both hid themselves, and as the Spirit woman passed along, the brother shot her also, and cut up the bodies. When they both got home, they told their friends and relatives about all that had happened, and everybody was delighted. . . .

All such stories belong to the new home of the Arawak. There is no indication of their ever having existed in the Antilles or in North America.

The higher orders of priests so characteristic of the Arawak apparently never reached the Orinoco. Their absence is not so strange when it is remembered that they were closely bound up with the ceremonies connected with the more elaborate of the cemis and, as we have pointed out, no cemis, elaborate or otherwise, are found anywhere among the continental Arawak. The functions of the ordinary Arawak medicine man did not change much in the transfer from the islands to the South American mainland. But apparently they differed after all little from those of other tribes.

Now, it may justifiably be asked, if so much of the original Arawak culture was lost, how are we to explain the fact that they retained, at all times, their distinctive social organization, their agriculture, and their language?

The answer is comparatively easy. Their conquests and displacements were over simple peoples, be it in the region of the Orinoco, the western Amazon, or the southern Xingu. Where they came in contact with more complex cultures, like the *Chiriguano* of Bolivia, they could impose little and indeed almost lost most of their identity. Even the Carib, who had probably originally borrowed so much from them, were able, after they had assimilated these elements, to turn on them and practically drive them out of many of their island possessions. The same lack of resistance held true in an even more catastrophic degree when they encountered the Europeans.

Yet in spite of all these weaknesses, their role of culture-bringers to an area of tremendous extent in South America is in no way diminished, nor can their cultural virility be questioned. Even more important than all this, however, is the seemingly indubitable fact that they represent the link between the two continents, the north and the south, and that, even more, they have, in an indirect manner, brought to the Orinoco influences from the Mexico of the twelfth to fourteenth centuries.

With the struggle of the Arawak and the Carib we began. With that struggle we can well end, and so I shall give the account of an Arawak from the Pomeroon district in British Guiana, the account of how his people had worsted the traditional enemy:[11]

An Arawak and a Carib were very friendly. This must needs be so, because each had taken the other's sister to wife. They regularly used to go hunting together. After living in harmony for a long time, they went out hunting, but on this occasion, they did not go in company, and they both stayed away longer than usual, and their friends were beginning to wonder what had happened to them. The Arawak, having finally returned, went to see after his brother-in-law, followed his tracks into the bush, and came on the *babracote* upon which he found the dried body of his sister whom her husband had evidently killed. He went home, but did not speak for some time. He then told his wife, the Carib's sister, to come into the bush and hunt with him: when he got her away, the Carib's sister, he killed and *babracoted* her. The Carib next came along to see what had happened, and he soon saw. He also went home again, but did not speak for some time. Finally, he expressed a wish to fight and kill the Arawak, but the *Nafudi* said, "No. All the Caribs together must fight the Arawaks together." So both sides cut a big field and planted plenty of the particular canes required for making arrows, and when these canes were full grown, they cut them down and completed their weapons, and both sides erected a strong house, *Waiba*, to store them in.

Up at Jack Low, on the left bank of the Pomeroon, is still to be recognized the site of the old settlement and fortress, the place itself even to this day being known as *Waiba-diki*.

Furthermore, it was arranged by both parties that as they intended fighting their battle at sea, and not on land, they would allow themselves time to build a large number of canoes. This being done, they filled their boats with arrows: twenty canoes were paddled by Arawaks, and forty by Caribs. They all went down the river, out to sea, at the Pomeroon mouth, each taking up such position as

Typical Baniva House from the Upper Amazon

would permit of the intervening distance being just sufficient to allow of the arrows thrown from one side reaching the other. The Arawaks, however, were shrewd. They made themselves corkwood shields. The Caribs let fly their arrows first, but these stuck in the shields, when the Arawaks broke them off with their *mossi* (the now almost obsolete club).

None of the Arawaks were slain, and it was now their turn to shoot. This they did, with the result that they killed all their enemy, except two, whom they purposely spared in order that they might go home and tell their friends what had happened, and what to expect should they ever dare to fight the Arawaks again.

The two who had been spared went away to the Cuyuni, to the Barima, and to the Waini, and remained three months gathering together all their people, who clamored that they would never rest until they had destroyed all the Arawaks. The Arawaks were waiting for them at Waiba-diki, their stronghold, and stretched a vine-rope across the river; and as the hosts of Caribs approached up the stream, the steering paddles of their canoes became entangled in this rope, and broke away; and while the occupants were looking after them, their canoes all tossed one against the other in dire confusion, and the Arawaks shot showers of arrows into the wavering multitude. Half the Caribs were destroyed; the other half effected a landing. But around their fortress, the Arawaks had already built a palisade, with just a few chinks in it to permit of arrows flying through; they were all well under cover, and though losing a few of their own people, massacred as before all their enemy, leaving but two to give the news to their friends. These two went to the east, to Surinam, and started collecting the remnants of their own tribe from those parts.

About three months passed. The Arawaks could wait no longer, so they traveled over to Surinam, and came upon the Carib forces collected in a fortress with enclosing palisade, similar to what they themselves had constructed for their own preservation at Waiba-diki. The Caribs were in overwhelming numbers. So the Arawaks hid themselves, and sent in one of their number to reconnoitre. This man, who could talk Carib, painted himself like one of that nation, and boldly entered the enemy's camp, where he found them all drinking. He said he was a Carib, and that he had just come from the Pomeroon looking for his family. He accepted a little drink and then took his departure, but not before discovering that very early on the following morning, long before daybreak, a crab whistle (i.e., made from a crab claw) would be blown as a signal for them to prepare for battle.

The scout returned to his people, with all the information that he had gleaned. That night, every one of the Arawaks made a crab whistle, and surrounding the Caribs while they were still drinking, blew their whistles, surprising the enemy, and slew them all, save one man and woman, who begged so earnestly for their lives that only their legs were speared. It is from this couple that all the present day Caribs are derived, and this is why there are comparatively so few of them. It was we Arawaks who broke their power.

CHAPTER IV

Cannibals and Adventurers

THE CARIB

CARIBS AND CANNIBALS! IT IS ONE AND THE SAME word. Yet these people meant more to the Europeans than as exponents of the gentle art of eating one's fellow men. We remember them in many other ways, less gruesome and more positive. We have incorporated their name into our geography, and some of their inventions—at least we obtained them from these Carib-cannibals—are part and parcel of our daily life: the hammock, the canoe. No sea perpetuates the memory of the gentle, hospitable, and cultured Arawak. But the man-eating Carib appealed to the European imagination, both to the northern and the southern. Possibly the Spaniards, the simple sailors and the more pretentious *conquistadores*, recognized the similarity between themselves and these naked aborigines. Both were daring individualists, both quixotic adventurers and colonists. And they were amazingly alike in the methods employed: terror, enslavement, death. The only new element the Carib added was anthropophagy. Yet the Carib had not always been adventurers, cannibals, and colonists. This belongs to the latest stage in their evolution. In attempting to characterize their culture and ferret out their origins, customs, and beliefs belonging to a stratum of the aboriginal history of South America much earlier than that of the Arawak will be revealed to us.

Columbus first encountered the Carib in the Antilles, but they were intruders and newcomers there. For that fact there were still extant traditions among the Arawak in 1492. Their incursions into the islands of the sea now named for them must, however, have begun early, although not until they had been thoroughly saturated with Arawak culture did their depredations take on a serious character. Yet at no time was their culture essentially anything else but South American. It is consequently in South America that we must look for their ancient home. But where? Here the distribution of Carib-speaking tribes in South America gives us some clue, some indication.

The area they inhabited was far more circumscribed than was that of the Arawak. A not inconsiderable part of it lay in a region into which the Arawak had never penetrated or where their penetration had been very partial and very late, between the rivers Xingu and Tapajos. There are ample reasons for believing that the Carib themselves have not been in the southern parts of this region very long, but clearly they considerably antedated the Arawak. Nor are the Carib to be found along the western affluents of the Amazon where the Arawak had penetrated in considerable force. Their older habitat must thus be pushed northward, to the area north of the Amazon and to the Guianas. Whether this was their original home may be left open to question, but they must have lived there long. It is certainly that section of South America where they evolved whatever was distinctive in their culture.

The language of the Carib is quite distinct from that of the other two linguistic stocks, the Arawak and the Tupi-Guarani, that have swept over so large an area of South America. For the possible relationship of the latter two there is some suggestion. But the Carib language definitely does not belong with them. Now the region of the upper Amazon swarms with peoples speaking unrelated languages, and we can assume this to be the hearth from which the Carib ultimately came. A number of their traits, particularly their social organization, point in this direction. It will be well worth while then to keep this in mind.

Although the only Carib tribes who have been studied in any

detail are those of the Guianas, we shall begin with those found in the Antilles, for that is where South America properly starts.

The Carib of the West Indies differed from the Arawak in one of the basic characteristics of the latter's social structure—namely, the complete absence of a graded society and of an inherited chieftainship. Only in time of war did a chieftain have any considerable power. In short, he differed little from the generality of chiefs throughout northern South America. At times, however, heads of families were given special position and accorded the title of chief of a *carbet*, the carbet being a community house without which no Carib village was thinkable. In contradistinction to the community house of the island Arawak, it contained no idols and was never used as the residence of the chief.

Such a carbet and its surrounding was described as existing as late as the year 1696 on the island of Martinique. It was sixty-four feet long and about twenty-four wide. "The posts on which it was erected," says William Sheldon,[12] quoting from this older source, "were rough, forked, and the shortest of them about nine feet above ground—the others were proportioned to the height of the roof. The windward end was inclosed with a kind of wicker work, of split flags; the roof was covered with the leaves of the wild plantain, which are very large, and much stronger than the leaves of the plantain which bears fruit. The laths were made of reeds. That end of the carbet which was covered had an opening or doorway for a passage to the kitchen; the other end was nearly all open. Ten paces from the great carbet was another building, about half the size of the large one, which was divided by a reed partition. The first room served for a kitchen where six or eight females were assembled and employed in making cassaba. The second room served the women and such of the children as were not admitted into the great carbet, to sleep in. All the rooms were furnished with hammocks and baskets. The men had their arms in their rooms. Some of the men were making baskets—two women were making a hammock."

The foregoing facts show the extent to which these island

Carib, even under the most unfavorable conditions, still ad-
hered to their old manner of life whether in an Arawak or a
French colonial surrounding. And this indeed was to remain
one of their salient traits. All the more remarkable consequently
must the impact of Arawak culture have been upon them if it
could impose both the matrilineal clans and agriculture upon
these stubborn marauders.

In most parts of British Guiana, which had certainly been their
home for many hundreds of years before the Arawak arrived
there, the Carib likewise succumbed to the influence of these
hereditary enemies in the matter of clan organization and the use
of maize. Yet the hold of these two elements so essentially alien
to their culture was tenuous, and among the tribes along the
Barima River, in western British Guiana, there is no indication
of them. What is it, however, that these Barima Carib possess
in common with their kindred to the east? An enumeration of
these possessions is quite illuminating. It includes the intensive
cultivation of the bitter cassava, the hammock, simple pottery,
basketry, the imbibing of tobacco juice by the medicine man,
the couvade, elaborate methods of taking revenge, a highly
systematized magical apparatus, a belief in numerous spirits in-
hering in all objects and infesting every nook and corner of
nature and, lastly, the high position assigned the priest or medicine man. There is no blowgun and there is little cannibalism.

These are all old possessions of the Carib. They are also old
possessions of the whole area watered by the Amazon and its
affluents. Indeed the Carib have no tradition of their having been
without them. They have, apparently, been theirs from time
immemorial. The origin of cassava, for instance, is ascribed to
a bird called *Bunia* and the story of how they obtained it is
worth repeating:[13]

Time was when the Indians had no cassava to eat; they all starved.
Animals and birds also had nothing to eat; they likewise starved. It
was the *Maipuri* alone who, going out regularly every morning and
returning home of an evening, always appeared sleek and fat. The
others, noticing his droppings—banana-skins, cane strips, etc., talked
to one another after this manner: "Maipuri must have found a good

place to get food. Let us watch him." So next morning they sent the bush-rat to dog his footsteps, and find out how he managed to keep in such good condition. The bush-rat did what he was told and followed Maipuri a long, long way into the bush, when he saw him pause under the shade of an immense tree and gather the fruit that had fallen. This tree was the *allepantepo*, and very wonderful, in that everything you could wish for grew upon its branches—plantains, cassava, yams, plums, pines, and all the other fruits that Caribs love.

As soon as Maipuri had had his fill the bush-rat climbed the tree, and picked upon the corn to satisfy his hunger; when he could eat no more, he came down and brought with him a grain in order to show the others what he had succeeded in finding. The Indians thereupon followed the rat who led the way back to the tree, and by the time they reached it, many plantains, pines, and other things had fallen on the ground. After they had cleaned up everything, they tried to climb the tree to get more, but it was too big and smooth, so they all agreed to cut it down. They made a staging around the trunk, and began hacking with their stone axes, and they cut away there for ten days, but it would not fall—so big was allepantepo. They cut away for another ten days and still it would not fall.

By this time their work had made them thirsty, so the Indians gave calabashes to all the animals except the Maipuri, to go fetch water; to the Maipuri they gave a sifter. When they all reached the waterside, they of course drank out of their vessels, except Maipuri out of whose sifter the water poured as fast as it was poured in: this was part of his punishment for being so greedy in keeping the secret of the bountiful tree all to himself. At the expiration of another ten days, cutting continuously, the tree at last fell. The Indians took away as their share all the cassava, cane, yams, plantains, potatoes, bananas, pumpkins, and watermelons, while the acouri, labba, and other creatures crept in among the branches to pick out all they wanted. By the time the Maipuri had got back to the tree from the waterside only the plums were left for him, and with these he has had to remain content even to the present day. What the Indians took they brought home with them and planted in their provision fields. But it was the Bunia bird who spoke to them and explained how each was to be propagated and cooked, and how some, like the bitter cassava juice, had to be boiled before drinking, while others could be eaten raw.

We are here in a mythological world utterly distinct from
that of the sophisticated island Arawak. All its affiliations are
with the interior of the southern continent. And yet after we
have almost succeeded in convincing ourselves that we must
never look to the north of the Caribbean Sea for anything connected with the Carib, we come upon a tale that has themes and
incidents that seem to transport us much farther, across the Gulf
of Mexico, to the Puebloes of the southwest and the upper
reaches of the Mississippi. This is the tale of the twins, Pia and
Makunaima. We give it in full, for from it we shall learn not
only how closely interwoven was Carib culture with South
America as a whole—that is, South America east of the Andes—
but what strands bind it, however tenuously, and indirectly,
with the great continent to the north:[14]

A long time ago, there was a woman who had become pregnant
by the Sun, with twin children, Pia and Makunaima. One day the
as-yet-unborn Pia said to his mother: "Let us go and see our father.
We will show you the way, and as you travel along pick for us any
pretty flowers that you may come across." She accordingly went
westward to meet her husband, and plucking flowers here and there
on the pathway, accidentally stumbled, fell down, and hurt herself.
She blamed her two unborn children as the cause.

She became vexed at this, and when she next asked them which
road she was to follow, they refused to tell her, and thus it was that
she took the wrong direction, and finally arrived, foot-sore and
weary, at a curious house. This belonged to Tiger's mother, Kono
(bo)-aru, the Rain-frog, and when the exhausted traveler discovered
where she was, she told the old woman she was very sorry she had
come, because she had often heard how cruel her son was. But the
house-mistress took pity on her, and telling her not to be afraid,
hid her in the big *casiri* jar, and popped on the cover. When Tiger
got home that night, he sniffed up and down and said, "Mother, I
can smell somebody! Whom have you here?" And though she denied
having anybody on the premises, Tiger was not satisfied, but had a
good look around on his own account, and peeping into the casiri
jar, discovered the frightened creature.

On killing the poor woman, Tiger found the two as-yet-unborn
children, and showed them to his mother, who said that he must

now mind and cherish them. So he put them in a bundle of cotton
to keep them warm, and noticed next morning that they had already
begun to creep. The next day, they had grown much bigger, and
with this daily increase in about a month's time they had reached
man's size.

Tiger's mother told them that they were now fit to use the bow
and arrow, with which they must go and shoot the powis because
it was this bird which had killed their own mother. Pia and Makunaima therefore went next day and shot powis, and these birds they
continued shooting day after day. When they were about to let fly
the arrow at the last bird, the powis told them that it was none of
his tribe who had killed their mother, but Tiger himself, giving
them both full particulars as to how he had encompassed her death.
The two boys were very angry on hearing this, spared the bird,
and coming home empty-handed, informed the old woman that the
powis had taken their arrows away from them. Of course this was
not true, but only an excuse. They had themselves hidden their
arrows in the bush, and wanted the chance of making new and
stronger weapons. These completed, they built a staging up against
a tree, and when Tiger passed below, they shot and killed him. And
when they reached home, they slaughtered his mother also.

The two lads now proceeded on their way and arrived at last at a
clump of cotton-trees in the center of which was a house occupied
by a very old woman, really a frog, and with her they took up their
quarters. They went out hunting each day, and on their return
invariably found some cassava that their hostess had baked. "That's
very strange," remarked Pia to his brother, "there is no field anywhere about, and yet look at the quantity of cassava which the old
woman gives us. We must watch her." So next morning, instead of
going into the forest to hunt, they went only a little distance away,
and hid themselves behind a tree whence they could see everything
that took place at the house. They noticed that the old frog had a
white spot on her shoulders: they saw her bend down and pick at
this spot, and observed the cassava-starch fall. On their return home
they refused to eat the usual cake, having now discovered its source.
Next morning they picked a quantity of cotton from the neighboring
trees, and teased it out on the floor. When the old woman asked
what they were doing, they told her that they were making something nice and soft for her to lie upon. Much pleased at this, she
promptly sat upon it, but no sooner had she done so than the two

lads set fire to it; thereupon her skin was scorched so dreadfully as to give it the wrinkled and rough appearance which it now bears.

Pia and Makunaima next continued their travels to meet their father, and soon arrived at the house of a Maipuri, where they spent three days. On the third evening Maipuri returned, looking very sleek and fat. Wanting to know what she had been feeding on, the boys followed her tracks, which they traced to a plum-tree; this they shook and shook so violently as to make all the fruit, both ripe and unripe, fall to the ground, where it remained scattered. When Maipuri next morning went to feed, she was disgusted to see all her food thus wasted, and in a very angry mood quickly returned home, beat both boys and cleared out into the bush. The boys started in pursuit, tracked her for many a long day, and at last caught up with her. Pia now told Makunaima to wheel round in front and drive the creature back to him, and as she passed, let fly a harpoon-arrow into her; the rope, however, got in the way of Makunaima as he was passing in front, and cut his leg off. On a clear night you can still see them up among the clouds: there is Maipuri, there Makunaima, and below is his severed leg.

The Children of the Sun! It is clearly recognizable despite many transformations. How, we may indeed ask, did this favorite story of the Southwest of the United States, of the *Pawnee* and *Arikara* of Nebraska and North Dakota, of the *Winnebago* of Wisconsin, come here? Were it only found among those tribes with more complex civilizations, the assumption would be justified that it might have been brought over by the Arawak as part of that new wave of customs and ideas that had had their development in Mexico and spread from there in the twelfth century. But this tale of the two children who are found alive in the womb of their mother after she has been killed and eaten, and whose father is the sun, is known among the simpler tribes of North America as well, among the *Ojibwa* of Canada and, after a fashion, even in California.

The answer is that we are here in the presence of memories of the oldest culture stratum in the Americas. Pia and his brother represent the most typical creations of American Indian mythology, the heroes who transform the world and bring the arts of life to man. In a myth from a related Carib tribe, the brothers learn from the crane the art of fire-making when they see him strike his bill against a flint and the friction produce fire. "The brothers placed huge rocks in all the rivers to detain the fishes: the rocks thus placed caused the great waterfalls. Crane was at first accustomed to catch his own fish, but finding Pia and Makunaima more successful fishermen after the river had been dammed, kept near to them and took away their fish."

Their function is thus that of culture-transformers.

As they wander on with their mother, so the tale continues, she becomes tired and they convey her to the heights of Roraima, which is to be her final home. "Then came a change of occupation for Pia. He abandoned the hunt as the sole or principal occupation of his life, and traveled from place to place, teaching the Indians many useful and good things."

By him and his teachings we have the *piai* men. Thus did Pia pursue his course of benevolence until he disappeared finally from men and remained awhile with his mother on Roraima. And when his time of departure from her had arrived, he told her that whatever of good she desired, she would obtain if she would bow her head and cover her face with her hands while she expressed her wish. This she does in her need to the present hour. "Whenever the mother of these two heroes of our race is sorrowful, there arises a storm in the mountain, and it is her tears that run down in streams from the heights of Roraima."

Here Pia functions as a typical American culture hero. And since we have mentioned the piai, the medicine man, let us see what kind of person he was, what his functions were in a typical Carib community and what his position. Without that knowledge we can understand neither the Carib nor, for that matter, any of the tribes east of the Andes. Gillin has given an excellent account of such a piae among the Carib of the Barima River, and upon that we shall mainly draw. However, before we turn to the description of the functions of the typical Carib medicine man, it might be well to tell the story of how the first medicine man obtained tobacco and the various articles that form his paraphernalia. Only by keeping the words of the Indian will it retain its full flavor:[15]

Komatari wanted some tobacco, but as there was none about, he searched for it. He had heard of its growing on an island out at sea, so he went down to the shore, where he came across a house with a man inside. Approaching him, Komatari said: "I am poor, and want tobacco. I hear you have it growing on an island. Could you get me some plants?"

While thus engaged in conversation, the hummingbird came along, and said, "Hullo! What are you two talking about?" "Tobacco: we want tobacco," they replied. "Oh, is that all?" the little bird said; "why I'll go and fetch some for you. I shall be making a start before the morning, and you can expect me back just as the sun begins to turn that way" [pointing in a direction which would indicate about an hour after midday].

The hummingbird kept his word, and returned as promised, but when the house-master saw what he had brought back, he said, "Why, that is no tobacco leaf, it is only the tobacco flower," and, turning to Komatari, he said, "I will go myself." The house-master started next morning for the same island, telling Komatari to expect him back as soon as the hummingbird, that is, shortly after midday. But as a matter of fact, he never returned until the following morning. The cause of the delay was that so many people were watching the tobacco that he had to wait for nightfall before he could steal the leaves. However, giving Komatari some of the seed, he told him to go down to the waterside, where he would find his corial, and if he looked inside he would see two or three tobacco leaves, which he might take. Komatari did as directed, but instead of two or three leaves he found the whole corial full of them. He helped himself to as many as would fill a quake, and went home.

Before taking his departure, however, the house-master said: "I have a name, but will not mention it: when you know all about piai you will be able to find it out for yourself." At last Komatari reached home, and naturally all his friends came to pay him a visit, to get some of the tobacco; but he was shrewd, kept the tobacco under the roof, left home very early of a morning, and only returned late, so as not to be at home when anybody called. But at last a visitor came and made a very long stay purposely. They thus met, Komatari gave him three leaves, and sent him away.

Next day, another man paid him a visit, but Komatari had already left, and only *marabuntas* were there—many marabuntas, all of different kinds. The visitor went home, and, taking some fish with him, returned to Komatari's place and asked the marabuntas to let him have some tobacco, at the same time showing them his fish and saying, "Look! this is the payment." And so, while the marabuntas all swarmed down upon the fish, the man climbed up, got what tobacco he wanted, and cleared out. When Komatari got home, he also got up under the roof where the tobacco was stored, but found much of it missing, so he placed what was left elsewhere, and drove away all the marabuntas except one particular kind, a black variety, the *oro*, which he made his watchmen. Starting now on his field, he cut it day after day, and after burning it, at last planted his tobacco. When he saw that it was beginning to thrive, he built a piai-house, and going round his field, looked out for a calabash tree; he found one full of gourds. He took one, but on turning round, he saw a *Hebu*, who, after asking whether it belonged to him and getting "Yes" for an answer, said: "All right. So long as the calabash is yours, you may have the whole tree. I have a name, but will not tell it to you. I want to see whether you learn the piai business well. If you do, you will be able to find it out for yourself." On reaching home with the calabash, Komatari started cleaning it out. When cleaned, another Hebu came along and asked him what he intended doing with it, but Komatari would not tell him. You see this particular Hebu was the one who comes to kill people and so was afraid of the power of the *maraka* (rattle), which is made from this very calabash.

After scooping out and cleaning the calabash, Komatari went into the bush and, traveling alone, came upon a creek with swiftly flowing water; it was here that he cut the timber from out of which he next shaped the handle for the rattle and cut the sticks to make his special fire with.

Returning home once more, he fastened the handle in the gourd, but was not satisfied with the result: the rattle did not look as it should. So he hung it up on the beam of his piai-house, and went once more into the bush, where he again met the killing Hebu, who repeated his question as to what Komatari intended doing with the rattle, but, as before, the latter would not tell him. Passing along, and hearing a noise as of many people talking, Komatari proceeded in the direction whence the sound came, and found a number of Hebus fastening various parrot feathers into cotton-twine. How pretty this ornament would look tied on his calabash left hanging up at home, was Komatari's first thought when he saw what they were doing. On asking, the ornament was given him. The Hebu who gave it to him said: "I have a name, but I will not tell it to you. You can find it out for yourself, if you should ever become a good piai-man." Komatari next asked him for another kind of cotton-plait, with feathers different from those on the one mentioned, to wear as a hat, but the Hebu said he had none, though he could get it at the next house.

So Komatari went to the next house, saw the Hebu house-master, asked for the cotton-plait for the hat, and in the same man-ner as before, this Hebu also said to him: "I have a name, but I will not tell it to you. You must find it out for yourself when you are a medicine man." Komatari went home now, and arranged the feathered cotton on top of the calabash, when who should put in an appearance again but the killing Hebu! When he again asked Komatari what he intended doing with the calabash, the latter refused to tell him as before. But Komatari was not satisfied even now, because when he shook the gourd it did not rattle. As yet it had no stones in it. So Komatari went into the bush again, and followed creek after creek, and at last came to a big river. There he met another Hebu, who got the proper stones that were wanted. When he had given them to Komatari, he said, like the others: "I have a name, but I will not tell it to you. You must find it out for yourself when you are a medicine man." Komatari again made his way home and put the stones into the calabash. Just as he was finishing the work the killing Hebu appeared again, asking him as before, what he intended doing with the calabash. The answer was, "This is to kill you with, and to prevent you killing other people," and as Komatari shook the calabash, which was now a finished maraka rattle, the Hebu begun to tremble and stagger, and almost fell, but he managed to pick himself up and get away just in the nick of time. He ran to his *aijamo* and said: "There is a man who has an object with which he nearly killed me and I must get my payment. I am going back to kill him." "All right!" said the aijamo, "I will go with you." So they went together, and brought sickness to a friend and neighbor of Komatari's; for they were afraid of attacking Koma-tari himself. However, his sick friend sent for him. Komatari went, and played the maraka on him, and took out his sickness. So the killing Hebu made another man ill, but Komatari took the disease out of him also.

The Hebu next afflicted a third victim, and again Komatari was victorious. But when he attacked a fourth one, Komatari was out hunting. When he returned, the poor fellow was in a bad enough condition: so strong did the sickness come, and Komatari could not cure him—he "stood too long." The killing Hebu then explained to Komatari that it would always be thus: some patients he could save, and other patients he could not. Of course Komatari has been able to find out the names of all the Hebus that had lent him assistance in the manufacture of his maraka, and it is to these different Hebus whom the present-day medicine men are said to "sing" and call on when they cure the sick. For instance, the name of the Hebu that procured the tobacco seeds for Komatari was Wau-uno, "the white crane."

Initiation into the priesthood was not easy and required considerable fortitude. It took place in a small house made of palm leaves plaited together so tightly that no light could enter the interior. The various candidates all appeared with their hammocks, for they had to sleep there, and the instruction began. The first thing the instructor prepared was some tobacco juice, and each candidate was then given a large calabash of tobacco-water to drink and a cigarette to smoke. Before the effects were apparent, they were then taught how to make the rattle. As soon as the tobacco juice began to take effect, the instructor gave each one of them two small pieces of black stone to put in the rattle.

At this moment, according to Gillin's informant, he swooned, and in his hallucination dreamed that he came to a place where beautiful women were singing songs he had never heard before. He was in the land of the spirits. The women took away his cigarette and gave him one of their own making as well as their own tobacco juice, all this to the accompaniment of songs. Then he came to. By this time both he and the other candidates were sick and vomited. However, they felt that, if they had any luck at all, they had secured songs that would be of value to them in the future.

The second day they again imbibed tobacco juice and again

lost consciousness. This time they were formed in a line by their instructor and made to dance in a circle always to the left of the fire which was in the center of the floor. They rattled their marakas in their right hands and supported themselves with arrow sticks in their left hands because they had now become weak from their ordeal. After recovering from their swoon all lay down in their hammocks to snatch some sleep.

Early the next morning they were awakened by their instructor. A very important test was before them. They were told that they had to pass through a fire which had been built by the villagers. The instructor himself began the ceremony. He dropped on all fours, and started to imitate the actions of a tiger, clenching his fingers under the palms of his hands just as the tiger holds his claws, and growling. Thus he approached the fire and passed through it, followed by the neophytes. Then he reversed his steps and went through again. "The flames licked them," said the informant, "and some came out with their skins blazing."

They then returned to the initiation hut, where more tobacco-water was imbibed and another test awaited them. This time they were told to go to the creek and bathe. Weak and exhausted, they made their way there, and while they were bathing, the women pelted them with mud and taunted them, telling them to throw mud back at them, the one thing which they were unable to do because of their extreme weakness. The instructor then told them that they must try to catch whatever they could in the water—fish, worms—for if they were successful this would give them added power. Finally all returned to the village, the spectators to carouse, the candidates to the initiation hut. There they were given a large calabash of *casiri* into which large ants had been thrown. After consuming it, they were allowed to drink some sweet casiri "to cool them down." The initiation rites were now at an end, and those unfortunates who possessed the requisite strength were encouraged to participate in the festivities going on.

Although the initiation proper was over, the yet new piai were, by no means, free to act as they liked. For three months

Carib Village along the Coast

more they were subject to numerous restrictions: they could eat no meat or flesh, had to practice sexual abstinence; must not allow smoke or flames to touch them or come into contact with the steam rising from a cooking pot. In those extreme cases where a man had to have some meat he had to take it in the following fashion: first it was cut up into small pieces and then roasted over a fire on the end of the stick. This was, of course, to prevent the medicine man from getting into the smoke. The meat, wrapped in a tobacco leaf, was then swallowed. Since this was to be an offering to the spirit presiding over them, any difficulty in swallowing—for instance, if the meat-pill stuck in the throat of the piai—was interpreted as signifying that the spirit did not want it. However, as Gillin adds, the procedure would be repeated until the pill went down. Thus, with some persuasion, the spirit would always, in the end, accept it or, more properly, get accustomed to it.

The final and last rite in this elaborate initiation is the squeezing, by the instructor, of tobacco juice into the eyes of the new piai. They are then regarded as ready to practice on the community, and they do.

Now of what does their practice consist? What precisely is it they have learned? Basically they are three things: a knowledge of the action of certain herbs, the ways of the spirits, and the technique of shooting stones into other individuals. These three things, we shall see later on, constitute the *sine qua non* not only of the Carib medicine man but of all South American medicine men. For all three, but particularly for the last two, detailed instructions are always given.

"[To obtain control] over spirits," says Gillin,[16] "the teacher takes a long cigarette of tobacco wrapped in *kakarelli* bark and tosses it to the novice. If the latter is able to catch the cigarette between the second and third fingers (where the muzzle of the shooting tube is located), it is a sign that as time goes on he will be able to get into communication with any spirit at all."

However, it is with the concrete needs of the community that the medicine man, after all, is mainly concerned; such matters, for instance, as how to ensure a good cassava crop. Here, as we might expect, the procedure of communicating with the proper spirit is very specifically prescribed. Among the Barima the spirit presiding over the cassava is called *pinku*. First a "consulting room" is constructed. It must be made of the *manicol* palm. Then a cup of casiri, made by a preadolescent girl, is presented to the priest. He enters the structure while the villagers gather around. Once inside, the medicine man places the drink in the middle of the floor and drinks an infusion that has been prepared, made of green tobacco leaves in water. It is the drinking of this infusion that is supposed to enable the practitioner to converse with the spirits. The piai squats on the side of the hut opposite the door and chants a song to pinku, trying to induce him to partake of the offering so solicitously provided for him by the people. No rattle is used, because pinku is not included among those particular spirits ever represented by spirit stones. Tobacco, likewise, is not smoked.

It does not take long for pinku to make his appearance, and his coming is made known to those outside by a low humming noise, supposed to be the voice of the spirit. Then a strange thing happens. Not the priest inside the hut but the assembled people outside speak to him, each one individually and without the employment of any specific or traditionally prescribed formula. They implore him to drink the casiri and ask him for a good crop of cassava. The pinku answers. The answer, however, only the piai can understand. This is a division of roles that has had a long history in religion and has, we know, persisted even in our own. The people just hear the humming noise which signifies that he has indeed answered. Soon the sound of drinking is heard, and thereupon the medicine man emerges from the hut holding in his hand the goblet for all to inspect. The contents of the vessel show that all is well. It is clear as water and icy cold, proving beyond the shadow of a doubt that the pinku has indeed drunk the very essence of the inviting brew. The priest now returns to the hut to thank the spirit with a song and tell him to return to the field from which he has come. After he has finished his speech to pinku he emerges from the hut again, this time to inform the expectant people what is in store for them; whether, that is, the words of the spirit have been favorable or unfavorable.

More dramatic both for the natives and white observers is the role of the piai in connection with the shooting of stones into other individuals. Theoretically, of course, he is not supposed to indulge in this latter practice for mere pastime or as the agent of someone else; that is, as a hired assassin, but only for a justifiable and properly sanctioned cause. Probably in the days when Barima culture was still functioning normally and healthily, it rarely happened. Today that is different, although, in such matters, it is always best to guard against accepting uncritically the statements of native informants and the white settlers of the community.

In the instructions given the newly initiated piai, the following are the most important. According to Gillin they are:[17]

The neophyte must practice under the supervision of his teacher with a small arrow made of the central rib of the *kokerite* leaf and a small bow of *yarri-yarri*. A small cotton ball, about one-and-a-half inches in diameter, which serves as the target, is suspended from one of the cross-pieces of the house by a piece of string. While the novice shoots at this target with the bow and arrow the teacher tickles him in the ribs from behind. The novice must prove his marksmanship in this way before he is able to shoot spirit stones. If he acquires enough proficiency so that the cotton ball stops dead when he hits it with the arrow he will be able to kill when shooting with spirit stones; if, in his most successful attempts, the ball and arrow turn around a number of times after a hit is made, his future victims will recover in as many days. Next the teacher places a spirit stone in the novice's mouth and draws it from the mouth through the shoulder and through the arm three times, in order to make the tube in the arm through which the shooting is done. The fourth time the stone is drawn through the arm it lodges above the elbow joint.

Thus prepared, the priest can go to work. The precise type of shooting he is going to indulge in will depend upon what he has in view. If he desires actually to kill his victim, the stone must pass entirely through the body of the intended victim. If, however, all he wishes to do is to cripple him, the stone remains in the victim's body. The wound will be visible in either instance.

Having decided upon his objective, the medicine man removes one of the small spirit stones from his rattle and swallows it. Then he takes a long puff of tobacco smoke and points in the direction of his victim. As soon as he has swallowed the missile, he moves his left hand from his neck to his right elbow joint. There the stone is held as in the magazine of a gun. It is a general belief that a tube similar to the barrel of a gun stretches from the priest's neck right to his elbow joint and thence to a small opening between the bases of the first and second fingers. He now takes a long inhalation of tobacco smoke and then extends the right forearm in the intended direction. It is the force of this smoke that is regarded as the necessary physical agency for the ejection of the shot.

As in all such cases, the victim has his own means of combating and neutralizing the spirit stones that have been shot at him. That he has been so shot he knows from the feeling of pain he suddenly experiences in some part of his body. He immediately calls a practitioner, who locates the spot where the missile has entered. Upon this spot the latter blows smoke and sucks out the stone. That is if it is there. The situation is, of course, more desperate if the stone has passed through his victim's body. No amount of sucking will then do any good. All the practitioner will get for his pains is blood. An entirely different kind of treatment is, accordingly, necessary. The priest retires to his consulting hut and summons the spirit who is causing the harm. Unless he desists, he is told, he, the priest of the patient, will summon to his aid the tiger spirit, who will then devour the offending spirit.

Apparently the theory behind the shooting is that a piai who has shot his spirit stone in the direction of the victim ceases to be an active agent after the missile has been discharged and he has evoked the spirit of the stone. It is the spirit then who takes over, and the struggle consequently is no more one between this and that medicine man but between this and that spirit. The man controls the spirit and the spirit controls the man. It is an old and well-known formula throughout the domain of religion and, as the religious-magical formula *par excellence,* is the specific characteristic, almost always, of peoples without cultivated plants and without a highly organized religion and chieftainship.

I have gone into this very detailed description of the initiation, the practices, and the role of the medicine man because, as indicated before, it must serve for most of the tribes to be discussed in the succeeding chapters, with the exception always of the great Andean civilizations, of course, and the marginal peoples of southeastern Brazil, Matto Grosso, the Gran Chaco, and Tierra del Fuego. Naturally the initiation will not always be the same nor will spirit stones be always the missiles that are shot. The theory behind the shooting, official and unofficial, that will necessarily be different from tribe to tribe. But the general picture will be much the same.

In the foregoing description of the initiation and functions of the medicine man, in many ways the most interesting element is the role played by tobacco. Its use here as, prevailingly, a method of intoxication for special occasions is completely distinct from that which it enjoys in most of North America. Here it is not, as it is there, the one great boon which the spirits and deities desire with so intense a craving that, if necessary, they will sacrifice themselves for it. In the North American Indian cultures the spirits are overcome by tobacco, whereas here the suppliants of the spirits are. So fundamental a distinction, one definitely feels, must, in some manner or other, be connected with the length of time the people of these two continents have known and used it.

We know that tobacco did not originate in the northern continent, and the legends of the Arawak, Carib, and other tribes of British Guiana all insist that it came from the Antilles. Evidently that is the source from which they received it. Botanists must, however, decide whether it was first domesticated there, and that, on the face of it, is extremely doubtful. Some part of South America is more likely to have been its homeland than the Antilles, and its employment as an intoxicant most likely to have been its original use. Indeed it is not speculating too unduly to assume that, in some fashion or other, it was associated from earliest times with the knowledge of cassava. The cultivation of cassava is after all only in a secondary sense to be regarded as an indication of a full-fledged agriculture, and the same holds true for tobacco. To find tobacco playing so great and special a role in the same region where cassava is the staple of life and where neither the potato nor maize are known except to the Arawak intruders and tribes who have been markedly influenced by them is therefore not likely to be due to mere chance.

Yet this still does not dispose of the fact that these tribes apparently did obtain their tobacco from the island Arawak. And this can only mean that, for reasons not clear to us, the Antilles at one time in their history became the center from which the various uses of tobacco were secondarily disseminated to British Guiana and more definitely to southeastern United States.

But let us now turn to one phase of culture with which the tribes of northern South America, but more particularly the Carib, were associated in the minds of the early white settlers: their apparently well-organized methods of revenge. This is indeed one of their most highly developed specialties. Now there are four media of action a man may resort to, to avenge an offense committed against him: violence, poisoning, sorcery, and what was called *kanaima*. The last three were secret, kanaima the most secret of them all, the most abhorred by the community, and the most dangerous for the particular individual who has taken it upon himself to employ it. Only when all other means of obtaining redress have been tried and have failed does a man decide to become a kanaima.

It is easy to understand the reason for the terror surrounding kanaima. Apparently it is properly applied not so much to the man who has dedicated himself to kill a particular person as to the death-demanding spirit under whose influence the individual acts and who possesses him. Such compulsions are by no means unknown to the Indians of North America, but nowhere is this compulsive drive so well systematized socially. If it were not for its socially systematized procedure, the resemblance to "running amuck" would probably have struck people long ago. Yet that is what basically it is, a socialized running amuck. The terror of all concerned—victim, aggressor, the community at large—stems from this fact. Compulsion and murder lust throw their destructive mantle across the activities of the kanaima in a fashion that should delight the psychiatrist and overwhelm the psychoanalyst with joy. Nor is the terror decreased by the doubt that enters the minds of the Indians as to whether the kanaima is a man or a spirit animal, one of those unfortunate animals indeed, who, as the well-known authority on the nation of British Guiana, Brett, observed, "are possessed by the spirits of men who have devoted themselves to deeds of blood and cannibalism. To enjoy the savage delight of killing and devouring human beings, such a person will assume the form, or his soul animate the body, of a jaguar, approach the sleeping places of men, or waylay the solitary Indian on his path."

And this is the manner in which the kanaima operates. Say a person has died. A piai is summoned to determine the cause, to discover whether the death has been due to the action of an evil spirit or by the desire for revenge on the part of another Indian. If the verdict is that he has been the victim of some other Carib, then the corpse is carefully examined. If something unusual or a blue spot is discovered, then the priest is satisfied that the deceased has been destroyed by an invisible poisoned arrow. This is the handiwork of the kanaima. The priest's function then ceases, for his powers are of no value where redress for such a death must be sought. Retaliation and revenge are matters for the victim's relatives and friends, not for a medicine man as such. Accordingly, they immediately set to work to attempt to discover who the criminal is. There are a number of different ways in which this can be done. Let me enumerate a few.

Among the *Makusi*, a Carib tribe living on the Essequebo River in British Guiana, Schomburgk relates how the father of a child who had died, suspecting it to be the work of a kanaima, cut from the boy's corpse both the thumbs, little fingers, the great toe, and the little toe, as well as a piece of the heel, and threw them into a pot of water. The water was then heated, and as it boiled, great attention was paid to which part of the body was first thrown out, for the kanaima was to be located in the direction in which it had been thrown. When this has been determined, a consultation of all the relatives takes place and the direction given in which to look for the murderer. The person who is to take upon himself the work of revenge is also designated at this time.

It is always a near relative to whom the dangerous task is assigned of becoming a kanaima, dangerous because he must allow himself to become possessed by the destructive spirit who presides over this cult of revenge and retaliation. The prospect before him is not pleasant or one to be envied. It is clearly a constraint placed upon him by tradition and enforced by the community, a constraint recognized by all. This explains, in large measure, the unusual tenseness characterizing every action of the kanaima. We are really in the presence of a long-drawn-out and ritualized murder-compulsion. A kanaima must lead an abstinent life. Among the Barima Carib, for instance, he may eat no meat with the exception of a single species of bird, and he may eat this bird only because it is believed that its consumption will make him invisible. The few things he does eat are supposed either to help him in his quest or injure his victim. For example, he may eat a pimpler palm called *kosako* because, by doing so, he will cause the one he is pursuing to have the sensation of being choked and pricked. He can eat a certain white fungus because it makes him light and he can thus run faster. He can drink only rain water, and then only such as has collected in a particular way. He may use no water from a creek, because it may be running too strongly and he may thus lose control of himself. That is why rain water is better, it is believed; it is clear, and thus the kanaima too will be clearheaded. At night no fire may keep him warm. Instead his skin is rubbed with pepper. It is not surprising then that after such abstentions and food no one is particularly desirous of eating the body of a kanaima.

The person charged with the obligation of avenging a death will disappear suddenly from the settlement. He is now a kanaima, and his life is that of a wanderer, one to whom rest is not permitted. He cannot return until he has slain his victim or shot him with a poisoned arrow. Such a search, it is believed, may take a long time, sometimes lasting even for years. During that period he must avoid all contact with other Indians. He is, in a sense, outlawed from the moment he leaves the settlement. As an outlaw, as one without social status, he is accordingly treated. Those who meet him in the bush are supposed to kill him.

Because of his abstinent habits he becomes emaciated, and that is the picture generally given of him. He is supposed to wear a curiously wrought cap and to decorate his body in a terrifying fashion, to paint red spots on his skin and thus to transform himself into a jaguar at night.

Let us assume that he has tracked down his victim. How shall he kill him? Whatever method he employs—poison, club, arrow —he must be careful not to bring about his immediate death. This is not to be interpreted as simply a desire to see him suffer. That may, of course, enter. But the real explanation is quite different. The kanaima-avenger has now to think not only of his duty to kill the man he has at last tracked down. He must also prepare for his own return to normal existence. To ensure this, three days must be allowed him to perform certain rites while his victim is still alive. Without this he could obtain no purification for himself, and if he is not properly purified he is doomed to become demented and to die a raving maniac.

Having assured himself that his victim will not die for three days at least, he takes precautions to prevent his identity being revealed by his captured prey in a most effective manner. He slits the tongue of the unfortunate man with the fangs of a poisonous snake.

As a rule the victim is found by his friends and, upon death, buried. It is imperative now for the kanaima to find the body. On the third night the kanaima will then visit the grave and stick a pointed staff into the body. If there is blood on it after being drawn out, he will lick it off. This licking off of the blood is vital, for by that one act the dangerous consequences of his deed are neutralized. His purification is complete, and he can return to his settlement and to normal life.

On the face of it such an institution as the kanaima reads as though it belonged to a completely diseased civilization or, if you will, to a people who possessed none. Yet it is hardly the prerogative of so-called civilized peoples to throw stones in the matter of organized terror and bloodshed, certainly not today. Relatively speaking, the Carib spent less time in murdering and retaliation than do we. That when first discovered they were marauders and terrorists is clear. But they were then unquestionably just at the zenith of their expansion, and at such times it is not the habit of peoples to be overdelicate in their methods of dealing with their enemies. This in turn must have reacted upon their own culture and emphasized its sadistic side. We do not have to look far to understand this. The Spaniards, Portuguese, French, English, and Dutch demonstrated within a few generations of the discovery of the Americas that the Carib were bungling amateurs at the game of torment and destruction and death.

With the mention of cannibalism as a Carib practice we began, and it is only meet that we end this chapter with some remarks on this much-understood custom and predilection.

Like human sacrifice, a shudder of horror runs down our spine at the mere suggestion of anthropophagy. Yet cannibalism manifestly is not the expression of a perverted mind. Where, as among primitive people, no clearly marked line of demarcation exists between human beings and animals, and no horror is evinced at eating the latter, there is logically no reason why there should be any at the thought of eating the former. Indeed, a survey of the aboriginal world indicates that cannibalism was one of the most widespread of habits and indulged in by numerous aboriginal peoples extending from the most advanced, like the Polynesians and the East and West Africans, to the simpler Papuans of New Guinea and the North and South American Indians. The belief in the inviolateness of the human body or that there is something shameful in dismembering it after death or to use parts of it for food, ritual, or otherwise, all this is a very late development in the history of civilization. As a more or less general food staple the eating of human flesh was known, it is true, only to the natives of East Africa, and a number of the Melanesian tribes. As a ritual food, however, it was much commoner. The ancient Mexicans delighted in it and, in their codices, have left numerous pictorial representations of feasts where human flesh was consumed. As a method of expressing one's hatred and gratifying one's feeling of revenge it is still commoner, although there are only two outstanding centers for cannibalism of this type; Polynesia and South America.

Cannibalism may, in fact, be something secondarily acquired by the Carib and Arawak, possibly something that came to them from another group of tribes, the Tupi-Guarani. Certainly it is among the latter that we find its highest development. Yet, whether they borrowed it or not, the Carib soon became professionals in their own right. They indulged in anthropophagy for a number of reasons, so they claimed: because they liked the taste of human flesh, because they hated an individual, and for exactly the opposite reason, because they loved and respected him. This latter reason strikes us as somewhat strange and inconceivable, yet we know that a number of Carib tribes put the ashes and powdered bones of their deceased chiefs, friends, and relatives in their drinks to demonstrate their affection and regard.

Full-fledged cannibalism, however, is connected only with warfare and captured prisoners. According to a French source of the eighteenth century the Carib of French Guiana tied their prisoners of war to a forked stick or to a tree, "and having spat upon them all sorts of blasphemies they discharged a volley of arrows in different parts of their bodies and might let them die like that. Those who were more impatient of satisfying their vengeance cut the flesh off, bit by bit, and buccaned it."[18] Such human steaks are known in other parts of the world. There is, for instance, an excellent description of an almost identical impatience in the famous Chinese novel *All Men Are Brothers*, which Pearl Buck has translated into English.

For a more complete account of some of the details of cannibalism, the reader must wait until the next chapter for the Tupi-Guarani, more particularly, the *Tupinamba* were the past masters at anthropophagy and the well-known Belgian chronicler, De Bry, took great pains to describe these feasts and illustrate them for the delectation, morbid and ethical, of thousands of duly horrified and shocked Europeans, a few generations after the Hundred Years' War had ended, and only a few generations before the Thirty Years' War with its unspeakable horrors had begun.

This intimate connection of cannibalism with warfare must not be overlooked nor, for that matter, its equally intimate association with human sacrifice. All of these three aspects were fused into one whole among the *Aztecs* and, as we shall soon see, on a lower level, among the Tupinamba.

The Carib are among those tribes who never took kindly to European civilization. Wherever they could they withdrew from contact with it, and part of their spread over certain parts of South America may well be due to their desire to escape its utterly destructive and demoralizing effect. Where they could not do so they developed a negative compromise that consisted almost exclusively of loss of values and which gave them the most marginal of existences. It is characteristic of them that they never made any positive compromise or attempted any new synthesis of the old with the new as did the Arawak or Tupi-Guarani.

All this but confirms what can be gathered from other indications as well, that the Carib were fundamentally a simple non-agricultural tribe whose incursions into the new world as symbolized by the Arawak and the Tupi-Guarani were relatively recent.

CHAPTER V

The Wanderers and Eluders

THE TUPI-GUARANI

THE TUPI-GUARANI WERE, FOR A LONG TIME, the most enigmatic and puzzling of all South American Indian tribes. We find them everywhere and apparently possessed at all times by an all-consuming wanderlust. They were wandering when the Europeans first encountered them, and they continued wandering after that first encounter, at a redoubled pace in fact. This redoubled pace, so the well-known Americanist, Alfred Métraux, would have us believe, was due almost exclusively to the desire of one of their tribes, the Tupi proper, to escape from the loving but annihilating embrace of the white man. Yet this seems both too simple and too romantic an interpretation.

Whatever the reason, however, whether it was economically or climatically conditioned, whether they were fleeing from themselves or from their foes, they had developed one thing to perfection: the technique of covering long distances in comparatively short periods of time. An attempt has to be made, therefore, to explain this characteristic of the Tupi-Guarani if we wish to understand them, or South American ethnology at all. It is not easy. Most students have always insisted that the moment they come to concrete grips with the problems presented by the Tupi-Guarani, they seem to be faced by a blank wall. Where did their culture come from? A veritable *dolor de cabeza,* a headache, assails them. Even that most erudite, ingenious, closet-ethnologist, the famous Austrian theorist, Pater Wilhelm Schmidt, is perplexed and bewildered.

Yet Métraux has shown definitely that some of our bewilderment is unnecessary. The distribution of the Tupi-Guarani in precolumbian times, as given by him, places practically all the tribes of this very extensive family in eastern Brazil and west of the Madeira River. There is a narrow tongue of them extending along the Marañon and reaching as far as the Andes; there is a thin extension into Bolivia and another narrow tongue that goes as far as Buenos Aires. Roughly speaking, the Tupi-Guarani are to the south of the Amazon and the Arawak to the north. The Carib are on both sides of the river, but their area is much more circumscribed than either of the other two. Now the assumption has always been that the Carib belong in the upper drainage of the western Amazon and that they are intruders in the southern drainage of the great stream. That seems a practical certainty to the author. If distributions mean anything, and sometimes they do, the Tupi-Guarani should then have their main cultural affinities with the tribes between the Madeira, the Tapajos, and the Xingu, their secondary affinities with the tribes along the Marañon, and a somewhat marginal connection with the peoples who lived on the Atlantic littoral. The situation turns out exactly to be this, except for their possession of two traits: namely, an intensive maize agriculture and institutionalized cannibalism.

Everyone seems to be agreed that they are intruders. But intruders from where? If their ancient home lay in eastern Brazil, how did they get their maize agriculture and their cannibalism? Maize they could have obtained from two sources, the Arawak and the great Andean civilizations. A Tupi-Guarani tribe, the *Chiriguano,* in Bolivia, did actually come under the influence of the Andean cultures. But the Chiriguano represent the extreme western expansion of the stock, which did not take place before 1500. They have not been in Bolivia then long, and certainly did not relay anything back to eastern Brazil. With the Arawak on the other hand, they were in contact only along the Marañon, and the Tupi-Guarani expansion in that direction was also very late, probably even postcolumbian.

Thus the dilemma does exist. Yet one hypothesis for their acquisition of maize exists that has hitherto been strangely neglected: namely, that, like the Arawak, according to the interpretation advanced in a previous chapter, it came to the Tupi-Guarani ultimately from Mexico, being relayed to them first through the Southeast of the United States, thence to the Antilles, and finally to the northern coast of South America between the mouths of the Orinoco and the Amazon. It would then be easy for these influences to be carried down both the Araguaya River and the Xingu. Métraux, one of our leading authorities on the subject, believes that the expansion of the Tupi-Guarani to the north coast of Brazil is postcolumbian. Yet there may have been, if we bear in mind the many migrations of this group—there must, in fact, have been—many forward thrusts and retreats in their history.

The merit of this hypothesis lies in the fact that within the area here indicated—that is, Mexico—both maize and some form of institutionalized cannibalism exist. The torture of prisoners in exactly the same manner as that current among the Tupi-Guarani was a trait of most of the southeastern United States tribes and extended as far north as the Hurons of the St. Lawrence River. The flesh of these prisoners was frequently eaten.

Nor is this supposition of Mexican influence via the southeast of the United States wholly without corrobation. Influences spreading from the Antilles to the northern coast of Brazil are now generally admitted. Indeed some striking resemblances between objects found along the Tapajos River and the Mound area of the United States have been pointed out.

So again we must go back to that eventful turn of affairs around 1000–1100 A.D. that sent cultural elements flying from one end of Mexico to the other and scattered them throughout the region of the Gulf of Mexico. If we insist so vehemently that many of these traits were first disseminated along the coast of the Gulf as far as Florida, it is because there exists ample evidence for this. That the contact with the southern coast of the United States may have been slight and of short duration is admitted. Certain objects and customs and ideas have clearly spread to the Antilles without any previous passage through the southeast. That any, however, came to the northern coast of South America from Mexico directly is quite unlikely.

How they may have come, whether by trade or by a militant expansion—whether individual traits were disseminated or whole culture-complexes—here again we must fall back upon surmises, more or less reasonable. But everything militates against a gradual infiltration of the new culture elements; everything favors the hypothesis of an aggressive sweep of peoples carrying with them a new order of things. The Gulf and the Caribbean were in turmoil for almost a half a millennium before Columbus arrived. Its waters and its coasts must have been seething from the conflict of the new ideas with old traditions and old ways of life.

In a fashion, the situation must have resembled that which existed in the plains of the United States when, somewhere between 1200 A.D. onward, extending into postcolumbian times, peoples from all directions of the continent converged upon it. There was little time and, for that matter, little opportunity, for cultures to become integrated. Indeed those cultures that had started as integrated ones lost much of this integration on the trek to their new home, as they were forced to adjust themselves to new conditions, and they were often completely transformed by the peoples with whom they had to mingle and who, not infrequently, outnumbered them.

This, too, we can surmise, is what must have happened to those peoples who landed at the mouth of the Amazon and who carried with them maize and the custom of torturing and then dining upon their war captives. Evidently they preceded the Arawak, although we need not assume that this was by a long period of time. Their function was to be the same, that of culture carriers. Throughout, with few exceptions, they clung to the rivers, the Araguaya, Tapajos, Xingu. This was a region inhabited by peoples of much simpler cultures and speaking many and diverse languages. We can allow a sojourn of two hundred years among them and still give these Tupi-Guarani

Chuncho Chief in Ceremonial Attire, Upper Amazon

speaking peoples ample time to spread to their extreme limits. In two hundred years many new customs can be learned and adopted and many old ones forgotten or discarded.

And so our dilemma disappears. The Tupi-Guarani peoples then are to be regarded as newcomers from the north who became largely absorbed, culturally and probably physically, by the peoples living between the Tapajos and the Xingu but who kept intact a number of their basic possessions, material and intellectual.

What, however, impelled them to become such wanderers on the face of the earth? What lay behind their seeming restlessness?

Whatever it was, let us not overestimate or overemphasize it. From the mouth of the Amazon to the Chiriguano in Bolivia is not much more than 1500 miles. In no direction did the Tupi-Guarani ever spread much more than that. Why should such an expansion overwhelm us with amazement? The Mound-Builder civilizations of the United States covered that and more; the migrations of Siouan-speaking peoples extended from Louisiana and the South Atlantic to Alberta, Canada. For the first, four hundred years sufficed; for the second, probably not as much.

The Tupi-Guarani are, in fact, very much akin in spirit to the great Siouan-speaking group, and as a tribute to this spiritual kinship, let us begin our concrete discussion of Tupi-Guarani culture with their basic myth, the story of the twins who are sometimes the Children of the Sun, or moon, at other times the children of culture-bringing heroes and deities. This, incidentally, is also one of the basic myths of the Siouan group and of the Iroquoian and Caddoan peoples, all of whom belong, let me add, originally to the east and the southeast and all of whom, together with the Mushkogean (*Choctaw, Creek,* etc.), participated in some fashion, immediate or indirect, in the civilizations of the Mound-Builders.

Now the twins, in this myth, are always depicted as concerned with one primary object, the completion of the work begun by their father, the culture-hero divinity. Their primary function is to come always to the aid of mankind. The plot of the story

among the various Tupi-Guarani tribes is practically everywhere
identical, and it is only among the distant Chiriguano in Bolivia
that any of its distinctive features fade away.

A reference to page 54 will make it clear that the story of
the adventure of the twins is not in South America confined
merely to the Tupi-Guarani but that it is known in very much
the same form among the Arawak and Carib. Wherever, in fact,
these tribes are found, this tale is found. As soon as we leave them
and their neighbors it disappears. This is not to imply, of course,
that all tales concerned with the deeds of two heroes, twins,
are necessarily identical.

There are in fact two distinct twin cycles. The first deals with
two brothers, born either of one or of two fathers, who have
been taken from the womb of their dead mother after she has
been slain by an ogre or evil spirit. These children are always
depicted at strife of some kind with each other, although it is
always settled. They grow to maturity rapidly and then embark
on a series of adventures which includes the avenging of the
death of their mother. The second cycle deals specifically with
the Children of the Sun, born miraculously of a virgin. They too
grow up to maturity rapidly and embark on a series of adventures, the most distinctive of which are the search for their father
and the many difficult tests to which they have to submit.

Both of these cycles seem to have been confused with each
other from time immemorial, particularly in North America.
This confusion may be interpreted in two ways. Either it has
resulted from confusion on the part of the narrators—that is,
from essentially literary-traditional causes—or, secondly, reflects,
as tales often do, historical-cultural facts. The distribution of
these two distinct cycles and the distribution of their confusion
is such as to suggest that the second interpretation is, by far,
the more likely. The first version can then be taken to represent
one culture stratum, the second, another.

Now the Arawak, Carib, and Tupi-Guarani possess what must
be called the confused or mixed form of this tale. The children
are torn from the womb of their mother, who is then devoured.
Their task is to avenge her death and kill her slayer. They are in

no sense culture-heroes. Yet at the same time, in all these Arawak, Carib, and Tupi versions, they embark on a series of adventures in search of their father in which tests of identification play a most significant part. In short they are also Children of the Sun, the divine bringers of civilization. They are also culture-heroes. The intermingling of the episodes of the two cycles is complete.

Can any reasonable and satisfactory explanation be offered? I think so, one both satisfactory and of great significance for an understanding of aboriginal American history.

The first of the above versions is known in a fairly pure form practically all over North America except the Southwest and California. It can confidently be taken as belonging to a very old cultural stratum. Its mixed form is found *only among those tribes that have been in contact with the so-called Mound-Builder cultures.* Indeed among these tribes not only does the mixed form occur but both versions often exist unmixed and side by side. The second version exists in practically unmixed form and alone in the Southwest of the United States, in Mexico, and in Central America.

Where, consequently, a vast region is found in which the two cycles occur with their component elements inextricably intermingled, the one with the other, we are forced to conclude that the same influences that brought about the situation in North America are responsible for the situation in South America. In short, we have another corroboration for the spread of culture from Mexico around the Gulf between 1000 and 1400 A.D.

Bearing this in mind, let us retell, in some detail—for it is important—the adventures of the twins of the *Tembé* tribe, an important division of the Tupi-Guarani:

THE STORY OF THE KARUWARA[19]

The Indians in the beginning had no manioc. They planted only *camapu* berries. It so happened that an Indian was in the process of planting these berries when Maira suddenly appeared before him and asked him what he was doing. "That's no concern of yours," came the answer. "I'm not your son that you have the right to ask me what I am doing!" Maira said nothing and left, but ere he had gone a few steps, he turned around and behold! the forest had suddenly overwhelmed the man's plantation and buried him beneath the trees.

However, the man managed to extricate himself and was soon on his way home. He purposely left, somewhere on the trail, a calabash which he had found on his plantation. Then having arrived at his home, he seized his knife and went in pursuit of Maira to kill him. Soon he arrived at a hut and asked whether Maira had been there, only to be told that Maira had already left. Thereupon the Indian picked up a calabash he saw lying near the hut and muttered these words into it: "If I could only find that rascal Maira, I would kill him in the following manner." Then he threw the fruit up in the air and stood ready to catch it on the point of his knife. However, the falling calabash struck the man's hand and pushed the point of the knife into his neck and he died.

Maira continued going along the road until he came to another Indian planting his field. As in the first case, he asked him what he was doing, and the Indian answered, "I am cleaning my *camapu*," and added, "If only our father Maira would visit us, for, assuredly, he would bring us many of the things we want!" "He whom you see this moment standing before you, he is your father," answered Maira. "Do you wish some manioc?"

The man said, "Indeed I do," and Maira transformed the fallen trees on the plantation into manioc stalks. He then told him how to plant them, and when he was finished both proceeded onward toward the Indian's house. Hardly had they arrived there before Maira ordered the Indian back to the plantation to fetch some manioc roots so that they could prepare some *manikwera*. However, the man protested that since the manioc had but just been planted there could as yet be no roots. "Well and good," answered Maira, "in that case you will have to wait a year before you can gather your manioc," and he went on his way.

So Maira continued along his road till he met his companion and again traveled on. On one occasion he stopped in front of a *pitywe* tree, and contemplating its straight, beautiful trunk he leaned against it and said, "I wish that this tree could become transformed into a woman who would be my wife!" And, then, suddenly, there behind his back, the branches of the tree were transformed into a hut and the trunk into a girl who asked him to enter. With her he lived a very long time, but after a while he continued on his wanderings again.

Now the young woman had become pregnant, and when Maira left the child within her womb spoke to her and said, "Let us follow after our father!" The woman was much astonished to hear her son speak before he had been born and asked him, "Do you know the way?" "Of course I do." "Good, then, let us go!" And so they went on, the child within the womb telling his mother to pluck whatever flowers they encountered. But as she was plucking one a wasp stung her hand and thereupon she struck her abdomen with her hand and exclaimed angrily, "Why, indeed do you always want to have flowers. After all you haven't been born yet!" Because of this Maira's son became angry.

"Well, which trail did your father take?" she suddenly asked her son, and the son in his anger directed her to the house in which Mykura lived. They arrived there in the evening just as a torrent of rain was approaching. Mykura then asked the woman where she wished to go and she told him that she was in search of the father of her child. She begged him for a place to sleep, and he bade her enter. While the young woman hung up her hammock, Mykura climbed on the roof to make certain that it was firm and would protect them against the oncoming rain-storm. At the same time, however, he opened a rain spout that was just above the woman's hammock, and the water came pouring over her. "Why, it is raining here in your house," exclaimed the woman. Thereupon Mykura bade her hang her hammock closer to his where no rain would enter. Secretly, however, he climbed on the roof and repeated what he had done before. Again the rain poured over the woman, and she had finally to place her hammock close to that of Mykura and sleep with him the whole night. The next morning she found that she had become pregnant for the second time. Indeed within her womb Maira's son was already exclaiming to Mykura's son, "I don't want you so close to me! Keep on the other side!"

The following day the woman continued on her way, and when she asked him the path her husband had taken, Maira's son directed her to the dwelling of the tigers. There she found only an old woman at home who spoke to her and told her, "Where do you come from, my daughter? My sons are very evil beings, particularly when they return home hungry and find nothing to eat!" So the old woman hid her under a large basket.

Soon the sons returned and immediately asked, "What is this strong smell?" "Nothing," answered the old woman. They turned the basket upside down, but Maira's son changed his mother into a doe that immediately fled. However, the two tigers soon overtook it and tore her to pieces. "Look," they called to their mother, "there are two young ones here!" "That is good," exclaimed the old woman. "Let me have them so that I can cook myself a porridge of *mojyka*." She immediately threw the two infants into a pot of hot water but, in doing so, burnt her hand. Then she attempted to cut them up with a knife, but she cut her own finger. When she tried to throw them into the fire, again she burnt her hand. Finally she attempted to grind them in her mortar but only succeeded in striking herself with the pestle. So she gave up and decided to keep them and stuck them under the basket. The next morning she found two young parrots in their place. "What beautiful parrots," she exclaimed. "I am going to rear these as pets!" She fed them and put them back. The next morning they had become transformed into two children. "Look," she exclaimed bewildered, "they have now become two young human beings! These indeed will I keep as my grandchildren so that they can accompany me to the fields." And so she reared them carefully.

The tigers would make them little arrows with which to shoot birds, and then they would accompany the old woman to the plantations and play. At times they would call the old woman and delouse her and if she fell asleep they would unfasten her head, roll it on the ground, and then attach it to her body again. Then the old woman would wake up and ask, "Did I sleep long?" and the children would answer, "Yes, indeed, you slept long. Let us go home!"

One day the old woman said to them, "Don't go far away, children, for some evil thing may come upon you!" But they would pay no heed and go right on, and one day they came upon a *Jacuacu* who addressed them and said, "Ha-ha-ha, why you are living with the tigers who devoured your own mother!" Then Maira's son spoke to his brother and said, "Did you hear what the *Jacuacu* just told us? He said that the tigers had killed our mother!" And they both began to weep.

When they finally returned to the old woman, she asked them, "Why have you been crying?" "Wasps stung us," they answered. "Why, grandchildren, there are no wasps around here," said the old woman. "Yes, there are," they insisted. "No, there are none

around here." "All right then. You go and get that wasp nest," said
Maira's son to his brother. He went out, mixed *manigwa* leaves with
clay, blew upon them, and transformed the whole into a wasp nest.
This he took to the old woman. "Here are the wasps," he said to
her and threw the nest at her head. "Yes, yes, you were right, after
all, my grandchildren," yelled the old woman in pain.

When the children were sufficiently grown up they wandered
frequently into the forest. They would tell the tigers that they were
off to shoot deer. They would pitch their camp near a creek. Once
they stayed there five days, one of them making fire fans and the
other manioc presses which they then threw into the water. The fire
fans became transformed into *pirantras* and rays and the manioc
presses into watersnakes and eels. After having done this they said,
"Let us see what happens now." So they killed five wild pigs and a
tapir and threw them down to these water animals so that they could
accustom themselves to eating meat and becoming wild. Then
Maira's son built a path from one shore of the water to the other by
shooting two arrows across which united and so formed a safe
passageway. This path they then crossed and finally returned to
the tigers.

They told the tigers that there were many *anajas* on the other
side of the river and the tigers immediately said, "Let us all go there
tomorrow." "Yes, indeed, let us all go," answered Maira's son.

The following day they all went there. "Where are the anajas?"
asked the tigers. "Let us first hunt," replied Maira's son. So they
hunted and threw the intestines of the animals they killed into the
water for the fish to eat. "My but there are many fish here! Tomorrow we must have broiled fish!" so spoke the tigers. "Yes," answered Maira's son. "Tomorrow you'll have enough fish!"

The next morning Maira's son awakened the tigers and shouted,
"Come we must now go and get the anajas." All immediately started,
and soon they came to the little bridge across the stream. The tigers
ran on to it, and when all three were there, Maira's son caused the
waters to rise high and rapidly. The creek became an ocean. The
waves rose and carried the tigers into the raging waters, where they
were devoured by the meat-eating fish.

The twins took the weapons of the tiger-chieftain, and when they
returned to the home of the tiger woman, they threw them into the
fire. An explosion took place, and a firebrand flew out far into the
distance.

"Well, let us now look for our father," said Maira's son. So they spent a day and a night on the trail until Mykura's son asked his brother, "Where, indeed, will we find our father!" "Why, he is very close to us," answered Maira's son. And indeed they arrived at his place very soon thereafter. He had known all the time that the tigers had eaten his wife. In appearance he was an old man and carried a band across his forehead. The twins greeted Maira, and he responded: "So you have come, my children."

The rest of the story can only be summarized here. The most important incidents are the tests of strength and cunning between Maira and his sons. He asks them to find out where the mythical being called Azan sharpens his bow, where he makes his weirs, where he bathes, where those with long hair live, and where those with long legs live. The sons succeed in all five, and then challenge him to a shooting contest, which is to consist of transfixing a mountain with their arrows. The twins succeed, the father fails. And the story ends with the omnipresent "wandering" theme. "We are going to leave you now father." "Why, where are you going to go!" "Oh, anywhere."

Turning now from the mythology to the social organizations, religion, and general culture, a curious contrast confronts us. These last three are almost as unintegrated as the former is integrated. This is all the stranger in view of the multiplicity of economic bases of their life, in view of the domesticated plants they seem to have possessed. They had, for instance, according to the older observers, twenty-four varieties of manioc, five varieties of maize, potatoes, beans, etc. With the emphasis on sedentary life that this presumably presupposes, one might have expected a highly organized chieftainship at least. We must assume that they once had it, in fact had much more possibly. However, a wandering life, an enforced nomadism, is most destructive of the power of chiefs and plays havoc even with an intricate and well-integrated social organization. This, North American ethnologists know only too well. Much the same thing, in fact, happened to the Dakota division of the great Sioux family in their trek from the forests of Michigan and Wisconsin across the Western plains and northward to Alberta.

An excellent indication of how relatively simple their general culture was is afforded by the delightful account of the Tupinamba group that was written by a young German, Hans Staden, who was captured by the natives in 1549, while employed by the Portuguese, near the present location of Santos, Brazil. The red-bearded young man from Homburg in Hesse seemed doomed. Eyebrows and beard had already been shaved, and he was being properly prepared for roasting. His indignant protests that he was not a Portuguese, with whom the Tupinamba were at deadly enmity, but a German were rejected by the native chief. He had heard that defense a number of times before, poor Hans was told. The fact remained that he had been captured working for the Portuguese. Five former Portuguese whom he, the chief, now had stored away in his stomach out of harm's way had tried the same excuse and pretended they were French. They had lied egregiously, as subsequent events proved.

Fate, however, was with Hans, and he was saved. One of his masters took ill and called upon Hans for help. The red-bearded gunner from Homburg proceeded to lay his hands on the sick man, and he recovered marvelously. The chiefs began to tell him their dreams. Particularly urgent was the appeal of one chief who had partaken too freely of broiled Portuguese and feared that his digestion had been permanently impaired. To him and to all the others Hans ministrated energetically, and mildly suggested to them that they had better desist from eating any more Portuguese, that it might be just as well, indeed, if they changed their meat diet completely.

And so Hans Staden became a prophet. In 1557 he published an account of his captivity and adventures. Let us quote in some detail from this delightful little work. It is better than any summary a trained ethnologist can give:[20]

America is a large country inhabited by many tribes of savages who speak several different languages, and there are many curious beasts there. It is a pleasant country to look at, the trees are always green, but there is no wood there like our wood, and the savages are naked. . . .
There is a range of mountains which reaches to within three miles

of the sea, more or less, and begins to rise in the neighbourhood of Boiga de Todolos Sanctus, which was built by the Portuguese who inhabit there. The range of mountains runs beside the sea for about 20 miles, in latitude twenty-nine degrees south of the equinoctial line, and is in places eight miles from the sea-ports. The land on both sides is similar. Many beautiful rivers flow from these mountains, and there is an abundance of wild life in the heights.

A nation of savages lives on the mountains called *Wayganna*, and these savages have no fixed dwellings like the other nations living on either side of the mountains. The Wayganna wage war against the others, and when they capture them they eat them. This practice is also followed by their enemies. The Wayganna are great hunters in the mountains and are very skillful in shooting game with their bows, and have much cunning in the use of slings and traps, wherewith to take the animals. There is an abundance of wild honey in the mountains, which they eat, and they learn the cries of the beasts and the notes of the birds in order to track and shoot them. They make fire like the other savages with two pieces of wood, and roast their meat before eating. They carry their wives and children about with them. . . .

When they set up their camps close to the enemy's country, they surround the huts with hedges, so that they cannot be surprised, and to protect themselves also against wild beasts. They surround the camp with sharp thorns just as with us one lays down foot-hooks, and this they do for fear of their enemies. All night long they burn their fires, but they extinguish them by day, so that none may see the smoke and track them.

They wear their hair long, and allow their fingernails to grow to a great length. They have rattles called *maraka*, like the other savages, which they look upon as their gods, and they have their own dances and drinking ceremonies. They use the teeth of wild beasts as knives and chop with stone wedges, as did also the other savages before they commenced to trade with the ships.

They make constant war upon their enemies, and when they want to capture them they hide behind the dry wood near to the huts, so that when anyone comes to take wood they can fall upon him.

They treat their enemies with great cruelty and receive the same treatment when they are captured. For example, such is their hate that they often cut off an arm or leg from a living prisoner. Others they kill, before they cut them up for eating.

These people have their dwelling close by the sea, in front of the range of mountains of which I have spoken. Their dwellings extend also some sixty miles inland behind the mountains, and a river flows down from the hills to the sea, on the banks of which they also have a settlement called Paraeibe. They have settlements as well for some twenty-eight miles along the sea shore, and on all sides they are encompassed by their enemies. To the north they are bounded by a nation of savages called *Weittaka* who are their enemies. On the south are the *Tuppin Ikin*. On the land side their enemies are called *Karaya*, while the Wayganna inhabit the mountains, and between these two are the savages called *Markaya*. These tribes harass them greatly and make war also among themselves, and when they capture one of the others they eat him.

They prefer to set up their dwellings in places where they have wood, water, and game and fish close at hand. When they have exhausted one place they move to another, and their manner of settling is this. A chief among them collects a party of forty men and women, as many as he can get, and these are usually friends and relations. They set up their huts, which are about fourteen feet wide and quite 150 feet long, according to the number of those who are to inhabit them. These huts are about twelve feet high and are round at the top and vaulted like a cellar. They roof them closely with the branches of palms to keep out the rain. Inside, the huts are all one: no one has a separate chamber to himself. Each couple, man and wife, has a space in the hut on one side, the space measuring about twelve feet, and on the other side lives another couple, and so the hut is filled, each couple having its own fire. The chief of the huts has his dwelling in the center. The huts have generally three doors, one at each end, and the other in the middle, and the doors are so low that the people have to stoop to get in or out. Few of the villages have more than seven huts. Between the huts is a space where they knock their prisoners on the head.

The savages fortify their huts as follows. They make a stockade of palm trees, which they first split and then set up to a height of about nine feet. This they build so thickly that no arrow can pierce it, but they leave little holes here and there through which they can shoot. Outside this stockade they build another of higher stakes, which they set up close together, but so that the space between them is not sufficient for a man to creep through. Among certain of the savages it is the custom to set up the heads of the men they have eaten on the stockade at the entrance to the huts. . . .

They sleep in things which are called in their language *Inni*. They are made of cotton yarn, and they tie them to two poles above the ground, and at night they burn their fires beside them. They do not willingly go out of their huts at night for any reason without fire, so greatly are they in awe of their devil whom they call *Ingange*, and whom they often see. . . .

Wherever they go, whether in the forest or on the water, they are never without their bows and arrows. When in the forest they are perpetually watching, with eyes raised towards the trees, and when they hear the noise of birds, monkeys, or other animals in the trees they know well how to shoot them, following them unceasingly until they are successful. It seldom happens that a man returns empty-handed from hunting.

In the same way they take the fish by the sea shore. They have keen sight, and as soon as a fish jumps they shoot and seldom miss. When they have hit the fish they jump into the water and swim after it. Some large fish, on feeling the arrow, sink to the bottom, but the savages will dive to a depth of well-nigh six fathoms to get them. They use also small nets which they make out of long pointed leaves called *tockaun*, and when they fish with nets several gather together, each man having his own station where the water is shallow, and they beat the water, driving the fish down into the nets. He who catches the greatest number divides his catch with his fellows.

It happens at times that those who live at a distance from the sea come down to catch fish which they bake until they are hard, after which they pound them into a kind of meal. This meal when dried lasts a long time, and they carry it back with them to their homes and eat it with roots. Otherwise, if they took the baked fish home, it would not keep for long, since they do not salt it. Also the meal goes further than the fish if baked whole. . . .

The women prepare the drinks. They take the mandioca root and boil it in great pots. Afterwards they pour it into other vessels and allow it to cool a little. Then young girls sit round and chew the boiled root in their mouths, and what is chewed they set apart in a special vessel. When the boiled root is all chewed, they place it back again in the pot which they fill with water, mixing the water with the chewed root, after which they heat it again.

They have special pots, half buried in the ground, which they make use of much as we use casks for wine or beer. They pour the liquid into these and close them, and the liquor ferments of itself and becomes strong. After two days they drink it until they are drunken. It is thick, but pleasant to the taste.

Each hut prepares its own drink, and when the whole village desires to make merry, which happens generally about once a month, they go first of all together into one hut and drink there until the drink is finished. Then they go to the round of the other huts, drinking until they have drunk their fill and there is nothing left.

When they drink they gather round the pots and sit, some on the fire-sticks, others on the ground. The drink is served by the women in a very orderly manner. The drinkers sing and dance round the pots, and on the spot where they drink they pass their water.

The drinking lasts all night, the merry-makers continuing to dance between the fires, with shouting and blowing of trumpets, and when they are drunken the noise is terrible; but they quarrel little. They are also generously disposed, and when a man has more food than his fellow he shares it with him.

The men have a bare space on the head with a circle of hair around it like a monk. I asked them frequently from what they took this fashion, and they told me that their forefathers had seen it on a man called Meire Humane, who had worked many miracles among them, and this man is supposed to have been a prophet or one of the Apostles.

I asked them further how they contrived to cut the hair before the ships brought them scissors, and they told me that they used a stone wedge with another instrument underneath and so cut off the hair. The bare space in the middle they make with a scraper of transparent stone which they use frequently for shearing. They have also a thing made of red feathers called *kannittare*, which they bind round the head. . . .

They have a large hole in the lower lip which they make when they are young. They take the children and prick the hole with a sharpened deer's horn. In this they insert a small piece of stone or wood and anoint it with salve, and the hole remains open. Then when the children are fully grown and fit to bear arms they enlarge the hole and insert in it a large green stone. This stone is shaped so that the smaller end is inside the lip and the larger end outside. The result is that their lips hang down with the weight of the stones. They have also at both sides of the mouth, and in either cheek, other small stones.

Some of these are of crystal and are narrow and long. They wear also ornaments made from large snail-shells called *Mattepue*. These ornaments are shaped like a half-moon, and they hang them round the neck. They are snow-white and are called Bogesso. . . .

There is no community of goods among them and they know nothing of money. Their treasures are the feathers of birds. He that has many feathers is rich, and he that has a stone in his lip is also counted among the rich.

Each couple has a particular plantation of roots which supplies both man and wife with food.

Their greatest honor is to capture their enemies and to slay them; for such is their custom. And for every foe a man kills he takes a new name. The most famous among them is he that has the most names.

They put their faith in a thing shaped like a pumpkin, the size of a pint pot. It is hollow within, and they put a stick through it and cut a hole in it like a mouth, filling it with small stones so that it rattles. They shake it about when they sing and dance, and call it *tammaraka*, and each man has one of his own. . . .

There are certain wise ones among them called *paygi*, who are looked up to as soothsayers are with us. These men travel every year throughout the whole country, visiting all the huts and saying that a spirit has been with them from afar off, and that this spirit has endued them with power to cause all the rattling tammaraka chosen by them to speak and grow so powerful that they can grant whatever is required of them. Then each man desires that his tammaraka should have this virtue, and a great feast is prepared, with drinking, singing, and prophesying, and many other strange ceremonies. The wise men then ordain a day, and fix upon one of the huts which they cause to be cleared, no woman or child being suffered to remain there, and they direct that each man shall paint his tammaraka red and decorate it with feathers, and come to the place so that this power of speech may be conferred upon them. After this they all go to the hut, and the wise men sit down at the upper end, each one having his own tammaraka on the ground before him. The others place theirs also there, and each one offers a present to the wise men, such as arrows, feathers, and ornaments for the ears. . . . Then he (the paygi) seizes the rattle by the mouth, shaking it and saying: "Now speak and let us hear you: are you within?" Then he speaks a word or two softly so that one cannot know whether it is he that speaks or the rattle: but the people imagine that the rattle is speaking.

Nevertheless, it is the wise man that speaks, and so he does with all the rattles one after the other. Each one then thinks that great virtue has entered into his rattle, and the wise men command them to make war and take many enemies, since the spirit in the tammaraka craves for the flesh of prisoners, and so the people set off to war.

After the paygi (or wise men) have changed the rattles into gods, each man takes his rattle away, calling it his beloved son, and building a hut apart in which to place it, setting food before it and praying to it what he desires, just as we pray to the true God. These rattles are their gods, for they know nothing of the true God, the maker of heaven and earth, believing that the earth and the heavens have existed from the beginning of time. Beyond this they know nothing of the creation of the world.

They say that once upon a time there was a great flood which drowned all their ancestors, save those that escaped in canoes or on to the tops of high trees. This I imagine must have been the Deluge.

When I first came into their hands, and they told me about the rattles, I thought there must be a devil's spirit in them, for they said that they spoke often. But when I went to the huts where the wise men sat to make the rattles speak, and saw their tricks, and that everyone had to sit down apart, I went away marvelling at the simplicity of the people and the ease with which they were beguiled. . . .

They go first to a hut and take all the women, one after another, and fumigate them. After this the women have to jump and yell and run about until they become so exhausted that they fall down as if they were dead. Then the soothsayer says: "See now, she is dead; but I will bring her to life again." After the woman has come to herself they say that she is able to foretell future things, and when the men go out to war the women have to prophesy concerning it.

At one time the wife of the king to whom I had been presented to be killed began to prophesy and told her husband that a spirit had come to her from far away enquiring concerning me, when I was to be killed, and as to the club with which I was to be knocked on the head, and where it was. The king replied that it would not be long and that all was prepared, only he was afraid I was not a Portuguese, but a Frenchman. Afterwards I asked the woman why she desired my death, seeing that I was no enemy, and whether she was not afraid that my God would punish her? She replied that I must not be troubled since they were only strange spirits seeking news of men. They have many ceremonies of this nature. . . .

They eat one another not from hunger, but from great hate and jealousy, and when they are fighting with each other one, filled with hate, will call out to his opponent: "Cursed be you, my meat." "To-day will I cut off your head." "Now am I come to take vengeance on you for the death of my friends." "This day before sunset your flesh shall be my roast meat." All this they do from their great hatred. . . .

When they desire to make war in an enemy's country the chiefs gather together and take counsel how best to achieve their purpose, all which they make known in the huts, so that the men may arm themselves. They name the time of the ripening of a certain fruit as the date of their departure, for they have not the art to reckon by the day or year. They also fix their expeditions by the time of the spawning of a fish called *pratti* in their tongue, and the spawning time they call *pirakaen*. Then they equip themselves with canoes and ar-rows, and lay in stores of dried root-meal. After this they enquire of the paygi, their wise men, whether they shall return victorious. These will say "Yes," but will warn the enquirers to note well their dreams when they dream of their foes. If many dream that they are roasting their enemy's flesh, that signifies victory. But if it is their own flesh which they see in the pot, that is an evil omen and they had better stay at home. If their dreams are propitious they arm themselves and prepare much drink in the huts, after which they dance and drink with their idols, the tammaraka, each one beseeching his idol to assist him in catching an enemy. Then they set out, and when they draw near to the enemy's country, on the night before the attack, the chiefs once more direct their men to remember their dreams.

I accompanied them in one of their expeditions, and on the night before they intended to attack, when we were close to the enemy's country the chief went up and down in the camp, telling the men to note well their dreams that night, and ordering the young men to set off at daybreak to hunt for game and catch fish, which was done, and the food was cooked. Then the chief summoned the other chiefs to his hut and when they were all seated upon the ground in a circle he gave them to eat, after which they all told their dreams, that is, such dreams as were favorable, and then they danced and made merry with the tammaraka. They spy out the enemy's huts at night and attack at dawn.

If they take a prisoner who is badly wounded they kill him at once and carry home the meat roasted. Those that are unwounded they take back alive and kill them in the huts. They attack with loud

Chuncho Chief Playing the Panpipe

yells, stamping on the ground, and blowing blasts upon trumpets made of gourds. They all carry cords bound about their bodies to make fast their prisoners, and adorn themselves with red feathers so that they may distinguish their friends from their foes. They shoot very rapidly and send fire-arrows into the enemy's huts to set them alight. And if they are wounded they have their special herbs with them to heal their wounds. . . .

There are a number of features of Tupinamba culture Hans Staden describes that will immediately strike the reader as familiar, as similar to some we have already mentioned among the Arawak and Carib: the role, for instance, played by the rattle—*maraka* is, in fact, an Arawak word—and the all-important position occupied by the medicine man. The veneration displayed toward the rattle, the fact that it is kept in a special hut, all this reminds one somewhat of the island Arawak *cemi*. Hans, like his German descendants, was manifestly not too keen an observer of social organization, but still his failure to mention certain things, considering his long stay with the Tupinamba, must be given considerable significance. The complete absence of any reference to such matters as the clan, the dual organization, masked dances, initiation rites for boys and girls, etc., I consider very important. I take it to indicate that the contact of the Tupinamba with peoples where these customs existed could not have been very intimate. This may mean one of two things, either they had lost important elements of their old culture or some of the new traits that I am assuming had spread from Mexico never reached them. The latter, I think, represented the true situation. In this connection I cannot too strongly insist that I am not for a moment contending that the Tupi-Guarani were invaders from outside South America, as I believe the Arawak were. All I claim is that some of the Tupi-Guarani tribes were at one time living as far north as the mouth of the Amazon as early as the eleventh century, possibly before that, and were in intimate contact with elements that had been disseminated from Mexico. Not all of these were necessarily relayed to those members of their stock who dwelt far to the south.

But let us for a moment return to mythology and religion

again. The twin cycle is but one of many myths of the Tupi-Guarani group that are characterized by their elaborateness and the logical manner in which the various episodes and themes have been integrated. This holds even more markedly for a cycle as important and perhaps even more significant than the story of the twins; namely, that connected with the culture-heroes proper. The old French historian, Thevet, in an unpublished manuscript utilized by Métraux, insisted that there were many such culture-creator gods, but he probably confused different aspects of the same personage. For us the important thing is the role of this divine hero *Monan* among the Tupinamba of Thevet and his analogues in other Tupi-Guarani tribes, a role always the same. It is he who introduced agriculture and founded their whole social order. In some tribes as, for instance, the Apapocouva-Guarani of the southeast of Brazil, he is aided in his original creation by another hero-deity, a trait that has some interesting parallels among the Indian tribes of eastern United States.

Associated with this divine culture-hero is the incident of the destruction of the earth, once by fire and once by water. Both themes are very widespread in North America and, in general, it can be said that the first is more specifically the possession of tribes influenced by Mexico and that the second belongs to the simpler tribes of the northern continent.

One final feature of Tupi-Guarani mythology must finally be noted: the marked tendency to interpret their mythical heroes as celestial beings—the sun, the moon, the morning and evening stars. Here too the similarities with southeastern United States and Mexico are numerous and startling.

Hans Staden, in the passages from his book quoted above, has given us some idea of the religious beliefs he found among the Tupinamba. Clearly his account is too simple and he leaves out one spirit-deity of unusual importance to them, the great thunderbird god, Tupan. The missionaries, however, mention him at every point and emphasize his great importance in the religious beliefs of the Tupi. In fact they are fairly unanimous in insisting that term *tupan* actually signified "sacred, mysterious, and all-important." There seems no justification for regarding this identification of the thunderbird god with the word "sacred" as due to a misconception of the missionaries as Métraux does. The same identification has taken place among a number of the Siouan tribes of the United States. It testifies, in no unmistakable terms, to the importance and significance of the thunderbird among these people and thus adds one more link to the tie that binds them to the cultures of the Gulf of Mexico proper to the Mississippi and beyond.

We now come to that aspect of Tupi-Guarani civilization which, from their discovery, has been most specifically associated with them and which, because of the horror it evoked among Europeans as well as its dramatic side, has been most accurately and completely described—cannibalism.

On page 72 we pointed out first that cannibalism was widespread in the two Americas, and second that it is intimately connected with warfare. A third feature may now be properly added: its ritualistic character. This last aspect of the killing and eating of a prisoner has always been pictured as if it somehow appertained to every series of war rituals that has been highly organized and specialized. At any rate no ethnologist seems to have been particularly struck by its special significance or attempted to advance any coherent kind of interpretation. That the ritual and highly institutionalized anthropophagy of the Tupi-Guarani demand an interpretation is self-evident, and what is just as self-evident is the fact that a reasonably convincing explanation can be given. Before giving it, let us, however, first describe the ceremonies connected with the great occasion.

The ritual connected with cannibalism begins properly with the setting out of a war party. In Indian theory the main purpose of warfare was to secure prisoners. Actually you went to war, of course, to revenge the death of a tribesman or relative in order to attain status. Then when you have secured your prisoner you return home and the long series of rites and observances begins. We shall follow them point by point, as described by Métraux for the Tupinamba.[21]

As soon as the victors return to the village, they are surrounded by the friends, who despoil them of everything they have—their ornaments, weapons, hammock, eating utensils, and whatever food, human or otherwise, they may happen to possess. If a prisoner is particularly obstreperous, four cords are drawn around his neck and his hand is tied securely under his chin. It is incumbent upon everyone to insult and abuse him and everyone takes great pleasure in informing him of the fate in store for him.

The entry into the village is always in the nature of a triumphal march. The chief meets the victors and invites them all to bring their prisoners to the palisades surrounding the huts. There the victors and their friends form a circle around the prisoners, who are given a rattle and compelled to dance and deliver the following speech: "We left our homes as brave men should, with the intention of capturing you and eating you, our enemies. But you, on the contrary, triumphed over us and it is we who have been captured. We are not complaining about our fate. Real brave men are willing to die in the land of their enemies. Our country is large and our tribesmen will revenge us." To this a group of Tupinamba reply, "You have killed many of us and we will now take vengeance for it."

The captive's eyebrows are then shaved and his hair cut in front. He is made to look exactly like a Tupinamba warrior. He is then smeared with resin or honey, and covered and decorated with feathers of the most beautiful description. If he encounters a woman, he is obliged to say, "Your food has arrived."

The triumphal entry is made only after the captives have first been conducted to the tomb of the deceased relatives of their conquerors, which they must clean or, more properly, to follow the old French chronicler Thevet, "whom they must renew, just as if the captive were a victim who is to be sacrificed to the memory of these dead."

After the first outbursts of hatred, the position of the prisoner changes completely, and he practically becomes a member of the tribe. Theoretically the shadow of death is always about him, but his execution may be postponed for as long as five years and he may, in certain cases, never be killed.

It seems perfectly clear from what Thevet says, as quoted by

Métraux, that primarily the captive is regarded as a kind of substitute for some deceased person. For instance, he is always conducted to the hut that had been occupied by the man whose grave he had cleared off. Once arrived at the hut he is given the hammock, the weapons, the necklaces, the feather ornaments, in fact everything that the deceased had ever possessed. He can use them at his will. More than that. If all the near male relatives of the deceased have perished, their widows frequently marry the prisoner. In short, the captive represents a complete replacement of the dead man.

In spite of these facts he has, of course, no status, for after all, he is destined to be killed within a given time and according to specific rules.

When the time for his execution approached it was customary to march him, lavishly decorated with the feather ornaments used at the great tribal ceremonies, through the village. If, at such a ceremonial exhibit of the prisoner, perroquet feathers were thrown at the unfortunate man, this was a symbolic gesture indicating that his days were now numbered. Apparently just before the final preparations for the ceremony proper, a long carousal took place at which the portions of the body of the captive were symbolically distributed to their future recipients. It was then, likewise, that each individual was assigned the role he was to play: who was to shave him, who was to decorate him with feathers, who was to paint him, who was to wash him, who to kill him, and who, finally, was to take charge of his mutilated body.

The prisoner was specifically informed of all the preparations that were taking place, but there seems to have been no conscious brutality involved in this, and he was treated with kindness and affection. An old French source, Yves d'Évreux, quoted by Métraux, speaks of one case where the affection showered upon a captive and the sincere solicitude expressed by him were quite remarkable. The particular person he mentions had been captured when he was young. His mother had been killed and devoured, and the same fate awaited him. But this, in no way, affected his love for his adopted parents or theirs for him.

The actual death ritual begins by the despatching of messengers to all the villages of the tribes and friends announcing that a day had been set for the macabre festivities. Plenty of time was allowed, for much had to be done.

The first and most important matter was to begin the plaiting of the ceremonial cord with which the prisoner was to be tied. It had a special name, *musarana*. Its manufacture and the reverence in which it was held was a veritable cult. It could not be made by twisting but had to be plaited, a procedure that necessitated an enormous amount of work.

Next in importance was the executioner's club. This was six feet long, says Hans Staden, and was covered with a sticky mess, "after which they take the eggs of a bird called *mackukawa*, which they break up to powder and spread upon the club. Then a woman sits down and scratches figures in the powder while the other women dance and sing around her. When the club, *iwera pemme*, is ready, decked with tassels and other things, they hang it in an empty hut upon a pole and sing in front of it all night."

Throughout this time the victim behaves as though nothing were about to happen to him. Little attention is, in fact, paid to him except that at a number of intervals the women take the prisoner to the village square and dance around him.

On the first day they paint the musarana and consecrate the prisoners, for there were always more than one. They are taken from the houses where they had been so solicitously cared for and conducted to a hut at the south end of the village. There the front part of their head is shaved and their face is blackened with genipa. Many of the women of the village now join them and likewise paint themselves black. These women sling up their hammocks around those of the prisoners and rest in them, chanting all the time. Their songs express their disdain for the captives and the members of their tribe who had never been able to kill any of their friends. They mock the unfortunates and announce to them their fate and the revenge that they are about to take on them.

The men who are to play a prominent part in the subsequent rites spend the day decorating themselves lavishly and dancing.

The second day is taken up with gathering bamboo for the construction of a conical hut in which to prepare the oven or fire. When it is finished, all the people, both men and women, dance around it, carrying bundles of arrows on their shoulders. The prisoners, who are placed at a distance from the dancers, throw them whatever they find at hand.

On the third day everyone assembles in the village square, trumpet in hand, to the sound of which they dance all day.

On the fourth day the prisoner is taken early in the morning and conducted to the river bank, where he is carefully washed. His few remaining hairs are shaved off, and he is thoroughly cleaned. On his way back he is attacked by an Indian who attempts to overpower him, while other Indians tie him with the musarana. The captive is supposed to defend himself vigorously to prove that he is a valiant man, and the assailant tries to attain his goal without calling in the aid of his fellows. Often the assailant is beaten off, and then another one must take his place.

As soon as the prisoner is subdued, some young girls approach with the sacred and ominous cord, painted white, which is passed around his neck. While the men tie up the prisoner securely the young girls intone a mocking song. The ends of the cord are then thrown around the arms of a woman who walks behind the prisoner. However, this is not always done, for sometimes the two ends of the cord are seized by the two men whose duty it is to attend to the captive closely. The latter is then given some genipa fruit, which he is supposed to throw at all those within reach. Or they may give him a bow with blunt arrows to shoot in whatever direction he wishes. His wife stays with him throughout all and supplies him with new arrows, etc.

When all have had enough of this game, the prisoner is taken back to his hut to be then escorted at five in the afternoon to the provisional hut erected in the village square—all this, of course, to the accompaniment of the maraka.

At some period during the day the club has been transferred to a special hut built for it. It has now to be decorated and consecrated. After being, as described above by Hans Staden, smeared with honey and plastered with powdered egg, it is

allowed to rest flat upon a receptacle to dry. Finally it is carried
to a hut from which the residents had been removed and it is
suspended from the roof. A group of women then guard it
throughout the night, dancing and singing without interruption,
in order to lull the terrible and sacred implement to sleep as they
said. Before the club has been carried to this hut, some women
proceed to the final painting and decoration of the victim.

Soon after sunset the Indians gather for the final drinking bout
and festivities before the execution of the captives. These latter
must be present and participate, particularly in the great dance
that takes place then and is called "the dance of the hinds."
A very significant interruption must take place in this dance to
permit the captives their last gesture of hostility, which consists of pelting the dancers with a veritable hailstorm of missiles.
This is the last expression of freedom of action vouchsafed them,
for they are then brought back to the special hut in which they
have been confined, and strictly guarded. They lie in their hammocks, so securely tied that movement is practically impossible.
To prevent any great effusion of blood when they are killed,
they are given a special fruit to eat, which is supposed to possess
this virtue.

The final day has now arrived. At dawn the women arise, first
remove the club from the roof, and then wake up the prisoners
and destroy the temporary hut that had been erected for them.
They are then conducted to the place of execution, which is
generally in the center of the village. The victim is thrown to the
ground, and the cord which has been around his neck all this
time is removed and tied tightly around his waist. He then stands
up again, and the women dance around him mocking and taunt-
ing him. Then a fire is lit so that the victim can see it, and the
ceremonial club is brought and presented to a warrior so that it
can be shown to the captive.

The designated executioner, throughout all this time, stays in
his hut quietly. He is covered with the most beautiful ornaments.
On his head he wears a glorious feather dress, around his forehead is tied a red diadem of plumes, on his breast are suspended
necklaces of shells, and his arms and legs are covered with feather

clusters. An enormous "wheel" of ostrich feathers encloses his hips, and over his shoulders is thrown a long cloak made of the feathers of the red ibis. His face is painted red and his body is daubed with charcoal.

At the appointed time relatives and friends go to his hut. "Come," so they address him, "you to whom the great honor has been given to avenge the death of our ancestors, of our parents and our brothers and sisters." Then, to the accompaniment of dancing and singing, they conduct him to the center of the village. With dancing steps, twisting his body into all sorts of shapes and rolling his eyes in terrifying fashion, the executioner-avenger now approaches the place of sacrifice. In this manner he advances until he comes face to face with the victim. There he stops. He is now handed the sacred club. This is generally done by some old man who possesses a great reputation as a warrior. He is supposed to pass the club first under his arms and between his legs, and then to brandish it over the head of the victim.

As soon as the executioner-avenger receives the club, the following set colloquy takes place between him and the prisoner:

"Is not your nation our enemy? And are not you yourself the one who killed and ate some of my relatives and friends?"

"Most emphatically I am that one. Indeed I am the most powerful person imaginable and brave to boot. Were I not tied up here I would soon fall upon you and yours and destroy and then devour you as I have so frequently done in the past."

"Well that is over for you. Now it is you who are going to be killed, cut up, barbecued, and eaten by me and my relatives and friends."

"So be it. But my relatives will soon revenge me."

After this colloquy the executioner runs at him with his club and attempts to strike him in the nape of the neck. The victim must attempt to ward off the blow as long as possible. At times he is given a small club with which to defend himself. Instances have occurred where he actually succeeded in wresting the club from the hand of the executioner.

Everyone now watches the executioner intently, and as soon as he has delivered the fatal blow the bystanders pluck their bow-strings and raise great shouts of joy. The position in which the body falls is then carefully noted. This is important. If it falls face forward, no prognostication at all can be made, but if it falls backward, this is a good augury, for it signifies the near death of an enemy.

As soon as the man is dead, a few old women rush upon the body, drink the blood, and proceed systematically to cut it up and prepare it for roasting. The wife of the deceased also approaches, sheds a few purely ceremonial tears, just the proper amount, and then identifies herself with the rest.

Children are frequently forced to touch the body and moisten their hands in its blood. "You have revenged yourself on your enemy, my child," they are taught to say, "for this is the one who made you an orphan. . . . "

And thus this amazing ceremony ends—that is, except for the executioner. He has now to go through a number of rites to escape the vengeance of the dead man's spirit. He throws away his mantle and club as soon as the victim falls, and rushes head-long for his hut. Once in the hut, he runs around wildly to escape the spirit pursuing him. His sisters and female cousins at the same time rush through the village shouting, "This is my brother's name!" and proclaim the new name by which he must now be known. But not only the executioner must change his name. All those who have in any fashion whatsoever participated in the ritual must do the same.

These preliminaries over, the executioner takes to his hammock and lies there as though sick. His arms and waist are tied with cord for four days, and when he is untied he is blackened with genipa. He has now to submit to a rigorous fast. He cannot, of course, partake of the flesh of the man he has killed. He may eat no game or fish, use no salt. Above all he must speak to no one nor leave his hammock. Contact with the earth is particularly dangerous for him. Throughout the period of seclusion he amuses himself by shooting with a miniature bow at wax figurines placed in front of him, the figurines apparently representing the spirits of the dead. Finally the executioner must let his hair grow to a certain length as a sign of mourning. When it has attained a prescribed length a feast is given to indicate that the period of mourning is over.

At this final feast and carousal his hair is cut and he announces his new name. After this begins the painful operation of cutting deep incisions into his breast, arms, legs, and thighs. They are so treated as to permit characteristic cicatrices to develop. He then takes to his hammock again and observes certain dietary restrictions, at the end of which time his status becomes normal again and he receives a special title.

It is perfectly clear that the series of ceremonies here described does not center around the one thing that has made it famous—cannibalism. That constitutes but one act of this ritual drama. Actually there seem, at first blush, to be three distinct components involved here—the belief that the death of a tribesman must be avenged, the practice of human sacrifice, and cannibalism. But are they really distinct? Have these three essential components of our ritual no connection? To answer this question correctly, let us first pose a question. Is there, for instance, any civilization with which the Tupi-Guarani might have had some contact where all three exist and have been combined in a fashion reminiscent of what we find here? The answer must quite definitely be in the affirmative. We do find such tribes—the Aztecs and the Caddoan-Iroquoian tribes of southeastern United States. Among the Aztec the long preparation of the victim to be sacrificed and frequently eaten is quite well known. He is there supposed to impersonate a god, and the eating of his body is a sacramental union and identification with him. The cannibalism is quite secondary, however, the primary thing is the religious human sacrifice. Often, as the readers will perhaps remember, the necessity for such human sacrifice among the Aztec led to war expeditions that had only this one thing as their purpose.

The writer's suggestion then is that this highly intricate series of rites clustering around the Tupi-Guarani ritual anthropophagy represents this greatly distorted and remodeled Aztec ceremony. In short, I believe that its original purpose, that of a sacrifice, has been almost completely forgotten here. Not among all Tupi-

Guarani tribes, however, for it survives among the *Shipaya* division of that stock. So, likewise, it does among another tribe, the *Guarayu*, where the prisoner is killed in one of the specific Aztec sacrificial fashions—namely, with arrows.

We must then visualize this basic Mexican ritual as being secondarily combined with certain older war customs and beliefs and with the kanaima ritual, so characteristically developed, we saw, among the Carib, by whom, in fact, they have been greatly influenced (cf. pages 72-74). Because warfare and shamanism played so all-important a role in Tupi-Guarani life, the rituals connected with them completely overshadowed that particular aspect of it, human sacrifice, which must be regarded as historically oldest and fundamental.

Like the famous sun dance of the plains Indians of the United States, this ceremony thus proves to be a conglomeration of practices, customs, beliefs, and interpretations of the most varied mind. And just as certain groups who practiced the sun dance—the Dakota and Mandan, for instance—elaborated and overemphasized one element of the ceremony, namely torture, so most of the Tupi-Guarani overstressed the ritual eating of the captives to be sacrificed, an element which was, essentially, an unimportant detail among the Aztecs.

Such a secondary hypertrophy of a trait in a ritual whose original significance has been forgotten is quite common. In fact, among many of the southeastern Indians of the United States a derivative of this same Aztec ceremony is found, and stressing a different feature: namely, the prolonged torture of the prisoner. Since this is encountered among tribes lying definitely in the track of the Mound-Builders, we again are in the happy situation of attempting an approximate date. Sometime then between 1000 and 1400 A.D. this Aztec ritual swept around the Gulf of Mexico. In speaking of this ceremony as an Aztec one, all that is implied, of course, is that our only descriptions of it have come from the Aztecs. That they took it over from the Toltecs whom they conquered seems perfectly clear.

The exact fashion in which this, as well as most of the higher aspects of their culture, came to the Tupi-Guarani, must remain largely hypothetical. It may very well have represented a spread of Toltec-Aztec culture southward toward the coast of Venezuela instead of northward around the Gulf of Mexico and by way of the Antilles. That it necessarily antedated the spread of Arawak culture proper to South America by any great length of time may well be doubted. Indeed both peoples may have received these Toltec-Aztec constituents of their culture at approximately the same time.

The assumption that the Tupi-Guarani obtained the basic constituents of their culture, more particularly maize agriculture, the distinctive aspects of their mythology, religion, and ceremonialism at so late a date has a very definite bearing on their so-called wanderlust. As a particular tribe with a specific language, they may very well have dwelt at or near the mouth of the Amazon and southward for many generations, hundreds of years if you will, before these elements reached them. Indeed it is reasonable to suppose they did, but with a simple nonagricultural economy and only moderately nomadic. The extreme mobility that characterizes them must, however, have begun after the Toltec-Aztec influences had reached them. If they wandered so extensively after the discovery of South America, this constitutes a partial corroboration for the late arrival of these influences. Their post-columbian spread is thus simply a continuation of that "guaranization" of tribes which all ethnologists have noted. There is no need of overemphasizing special causes, such as their desire to flee from the Europeans or the influence of an old mythical search for the land where there is no evil, as Nordenskiöld and Métraux have done. Yet that they secondarily become eluders we do not doubt.

The Tupi-Guarani are the second of the two great culture disseminators of South America. It has almost always been customary to regard the Tupi-Guarani-speaking tribes as representing a very old linguistic stock of South America. That may be true. But their culture is very manifestly of mixed origin. One might indeed speak of two basic strata. The older stratum is identical with the culture of tribes of the north and east of Brazil and contains elements that belong to the oldest common

culture of the two continents. The second is that which came
from Mexico. Only after the two had been fully integrated did
the Tupi-Guarani migrations in South America begin. The real
spread of their culture may very well not have begun before the
fourteenth century and subsequent to that of the really fundamental culture bearers, the Arawak. Indeed it may even have
been subsequent to the spread of the Carib whose culture, we
saw, was largely conditioned and shaped by that of the Arawak.
Such an assumption—that is, the very late beginning of the actual
precolumbian spread of the Tupi-Guarani—would indeed account for the very clear influence that the Carib seem to have
had upon them.

And now before leaving these great wanderers, whose civilization had so many roots and assumed so many forms, let us recall
one other of their customs which so keenly excited the curiosity
of the early explorers and missionaries and which seems once
more to bind them to the heirs of the Mound-Builders—the tear-
greeting ceremony. When a guest arrived or a tribesman returned
from a journey he was welcomed not by laughter and smiles but
by tears and weeping. "When any guest doth come to the house,"
so says the anonymous *Treatise of Brazil*, which Purchas included in his famous collection of travels, "the honour and enter-
tainment they make him is to bewail him: Now the guest being
come into the house they set him in the net, and after he is set,
without speaking any word to him, the wife and the daughters
and the other friends do sit them down round about him with
their hair loose, touching with the hand the party: they all begin
to weep with a high voice and great abundance of tears, and there
they tell in a versified prose all things that have happened since
they saw one another to that hour and many other which they
invent, and the troubles that the guest hath suffered in his
journey; and all things else that may provoke pity and tears. The
guest all this time speaketh not one word, but after they have
bewailed him a good while, they wipe the tears, and remain so
quiet, so modest, so pleasant and merry that it seemeth they
never wept."[22]

From Rio de Janeiro to the delta of the Mississippi and north along the course of that river to the Dakota and the Assiniboins the custom extended. Assuredly this cannot all be chance, such a massing of similarities and such strange ones along the Mississippi and throughout southeastern United States—tears and human sacrifice, torture and ritual cannibalism!

PART II

The Old Stock

CHAPTER VI

The Melting Pot

THE TRIBES OF THE AMAZON BASIN

FROM ITS DISCOVERY TO THE PRESENT DAY THE
Amazon has filled the traveler who first beholds it with wonder
and admiration. "Each country," wrote Christoval Acuña in
1639, "has striven to make out a title to be the mother of such a
daughter; attributing to their own bowels, the first sustenance
which gave it being, and called it the river Marañón. . . . [It]
flows from west to east . . . and a few degrees to the south of
the equator. Its length, from the source to the mouth, is one
thousand three hundred and fifty Castilian measured leagues.
. . . It flows along, meandering in wide reaches; and, as absolute lord of all the rivers which run into it, sends out its branches,
which are like faithful vassals, with whose aid it goes forth, and,
receiving from the smaller streams the lawful tribute of their
waters, they become incorporated in the main channel. It is
worthy of remark that according to the dignity of the guest, is
the harbinger who is sent to receive him; thus with ordinary arms
it receives the more common rivers, increasing them for those of
more importance; and for some which are so great as almost to be
able to put shoulder to shoulder, it comes forth in person with
its whole current. In breadth it varies very much, for in some
parts its breadth is a league, at others two, at others three, and at
others many more; preserving so much more narrowness in a

course of several leagues, in order that, with greater ease, spread out into eighty-four mouths, it may place itself on an equality with the ocean."[23]

Ecuador and Peru might fight for the right of possessing the lake to which the mighty river owes its source, but the natives in the jungles that begin as soon as you descend the Cordillera to the east cared little for such matters and knew little about the great civilization to the west. The number of tribes to be found there, each distinct from the other in language and often in custom and tradition, was legion. Few other areas of the Americas can exhibit such a diversity. It is not surprising then to find that each tribe was interested primarily in one question: namely, how could it maintain its particular culture intact and how could it defend itself against its enemies.

Let us take the area that lies roughly between the Japurá and the Igaraparana, on the one hand, and the Igaraparana and the Issa, on the other, and whose inhabitants have been so well described by Whiffen.[24] Here those north of the Japurá will have no dealings with those south of it and regard them as savages. The *Maku* to the east are universally despised and regarded as slaves; the *Andoke* to the north of the Apaporis River, on the other hand, are the bullies, the terror of all the tribes around them. Peaceful tribes are practically nonexistent. For the most part these peoples are always at war. If people combine, it is not through love of one another but because of the mutual hatred they bear some other tribe.

According to Whiffen the constant state of warfare found here is based on fear of one another and the realization that the only protection any particular tribe can obtain is in the extermination of his neighbors. "Every ill that befalls a man they set down to the evil intent of an enemy. Death from whatsoever cause is invariably considered to be murder, and as murder it has to be revenged on some suspected person or persons. Hence it follows that blood feuds innumerable are carried on relentlessly. Any and every excuse serves for a fight. If a thunderstorm should wreck a house, it is more than sufficient reason for that household to attack another in reprisal of the damage done; for it is to them quite evident that the catastrophe was caused by the magic of some malicious dweller in the vicinity. . . . One result is that there are no recognized native trade routes or trade centers nor are there any markets where the tribes of any language group may meet and exchange their wares. Even local markets are nonexistent."[25]

While the statement just quoted may be somewhat exaggerated, still it holds to an amazing degree for most of the tribes of the Amazon Basin and particularly for those of the northwest section. Such a situation taken together with the jungle and the climate is bound to react on the social organization. Not only is it almost impossible to develop large and cohesive social units under such conditions, but new tribes entering the area would be likely to have whatever integrated and unified social organization they may have brought with them greatly modified if, in fact, they did not lose it entirely. Often to speak of "tribes" in the ordinary sense of that term would be somewhat meaningless here.

Yet lack of larger social units or a tribal cohesion and unity for those tribes who belong to what we must call the old stock does not imply a lack of cohesiveness and feeling of common kinship within these smaller units. Quite the contrary. We find, throughout the western Amazon region, social units forming an undivided household community varying from sixty to two hundred individuals, all of whom occupy a common house and live under a chief. At times there may be two or three of such houses, but never more. In normal conditions the chief of such a household has little influence except what he may exert due to his personal character. Certain privileges, however, are his. He has a special portion of the house assigned to him and his family, prisoners taken frequently belong to him, and he has a right to all the unattached women. He leads the tribe in war and has great influence in the councils. But any unusual power this may seem to give him is largely if not entirely neutralized by the fact that chieftainship is not automatically inherited. Although the son generally succeeds, he must be selected by the council, and the council consists of all the males of the household who have reached man's estate.

All this makes definitely for a type of economic communism. Among other things it means the use of a common fireplace, its preparation, and the grinding of corn where maize is used. But not only economic communism unites them. Another bond also exists, equally important: the feeling of blood kinship that expresses itself in local exogamy; that is, in the interdiction of marriage within the household or cluster of households. The cultural and religious implications of such a social custom and such a belief are naturally of the most far-reaching kind.

Whoever they are, these people of the jungle, whether invaders from the north, like the Arawak, or late intruders from the east, like the Tupi-Guarani *Omagua*, all the Indians in the western Amazon Basin live in such houses. Our first duty then must be to see what these houses and households are like. Let us take those of the *Boro* and *Uitoto* tribes as our example. Both the house and its setting in the jungle have been excellently described by Whiffen. Let us see what he says:[26]

Out of the silence and gloom of the forest the traveler will emerge into the full light of a clearing. Though it is the site of a tribal headquarters there is no village, no cluster of huts, except among some of the tribes on the lower Apaporis. There is but one great house, thatched and ridge-roofed like a gigantic hay-rick, standing foursquare in the open. This is the home of some three score Indians.

The immediate signs of their occupancy are but few. There is hardly any litter cumbering the homestead. Whatever of refuse there be is cleared more speedily by the ants than it would be by the most up-to-date sanitary authority of London. Back here in the untouched districts, away from the Rubber Belt and the commerce-bearing rivers, there are none of the leavings of civilization: no broken bottles, no battered tins, no torn and dirty scraps of paper—indeed if bottle or tin ever found its way to these wilds it would be esteemed a most rare and valuable treasure. No village dogs bark their challenge at the stranger's approach, no domestic fowls flutter away to safety. A naked child or a startled old woman may scurry into the murk of the maloka, otherwise the silence and solitude appear little less profound than in the forest.

That is the picture as the artist or camera would reproduce it. The details, the essentials, must be sought within.

First of all the characteristics is the fact that nothing makes for permanence. The house and its contents at the best are but made for temporary use. The possession of a central tribal house does not presuppose that these Indians remain for any length of time in one locality. After about two or three years the house falls into a state of disrepair, but the tribesmen will not patch and mend it. They will simply discard it like all useless things. The women will be loaded up with the few tribal possessions—not forgetting the inevitable burden of their infants—the house will be burnt, and the whole of this *grosse famille* departs to seek a new site on which to build another habitation.

Building material is easily come by, and though to clear the land for agricultural purposes from the virgin forests entails considerable hard work, it is periodically a necessary task. However rich it may have been in the first instance, successive crops rob the soil of its fertility, as the Indian is only too well aware, and fresh ground must perforce be broken up every few years. Then again, paths converging on the homestead in time are worn through the forest undergrowth, dense though it may be, circuitous though the trail of the Indian is invariably. Secrecy is security. A track-way is as good as an invitation, a sign-post, to the enemy. To move becomes a precautionary measure, even if the food supply be not exhausted— another reason that makes for unsettled conditions in forest life.

The site chosen is never near a river, for these are the highways for a possible enemy, and streams for ordinary purposes abound. Also—but this is an insignificant reason in comparison with the first —insect pests are not so abundant at a distance from the river-bank. With an eye to defense from hostile visitors, the Indian habitation is sedulously hidden, and the paths that lead to it are concealed also in every possible way. The track from the river especially may run more or less directly for, say, a third of a mile; then it is absolutely stopped by a fallen tree. No cleared pathway apparently runs beyond this, but the Indian, creeping through the thicket by devious ways, eventually reaches another comparatively cleared track. This will in turn be stopped in the same fashion, and thence lead more directly housewards. The river-path may be broken twice or even three times in little more than a mile.

At the same time that the ground is cleared on which the house is to be built, a plot immediately in front is also cleared for use as a dancing ground. This is customary, but not invariable, for some tribes are content with the dancing space inside the house. The outside dancing floor once cleared is quickly trodden down, and though no special preparation is attempted will soon be baked comparatively hard in the sun.

The construction of the great house is not complicated, but the workmanship is dexterous, and will bear the closest inspection. Four great poles, 20 to 30 feet high, form the main supports of the roof, which slopes down on either side tentwise almost to the ground from the central ridge-pole. More posts and cross-beams support it, and the whole is most adroitly lashed together. The forest supplies all the needed material. It is there ready to hand, growing where the house is to be erected. The straightest tree-trunks provide the posts and cross-beams; the creeping lianas serve to splice and bind the framework together; Bussu palm-leaves make the thatch, which, as the actual wall is but some three feet in height, is practically roof and wall in one. The *bejucos*, or lianas, used to tie the beams and poles are first soaked in water to render them supple enough.

To make the thatch the Indians slit bamboos and insert the palm-leaves doubled backwards. The strips are then laid on the framework of the house, one above another, so that the uppermost strips shall hang half over those below. They are piled on to a thickness of from a foot to eighteen inches, and when completed, this shingling is absolutely waterproof. When it ceases to be so, the house will be abandoned. The leaves are not plaited, or intertwined in any manner, so the roof consists only of loose fronds, row upon row, and these have more the appearance of tobacco plants hung in an open drying-barn than a reed or straw thatch.

All the native houses are made after much the same manner. They vary only in unimportant details. The shape, as a rule, is a rough parallelogram or square with rounder angles, but on the lower Apaporis the houses are circular. On the Napo River also they are hemispherical, but the section of a Witoto or Boro house usually would be a triangle some 30 feet high, with a 60-feet base. Witoto houses sometimes are more circular as to ground-plan, but always have the pointed roof, not a cone.

The house is not always roofed and thatched to the ground, the last two or three feet occasionally being made of a closely set palisade, lined with matting or thatch.

These houses have no windows, and the entrance is merely an opening in the palm-thatch eaves of some three feet by two. This most frequently is closed with a removable section of the thatch, which must be lifted out when any one enters, and replaced behind them; or it may be covered by a curtain of thatch, which is hung on a cross-piece of the eaves by a strip of liana, and simply is pushed aside and swung back into place. Whatever the "door" may be, the opening is invariably kept closed, and it is the duty of any persons coming in to fasten up the entrance as soon as they have entered. The consequence of this absence of any opening is that the interiors of the malokas are nearly as dark by day as by night. But this deep gloom keeps out insects—no small consideration in a land so infested with them.

The interior with its pointed roof resembles a circus at a country fair. The central space is usually kept clear, and is used by the children as a playing-ground what time it is not required for more serious tribal business, such as dancing or a tobacco palaver. The far end of the house—where there is usually another small entrance—is the portion reserved for the chief and his family. Neither the Boro nor the Witoto indulge in the cubicles of palm-leaf thatch found in Uaupes houses, nor are their habitations divided into two, with a small chamber at the end, as in *Tuyuka* houses. Each family has its own fire, but that is the only distinction, though on the lower Apaporis mats of beaten palm-leaf are used to form a sort of booth for each family. Such mats, *duriei* as the Witoto call them, are also employed in some houses for the protective purpose of securing the entrance.

The Apaporis Indians also make shelves or platforms on which they sleep, but all the other Issa-Japura tribes use the hammock slung about 2½ feet from the ground. One is hung for every man adjacent to his family fire—almost over it in fact. A second, placed rather less advantageously, in local opinion, belongs to his wife; while a third may be set between the two, close under the sloping thatch, for the children, when they are not asleep on the rough floor of uncovered earth. The family possessions are stored in places on the rafters overhead along with the hammocks, cooking-pots, and baskets with dried fish or smoked meat, the cassava-squeezer and personal treasures.

The chief has no other house, but any tribesman with a wish for one can build a small house for himself and his family in the bush, though he still retains his right to a corner in the common dwelling of the tribe. A temporary shelter is easily contrived by lashing poles to four trees, some seven or eight feet above the ground. On this frame-work branches for rafters and palm-leaves for thatch are quickly adjustable. This is the ordinary way of preparing a sleeping-place in the forest, and is known among the rubber-gatherers as a *rancho*, but the Indians' private houses are constructed more securely, and more like miniature editions of the central tribal house, although in this case no wall whatever supports the sloping roof as a rule. These may be called their country homes, and they may be perhaps as much as two days' journey from the great house of assembly.

These large house units with their economic communism and in which one extended family live, have a very interesting distribution. Apart from the western Amazon Basin we find them among the few divisions of the northern Ge people in north-western Brazil, in the Chaco, both the Bolivian and the Para-guayan, in Matto Grosso, and among the Patagonians. None of the Tupi-Guarani with the exception of the Chiriguano in the Bolivian Chaco have them, and very few of the Arawak tribes. They are utterly unknown among the Arawak of the Antilles. On the other hand, they are almost universally characteristic of the Carib and the numerous smaller linguistic stocks of the western Amazon. Most of these tribes have no clan organization, and their agriculture is limited to the cultivation of the bitter manioc. Where maize exists, it can be safely attributed to either the influence of the Arawak or the Tupi-Guarani, both of whom, we saw, are intruders in this area. The presence in Matto Grosso and the Chaco of these community houses can easily be explained as due to the penetration of Carib tribes into Matto Grosso, and of Arawak tribes who had taken over this trait from them, into the Chaco. We can thus confidently assign the western Amazon as the region where this type of household unit was originally elaborated.

Although, as we have just indicated, most of the tribes in this area had no clan organization, the household unit did possess one of the fundamental traits of a clan: prohibition of intermar-riage within the household—that is, exogamy. How are we to explain this? The question is again not a purely academic one but, on the contrary, vital for an understanding of aboriginal South America. There are only two possible alternatives. Either these peoples once possessed a clan or a dual organization and have lost all of its characteristic traits except exogamy, or exogamy has developed as a single factor. The second possibility seems altogether improbable for a number of reasons. First of all, no evidence for such a development is found in the aboriginal world and, secondly, and of far greater significance, this region is so crisscrossed with tribes who have either the clan or the dual organization that it is only natural to assume that all the tribes found there had, at one time, either the one or the other. In this belief we are reinforced by two marriage customs of the Carib, the almost universal obligation that a man marry his sister's daughter and the marked tendency for the husband to move his wife's home after marriage.

If all the non-Arawak tribes in the area under question did once possess the clan or dual organization, that would, roughly speaking, mean that this type of society was spread over the whole vast region watered by the Amazon and its affluents, actually everything from the Araguaya River west as well as over Venezuela and the three Guianas. There would thus be one continuous block of peoples with clan organization or clan and dual organization together, stretching from the Great Lakes of the United States and the Gulf of St. Lawrence southward to the Amazon Basin and beyond. But there is still another block extending from southern Mexico through Central America and then down the west coast of South America as far as Chile and including all the great civilizations of the two Americas, with the exception of the Aztecs.

Clearly, these must all be connected in some fashion. Clearly the picture presented by western and northwestern Brazil, where we find tribes with no clan organization alternating with others that have either matrilineal or patrilineal clans and with still others having both clans and the dual organization, is not a natural one but, on the contrary, one of confusion and bewilderment. Like a last refuge place, peoples and cultures seem to have converged upon this section of South America from all directions. The Arawak and Tupi-Guarani were comparatively late intruders. Many other peoples must have preceded them.

It is easy to see why this should be so. The Orinoco could bring them, the Amazon could bring them. They could come down from the Cordilleras of Ecuador, Colombia, Bolivia, and Peru. And they must have come not simply once but a number of times, carrying with them new customs and new ideas, many of which were subsequently lost or transformed beyond recognition yet some of which prevailed and persisted intact. But this incessant and aggressive impingement of peoples and cultures upon one another makes it impossible for highly integrated cultures to develop. The atmosphere is fundamentally that of the frontier and the melting pot. Along such open routes as were the Orinoco and the Amazon, nothing else could very well be expected.

To attempt consequently to determine what was possibly the original culture of the area is quite hopeless. We can, however, assume that, at one time, a hunting and fishing culture once prevailed here. That maize agriculture, with its accessories and implications, came from without, we know. The same holds for the sweet potato. But the cultivation of manioc and the technique for extracting the poison out of the bitter variety, that bears all the earmarks of being very old in this region. The same holds for the blowgun, the panpipe, the signal drum, puberty initiation for both sexes but more particularly for girls, the couvade, etc. Whether it also holds for the numerous and highly distinctive masked dances is an open question.

These traits can be roughly divided into three groups: those that have a much wider distribution over South America, those that have either developed in this area or been highly specialized there, and those that are clearly intrusive. We shall continue our description in terms of the first two and confine ourselves specifically to a selected number of customs. Let us begin with the panpipe and the signal drum.

Although panpipes of clay have been found in the ancient *Nasca* culture of Peru and stone panpipes in northern Argentine and Chile, the typical panpipe and the one from which the others undoubtedly originated was made of reeds and its home is the western Amazon. Such a panpipe is closed at the bottom and the proximal end has a fine thread wound around it. These windings are very important, for they prevent the pipe from cracking. The smallest crack, be it remembered, makes it practically impossible to produce sound.

The most important detail in construction is naturally the length of the pipes, since the notes tend in direct proportion thereto. To obtain the deep basic note generally desired, the pipe must have a specific length and yet not be too narrow. Otherwise there is produced instead of this deep basic note the third or fifth overtone which is, in fact, what happens in most of northwestern Brazil, where the panpipes are made of arundinaria. The closed pipes usually have the bottom covered by a natural septum, and to have this they must be cut very carefully *in* the septum.

When the pipes are finished and have their correct pitch they are joined together. How many are so joined varies from tribe to tribe. The smallest number is, of course, two. Among the ancient Peruvians there were at times thirty-four. However, the normal number is between five and ten. Before they are combind they are placed in a certain order, the usual manner being to arrange them side by side in a row, according to size. In binding them, different methods are in vogue, two types of ligature being in use, one of which is characterized by having only windings of thread, whereas the other has both the windings and a stick of slit reed, to give the instrument additional solidity and strength.

Each panpipe is generally played by itself, but there are numerous examples even today of panpipes being played in pairs. This was apparently the common custom in ancient Peru and Bolivia, and it is still common among the descendants of the *Aymara* on the plateau around Lake Titicaca. The reason for this antiphonal manner of playing was due to the fact that the two part-instruments complete one another, for every other note in the scale is found on one instrument and the remaining notes on the other. "That this curious manner of playing," so says our main authority, "is precolumbian is proved by the archaeological flutes on which the notes complete one another. On all Peruvian vases, musicians playing panpipes are occasionally portrayed. They blow in pairs, and the two instruments are united with a cord, which evidently serves to keep together the two instruments which really form a whole, and perhaps do not agree with any other panpipes."[27]

Panpipes tied together in this way still exist among certain tribes in the Rio Negro territory.

An interesting problem arises in connection with the panpipe. Apart from South America, it is unknown in the new world. It is, however, very characteristic of Melanesia. Are we here dealing with some far-flung influence from across the Pacific, or is this an independent invention? Taken by itself, it would mean nothing, but since there are other elements in the cultures of the western Amazon and other parts of South America, particularly among those peoples who belong to what is presumably the oldest stock, the question of such influence cannot summarily be dismissed. But one thing can be dismissed if they came here at all, and that is that they came as a specific Melanesian "invasion." Yet, if we care to play with such theories, one thing is clear. The panpipe and the blowgun did not reach the South Americans from the northern continent. If they are of foreign origin, they came across the Pacific. But such a possibility, while not entirely excluded, is on the face of it highly improbable.

We come now to the signal drum that plays so important an element in the life of these people. What its role is, Whiffen has well indicated.[28]

The Indians have no cymbals, gongs, or bells; but the drum is an important factor not only in native music, but in native life. The drum is the telegraph of the Amazons. In fact, the most remarkable of all the native instruments is the *manguare* or signal drum. Although the primary use of this drum is to signal, it is utilized on great occasions as an addition to the aboriginal orchestra. To make this important adjunct of the maloka two blocks of hard wood are chosen, some six feet in length, and about twenty-four inches in diameter. These blocks are very carefully hollowed out by means of heated stones that are introduced through a narrow longitudinal slit.

Instead of endeavoring, however, as would be the case with an ordinary drum, to contrive as nearly perfect a cylinder as possible, the object of the signal-drum maker is to obtain a husk of varying thicknesses, so as to secure differences in note. Accordingly, with his rude implements, hot stones, capybara-tooth borer, and stone axe, he fashions the interior of the drum in such a manner that the outer shell, the sounding-board, varies in thickness from half an inch to four inches. Two blocks are used; the smaller is called the male, and the larger the female. The ends are simply the wood of the tree which is not removed, all the hollowing being accomplished by means of the grooved slit. When finished these are suspended by withes at an oblique angle, one end much higher than the other— say six feet and three feet respectively from the ground. They hang from the rafters of the maloka, or from an upright frame, and present the appearance of two barrels surmounted by a narrow slit.

The musician takes his stand between these drums and, with a wooden mallet headed with a knob of rubber, beats out his message or his tune. Altogether he has a range of four notes—two low ones on the female manguare and two high ones on the male. On these he rings the changes with great rapidity, and produces a sound which, though not startlingly loud, has such penetrating qualities that it can be heard twenty miles away. He beats very quickly in short and long strokes, not unlike the Morse code. By means of the manguare a skilled signaler can carry on a conversation as accurately as a telegraph operator at St. Martin's-le-Grand, or a soldier with a heliograph—but how he does it is another secret of the Amazonian bush. When used for its proper purpose as signal drum, the Boro and the Okaina can carry on conversations upon almost any subject within their ken. Other tribes are only able to distinguish between a warning of danger and an invitation to a dance. Brown could use the drum for small matters—he could hurry the bearers out of the bush for example. He said there was no code, but that the signaler tried to represent the sound of words with the drum, and Indians invariably told me that they made the words with the drum. However, with a language dependent on inflection, as theirs unquestionably is, there must be a code of some description.

India-rubber, which has added a new and awful terror to the life of the forest Indian, is only employed by these tribes to make the drum mallet, used with the manguare, and the latex for depilatory purposes. The Witoto call the mallet ouaki, the drum is hugwe.

These great signal drums have designs worked upon them in which the organs associated with the presumed sex of the instrument are prominent; and, after the manner of the natives, both instruments are invariably distinguished internally with the proper sexual characters, the female drum having two breasts pendant inside.

Even in the construction of a small playing drum much time and ingenuity are expended. First an aeta palm is selected, cut down, and a section of the trunk laboriously hacked off. This section in turn is carefully hollowed, until only a thin shell remains. Some tribes use a section of bamboo in place of the hollowed palm, but these never secure so fine an instrument or so fine a note as the palm trunk makes. Over the two ends of the cylinder dried monkey skin is tightly stretched—preferably that of the howler monkey, as it is popularly supposed to produce a louder and more rolling sound. Some tribes then fasten across one end of this drum a very tight cord, into the centre of which has been tied a fine sliver of wood. By this means two notes are obtained—the open note, where nothing interferes with the vibrations of the drumhead, and the closed note, where the vibrations of the splinter intersect those of the skin. A very inferior instrument is made with agouti skin over a bamboo cylinder. The drums made on the Napo River look very much like an English child's toy drum, rather high and narrow, and, of course, made entirely without metal. The sides bulge slightly, and have crossed threads of fiber string. The vellum of the drumhead is kept in its place tautly by a close-fitting ring. These drums are usually decorated, and are objects of barter among many of the tribes. They are played with the fingers only, not with drumsticks or mallet.

The western Amazon is, of course, not the only region where the drum plays the function it does there. It was equally, if not more, important in the Gran Chaco and ancient Peru. Among the *Mataco* of the Argentinian Chaco, Karsten says that the drum is at work almost every day and is used for all sorts of purposes —to conjure up the spirits of hurricanes, of disease or drought, or to frighten away the spirit of some dead Indian. In a neighboring tribe, the *Choroti*, so Karsten continues, it is employed to produce an abundant harvest of algarroba. Night and day it is then beaten, to accelerate the ripening.

However, we are dealing here with a musical instrument and

its associated functions of much wider distribution than even South America. Although differing in some important details, we find it in central California with extremely sacred associations. Ancient Mexico and Central America likewise, as well as the Antilles, had it, although there the drum was quite open at the bottom and the upper side was H-shaped and had two longitudinal tongues. Finally, of course, we have the similarity between the signal drum of northwestern South America to those of Africa to add to our troubles.

Thus again we are brought back to North America and Mexico, and once more what seemed typical of our region turns out to have had its real center outside of it. For the culture trait now to be described, the puberty ritual for boys and girls, the same problems will come up again. Perhaps the best account we have for the western Amazon is that given by Koch-Gruenberg for the Carib tribe called the *Taulipang* or *Arekuna* living west of the Roraima Plateau in Venezuela, and this we shall now summarize.[29]

As soon as a boy reaches the age of puberty he is apprized of that fact by being given a highly specialized kind of a whipping with a lash made of the fibers of the mauritia. This lashing must begin with the left leg and gradually work around until the right foot is reached. Lacerations are produced that frequently swell and at times break out into an open wound. Following this, lashing incisions are made in both his arms, along his chest down to his abdomen, and vertically down his chin. The wounds are then treated with certain supposedly magical potions, prepared from special leaves, roots, and bark. The purpose of these incisions is to furnish the youth with the means for becoming a successful hunter and fisherman, each incision being associated with a specific kind of virtuosity. Thus the incisions on the arms and across the chest will enable him to be successful with bow and arrow, those on the chin with the blowgun.

Following the lashing and the incisions comes the very unpleasant ant test. Black stinging ants are applied to all parts of his body until he is practically overcome and is so weakened that he has to spend a week in his hammock.

Koch-Gruenberg believes that, like the whipping and the incisions, the ant test has a magical purpose, that it is a form of hunting magic. If he can endure the excruciating pains inflicted by the bites of the ants it is believed that his powers as a future hunter and fisherman will be increased and strengthened.

Throughout these tests the youth must remain quiet and give no indication of pain. Should he cry out, the whole success of the ordeal is nullified, and he must begin all over again. For a year thereafter he must observe certain food taboos. He can for instance only eat small fish and small birds and drink a warm brew called *mingau* and *kashiri* (cf. page 62). Only after he has successfully passed through these ordeals is he given the status of a full-grown man. He may not, however, marry until he is between twenty and twenty-five years, for otherwise the various magical powers he has received at these puberty rites will lose their potency and pass over to his wife. In such cases he will remain throughout his life an unsuccessful hunter and fisherman.

Girls at puberty have to submit to a similar ordeal. They also undergo the ant test, but with them it is confined to the palms of the hand, the arms, the soles of the feet, and the rump. Shortly before their first menstruation they are tatooed at the corners of the mouth. The coloring material used for this purpose is prepared from the ashes of burnt honeybees, on the theory that this will make the kashiri that they subsequently prepare as sweet as honey. After this the hair at the nape of their neck is cut off.

All this takes place before their first menstruation. At the first sign of menstruation they immediately retire to their hammocks and are regarded as unclean. Some old woman, generally the grandmother, now makes them some sandals and prepares the *urucu* paint, with which she covers the whole body of the young girl. On her face she paints special patterns. An old man then appears whose duty it is to strike her with the same type of a lash used for boys. This lashing begins at the shoulder and works down gradually.

Until the menstruation has ceased she must remain in her hammock. The space where the hammock has been hung is partitioned off from the rest of the hut so that no stranger upon entering can see her, for if that were to happen it is believed she would lose all sense of shame and womanly modesty.

Throughout her seclusion certain actions are forbidden her and certain food taboos imposed. She may, for instance, not run her hand through her hair but must instead use a kind of stick made from the stem of the *inaja* palm. She may eat only certain small fish. She must be particularly careful not to eat any fish that are very active in the water, for that would increase the flow of her menstrual blood. She may drink the mingau, mentioned above, but no kashiri under any conditions. These food taboos she must observe until she has passed her fifth or sixth menstrual period.

When her first menstrual period is over she may leave her hammock. Certain activities are, however, still not permitted. She may not go to the plantations, carry a burden basket, touch either a knife or an ax, cry out loud, or engage in any kind of quarrel. Nor may she blow on a fire directly. Instead she must use a fire fan. If she disobeyed any of the injunctions she would immediately be inflicted with pains or become faint.

After each menstrual period she is given a special name. After the fifth she is ordered to rub a specially prepared concoction into her hair so that it will grow long again. Finally, the objects that she is to use from now on—ax, various types of knife, baskets, etc.—are all subjected to certain magical spells so that no harm will befall her.

Although the puberty initiations just discussed play an important role throughout the western Amazon, they very definitely give the impression of having lost much of their older complexity and of having become subordinated to magical procedures, particularly those connected with hunting and fishing. Both to the north, among the Arawak of British Guiana, and to the east, among the Ge people, puberty initiation, each quite different in type from that of the other to be sure, is much more fundamental, especially among the latter. Since puberty fasting for both boys and girls is widespread in North America, there cannot be any question here of coastal Arawak influences as such. Rather we must regard these ordeals as survivals and modifications of a trait of an early culture that once extended from Alaska to South America.

The ceremonials, particularly the masked dances, to which we must now turn bring up problems of even wider scope than those just mentioned.

Although ceremonials accompanied, of course, by dancing are known throughout this region, the real ceremonial center for this region is the Rio Negro. These ceremonials fall into two main divisions: the dances without masks and those with masks. The purposes for which these dances are given are of the most varied type, but in general it can be said that they are principally connected with the propitiation of spirits, with the promotion of fertility, human and otherwise, with initiation into the men's tribal society, and with death.

For the latter, one example must suffice. Among the *Kobeua* there is a very peculiar feast in which the bones of a dead ancestor are first exhumed, then burned and ground to powder, and finally consumed in kashiri beer. At the dance performed on this occasion the participants wear long yellow strips hanging down from the neck and carry clubs adorned with bast pendants, which they hold in the left hand. In their right hand they hold wooden images supposed to represent different kinds of fish and which are tied to tubes of a certain kind of wood. The dance movement consists of a ritual movement, forward and backward and a stamping on the ground with the right foot. The rite is supposed to have as its object the imparting to the living of the spirit of the dead, to thus facilitate his rebirth.

To really understand and visualize these fascinating Rio Negro dance ceremonials, an eyewitness's description is necessary, and I shall accordingly summarize one of Koch-Gruenberg's.[30]

According to Koch-Gruenberg the dance to be witnessed at the village of Actiaru began at sundown. It was initiated by the appearance of two dancers wearing colorful feather dresses and with anklet rattles attached to their right feet, who danced in hurried steps up and down before the ceremonial hut. They dance side by side, each one placing one hand upon the shoulder

of the other while in their free hand they hold long flutes made
of the wood of the pashiuba palm, from which they extract somewhat monotonous tones. While these two are dancing, two other
Indians similarly bedecked, but without the anklet rattles and
also provided with flutes, climb into the branches of a tree and
accompany them.

After the dancing has lasted some time, the two dancers go into
the house to emerge almost immediately with two women. The
four now dance, the women in the middle, the men with their
arms around the necks of the women and the women with their
arms around the waists of the men. This dance comes to a conclusion with a sustained fortissimo note from the flutes. A rest
period follows, filled in with the music furnished by some youths
playing the panpipe and with the usual drinking of kashiri. But
let me continue in Koch-Gruenberg's own words: [31]

The guests from other tribes remain outside on the large, open
plaza where the posts have been driven to which the hammocks for
the women and children are to be attached. Numerous small fires are
scattered around to protect the participants and guests against the
cool full-moon night. Within the ceremonial house itself, the *Kaua*
Indians from the neighboring *Wirausa-Parana* stage a dance, an old
man with fifteen youngsters and boys. First they divide off, with the
old man as the leading dancer in the middle, and the two lines move
for a time backward and forward. Then they join together in circular formation, each one with his left hand on the right shoulder of the
person next to him. Each person holds in his right hand a calabash
rattle covered with decorations and with feathers suspended from it.
Every stamp of the foot is emphasized and punctuated by a staccato
jerking of the rattle. At the ends of the circle, in the small openings,
one can see half-grown boys jumping around in wholly unorthodox
fashion and attempting to imitate their elders as best they can. They
keep time with their little rattles quite encouragingly.

While all this is going on the guests have piled up their gift, a large
quantity of *inga dulcis* (from which a highly prized sweet juice is
obtained) at the entrance of the ceremonial hut and placed on top of
it a sort of doll made out of rags. A man now stations himself next
to it and remains there playing on a flute.

The dancers mentioned above, who have hitherto remained in the hut, are now joined by women and girls and emerge in rhythmical step on to the open square, where they circle around the heaped inga. They then re-enter the hut and dance there without the women. Finally they arrange themselves as at the beginning of the dance and, facing the kashiri trough, shout "he-he-e-e-e." Then there follows a loud bellow, a sharp and dissonant whistling through the teeth, one more energetic jerking of the calabash rattles, and the dancers separate.

Outside, in the meantime, much is happening. The guests have torn down the inga pile and seized the doll. Part of the fruits are carried into the house in large burden baskets, where they are welcomed with jubilant shouts of joy.

Around the inga that have not been removed, dancing is again resumed. Four dancers now appear, two men and two women, followed by four youths blowing into their panpipes with all the lung power they possess. Thus they circle the inga. My friend Mandu now appeared and danced a round with his people. In this dance the left hand rests upon the right shoulders of the man ahead of him, while in his right hand he holds the carved handle of his dancing stick, with which he rhythmically strikes the ground.

After a while the women join in these dances. They dance somewhat outside the circle, since their right hand rests on the left shoulder of their partners. Some of the women are accompanied by their children, whom they either hold with their free hand or who ride on their hips. Some even carry nursing infants who sleep very calmly despite the terrific noise. One woman lets out long shrill shrieks as an accompaniment to the measured and slow chanting of the men.

After each round, lavishly bedecked and painted youths, in goose trot, rush out, knees bent, to the thirsty dancers and bring them kashiri. "Tsa-ha-ha-ha!" they shout at them, to which the dancers answer, "he-he-he!"

And thus gradually the inga is carried into the house and, amidst loud and jubilant shouts, thrown on the floor. . . .

One of the aftereffects of such a round of dances and drinking is that not infrequently one of the participants is seized with violent crying spells. Koch-Gruenberg describes one. The shrieking man is immediately seized by the medicine man and helpers —for he will need them—and thrown to the ground. The treatment then begins. The medicine man, holding a calabash rattle in his left hand, shakes it continually over the prostrate patient. Then he takes occasional puffs at a large cigar, which he holds in his right hand, and blows the tobacco smoke over the patient's body, particularly his head, which he holds in both hands. Slowly and rhythmically he strokes the patient so that he can draw the "disease matter" out of his body. Having seized this disease matter, he throws it into the air and then disperses it by blowing tobacco smoke in its direction; throughout his ministrations the medicine man intones a slow, monotonous chant.

However, the most important and dramatic dances are not the more or less open and profane ones, without masks, but the more private, secret, and sacred masked dances. For our knowledge of these we have again to depend upon the indefatigable Koch-Gruenberg.

In one of the villages, Iyaipana, on an affluent of the Rio Negro, he witnessed a whole series of masked dances representing a most disparate assortment of animals and spirits. There were dances depicting the butterfly, regarded as the most important, the buzzard, the jaguar, various fishes, larvae, alternating with those depicting evil demons who have taken on human shape, or representations of giants and dwarfs. As to the specific meaning of the dances at Iyaipana, that was not always clear. What was clear, however, was that the masks were not meant to be naturalistic, that the movements of the animals were symbolized, and that only men could participate.

The center for all these masked dances seems to have been among the Kobeua on the Aiary River, a northern affluent of the Rio Negro. There Koch-Gruenberg witnessed them in 1905 and described them for the first time with any thoroughness. Again I shall summarize his excellent and vivid account.

The great series of masked dances among the Kobeua shows a marked contrast to the one we have just briefly mentioned at Iyaipana. At this latter place there was a simple procession of masked dancers. Here, on the contrary, we are in the presence of a highly complex and dramatically interwoven succession of dances and interpretations.

It is generally late in the afternoon that the dances begin, and they are initiated by the sudden appearance of six figures covered from head to foot with fantastic masks. They emerge from the woods and, in goose step, approach the opening in the center of the village. They dance in groups of twos, while two other masked figures, clasping each other's hand, with fingers crooked, dance inside the hut. Suddenly those outside burst howling upon the entrance, strike against the wall with sticks and long hooked staffs, seeking to make their way in forcibly. They are repelled by the two guardian masks within. The attackers represent the evil spirits who wish to obtain possession of the maloka, the ceremonial hut.

While this is taking place, the mother and wife of someone who has recently died begin a piteous and loud ceremonial wailing. They know the danger. They know that, repulsed in the first attack, the evil ones will attempt to enter at the rear of the maloka. The scene grows wilder and more tumultuous. The attack on the rear of the maloka begins. The shouting and shrieking of assailants and defenders grow louder. The maloka echoes and re-echoes from the sounds of the sticks and hooked staffs grinding and beating against its walls. Part of the building is torn off. The evil spirits are about to enter. The wailing of the two women rises to new heights of horror and anxiety. Two of the attacking party have just seized the cross poles of the roof and stand there singing. The defenders continue singing and dancing. The wailing of the two women gradually becomes calmer. Sighs take the place of howling. Soon the wailing has become transformed into a gentle, melodic lament for the dead and then dies out completely.

When the dance is over, all burst out into laughter, and gaiety is the order of the day.

After this highly dramatic and intense introduction, the less serious dances begin. The most important of these are the vulture, the jaguar, the dorbeetle, the owl, and the bearded dwarf. The first four give amazingly accurate pantomimic imitations of the animals in question. The fifth, the bearded dwarf dance, is connected with an evil forest-spirit who is supposed to

Dancing Mask from the Western Amazon

mislead hunters and steal their prey from under their noses. The
dance portrays in pantomime all the details of a hunt. It shows
the hunter stealing upon his prey, the preparations for shooting,
and the final killing. Even the last gasping breath of the animal
is imitated.

Charged with humorous implications is the pantomime representation of an alligator hunt. The Indians make the figure of an
alligator out of bast and as soon as it is finished three masked
dancers pounce upon it and "kill" it with their sticks. The
"alligator" is then tied to long staffs and carried supposedly home
on their shoulders. There the make-believe continues in all
seriousness. After dancing within the house for some time, they
squat down, throw the "carcass" on the ground, and cut it up.
A make-believe fire is then kindled, and the "meat" is thrown in
the pots which the women have provided. The meal is ready,
and Koch-Gruenberg tells us that he was seriously asked to
share it.

We have but one more type of dance to discuss, really a series
of dances, known generally under the name of *Yurupary*. They
are by far the most important and are intimately connected with
initiation into the men's society so characteristic of the tribes
along the Rio Negro and which has features strangely reminiscent of customs in far-off Melanesia. As we shall see, later on,
however, these features also occur in a few other parts of South
America.

The Yurupary dances are supposed to vary markedly according to the type of special flute used. These flutes play an all-
important part in the ceremony, and not only are women forbidden to see them but the theory is that they are not even
supposed to know of their existence. They are to be kept in the
belief that the flute notes they hear at the time of the ceremony
are actually the voices of spirits who have appeared to the men.

But let us see what such a Yurupary dance is like.

The Indians, both men and women, arrive decorated in all
the gorgeous ornaments specifically appropriate to the occasion.
Their bodies are painted in black and red colors. After certain
preliminary preparations at which somewhat monotonous and

mournful songs are played, the women and children must leave. They are generally sent to the forest. As soon as they have left, three of the participants begin to blow on the large Yurupary flutes. After an interval, more dancers appear garbed in a peculiar mask-dress called *macacaraua*, which is supposed to resemble the principal deity of this region, Yurupary. These now perform a dance which consists of jumping on all fours among the other men and striking to the right and to the left with sticks. The flutes are then blown again for a short while, and soon the women appear on the scene again. Armed with whips, both men and women begin to lash each other. Small flutes are played, and kashiri beer drunk in large quantities far into the night.

When an initiation into the secret men's society is to take place, this occurs after sundown on the first day of the ceremony. The younger participants are then ceremonially lashed, this signifying their final admission.

Where these masked dances originated is a most difficult question to decide. Masked dances as such are not uncommon in North America, and many of the functions they seem to possess here in South America are found in the northern continent. The elaborate theory connected with the Yurupary flutes and the barring of women from participation in this fashion is, however, unknown north of South America with one great exception, the well-known male secret society of the central Californian Indians. However, that one great exception opens up some interesting possibilities. Are we not possibly dealing with another of the remnants of an ancient pan-American culture? The full answer to so fundamental a question we cannot discuss at length in this book, but we will touch upon it in a subsequent chapter.

Thus we see that, all in all, the Amazon, west of the Araguaya, contains a rather impressive number of features that presumably belong to the older residents of South America. This in spite of the fact that we are here clearly at the gateway to the continent and that culture wave upon culture wave must have beaten upon it again and again and given to the cultures elaborated there the most contradictory traits, merging elements belonging to the simplest with elements belonging to the most complex of aboriginal civilizations. Yet, in the end, it would seem that the essentially hunting-fishing basis of the older civilization, with its insistence on magical formulae and with its emphasis on the role of the medicine man and sorcerer shaman, with its truculent animism, always reasserted itself. Every aspect of life fairly reeks of it. Even when a mother laments for her child, her elegy must be framed in terms of magic and fear of the dead spirits as in the following touching song of the Carib Taulipang:[32]

You never went down the river, my child.
Where then did you obtain this illness?
Never, again, will I see you.
How should it ever have occurred to me that you would die
*   in this useless manner?*
Well, die then! Go your way!
I, too, someday, will have to go that way!
Do not complain about me when you reach your destina-
*   tion.*
Instead, tell your father all that we did for you here.
Remember, here on earth, I never maltreated you.

CHAPTER VII

Los de Abajo

THE GE TRIBES OF EASTERN BRAZIL

IT IS ONLY LOGICAL TO ASSUME ON THE FACE of things that, since America was originally settled from northeastern Asia, the peoples in South America would preserve more of the original culture that was brought here than did those in North America. The argument is clear. By the time a new group with new culture reached a given place, the older group would have moved on. This seems possibly a *simpliste* type of reasoning, but yet not wholly wrong essentially. The one, admittedly considerable, flaw in the argument is that the journey from, say, Alaska to southeastern Brazil or Tierra del Fuego, for instance, would be likely to so greatly transform a culture as to obscure its original possessions.

That a number of generations would be required for such a journey is clear. If, for the sake of argument, we assume that the original immigrants traveled 100 miles a year, 200 years will suffice. If they traveled 25, 1,000 years would be needed. It is far more likely that 1,000 years was required for the original journey than 200. Yet we know from controlled historical sources that certain customs and beliefs have remained unchanged in the Americas for the last 400 years, and we know that even in the advanced civilizations of Europe, Asia, and Africa, folkways have persisted for thousands of years.

Thus, on the face of it, barring the necessity to change due to geographical and climatic reasons—and, confessedly, that would be a factor of great significance in such a trek—the peoples in southern South America should have retained more of the basic culture brought here from Asia than did those in North America. The question then is have any of the South American Indians retained it, in part or in whole, and how are we to recognize the elements of that older culture?

We know roughly that the first people who crossed the Bering Strait were nonagricultural. We have good reasons for believing that they belonged to what approximated to the end of the Old Stone Age culture of Europe and Asia and that they did not enter America more than 15,000 years ago. Naturally then, the next question is who are the nonagricultural peoples of North and South America and where do they live? For North America, where most of the facts are known, the answer is simple. The nonagricultural tribes live, almost exclusively, along the western coast from Alaska to Lower California, in the plateaus parallel to that coast, and in the area north of the United States. In South America they live in the eastern and southeastern part of Brazil, the Chaco, and Tierra del Fuego.

If the absence of agriculture is the all-determining factor, then these should be the tribes where most, or at least, much of the oldest American culture has survived. This has always been the general assumption, particularly of European theorists. A fairly good case could be made for the existence, among just these tribes of South America, of what some have called the simple elements of culture, material and spiritual. But the term "simple" is, of course, highly subjective. We should have to include in it certain methods of curing and theories of disease, the couvade, secret men's societies, and the dual organization of the tribe, the last almost always implying a totemistic structure of society, or at least one where its salient characteristic, exogamy, exists. With regard to the dual organization, the problem that then arises is whether this trait is connected with a simple culture or a complex one, whether it has developed once or twice in the history of humanity, and whether it can, under certain conditions, originate anywhere and at any time?

These are the fundamental problems of anthropology with which the initiated scholars have now been wrestling many generations and upon which a relatively small number are agreed. They can hardly be discussed in a popular book. If they are brought up here at all it is because the tribes we are now to consider, the Ge, possess many of the traits that theorists, from time immemorial, have associated with the simplest of aboriginal cultures.

These Ge tribes are found in northern and north-central Brazil, between the Tocantins and Xingu rivers, to the west of this area, and in the extreme southeastern corner of Brazil. Beyond doubt these tribes are among the simplest in South America; that is, after we discard what are admittedly comparatively recent features, like the adoption by some of the Ge peoples of agriculture, which they have clearly borrowed from the Tupi-Guarani. Yet what remains after agriculture has been eliminated is quite remarkable not only because of the highly intricate and voluminous nature of the cultural detail but because of the amazing vistas on aboriginal America which it opens before us. If what then remains has always been associated with simple nonagricultural civilizations, then we shall have to regard such things as the clan, the dual organization, and age-classes as belonging to simple economies. Because of this fact we shall discard most of the other elements of Ge civilization and devote ourselves fairly exclusively to a discussion of them.

The best descriptions of the Ge are those of Nimuendaju,[33] and we shall summarize them at some length. Let us begin with the Canella in the north and confine our attention entirely to their social organization.

The village in which the Canella live had, some years ago, thirty houses arranged in a circle. Within the circumference of this circle runs a broad concentric "street." In the middle is a circular plaza. Each hut is placed at the fringe of the concentric street and is connected with the plaza in the center by a radial path. The houses are owned by the women, and a man lives with his wife.

The tribe is divided in double fashion: first, into two exogamous divisions, supposedly of equal rank, and called East and West, respectively; secondly, into two groups not coterminous with the first and not, of course, exogamous, which meet seasonally—that is, during the rainy season. At that time the village is bisected, the two divisions being called *Ka* and *Atuk* respectively. Membership in them hinges upon the personal names one possesses, the boys getting theirs from their matrilineal kinsmen and the girls from their patrilineal kinswomen. These names are transferred as a rule from one generation to another. As Nimuendaju and Lowie point out, the potential impermanence of individual affiliation with these groups thus contrasts sharply with the hereditary membership in the exogamous dual division. These same authors continue as follows: [34]

Not only the Canella and their name series are apportioned to the Rainy Season moieties, but all of nature is antithetically divided between them, as indicated by the following partial scheme:

Ka	*Atuk*
East	West
Sun	Moon
Day	Night
Dry Season	Rainy Season
Fire	Firewood
Earth	Water
Red	Black
Red plants and animals	Black plants and animals
Maize	Sweet Potato
Manioc	Cucurbit

Each Rainy Season moiety has a headman appointed by the chiefs and elders; and it is this headman's maternal home that serves as a place of assembly for his unit. In consonance with the above scheme the Ka use red paint for body decoration, the Atuk black paint. Each unit, moreover, has its own slogan; on the birth of a boy, e.g., his maternal uncle or mother's mother's brother—the prospective name-transferrer—steps in front of the door and by uttering the war-cry "wa-wa-wa!" or "ke-ke-ke!" announces to the village that a new Ka or Atuk, respectively, has seen the light of day.

These two complementary halves figure predominantly during the rainy season, and principally in two ways—in racing and hunting. The teams pitted against each other in relay races during the season are recruited each from the Ka or Atuk moiety, respectively. In these competitions each side carries a log, which is appropriately marked with red or black pigment. The two groups also go on joint hunting trips, accompanied by their female members. Continence is observed during these expeditions, but on their return there is an exchange of women.

After the beginning of the maize harvest, i.e., at the very close of the *Meipimrak* period, the men of each moiety assemble in the plaza, each accompanied by a sister's son. The Atuk lay down samples of the crop before the Ka, the last donor contemptuously throwing down an armful of cobs. Each moiety boasts of the number and appearance of their sisters' sons, simultaneously casting ridicule on their opponents' nephews.

During the dry season—that of ceremonialism par excellence—the Rainy Season moieties play a very subordinate role. In the *Pepye*, one of the two initiation rituals, the Atuk novices go to their individual seclusion huts at night, the Ka to theirs in the daytime, in accordance with the twofold scheme. Also on certain occasions the distinctive colors serve as badges of membership. . . .

Independently of both the exogamous and the Rainy Season bisection of the entire tribe, there is a dichotomy restricted to males, who are ranged into the two exogamous divisions. These appellations again, as in the case of the exogamous groups, refer to East and West. Each of these dual groups embraces three subdivisions, as shown below:

East	*West*
Giant Snake	Armadillo
Bat	Dwarf Parrot
Carrion Vulture	Alien Tribe

Membership in these groups, too, hinges on the acquisition of certain personal names. Just as every name, irrespective of sex, belongs to either the Ka or the Atuk Rainy Season moiety, so every masculine name belongs to one of the six Plaza subdivisions. Further, each of these Plaza names determines membership in two clubs, either in the Falcon and Jaguar societies or in the Duck and Agouti societies. On the other hand, affiliation with two other organizations, the Clowns and the King Vultures is quite independent of the personal names. . . .

Each Plaza group takes up a definite position in the village plaza and has an assembly house, whose location on the periphery of the village circle roughly corresponds to the position of the subdivision in the plaza.

The functions of the Plaza groups are ceremonial and largely relate to the two initiation phases, called *Ketuaye* and *Pepye*. Thus, in the Ketuaye initiation all offices are dual, one officer of each pair being recruited from the Eastern, the other from the Western Plaza group. Only in the case of the girl auxiliaries is this exclusive masculine dualism inapplicable. The Plaza grouping is very conspicuous in the Pepye initiation, where each of the six subdivisions uses a distinctive pattern in body painting. Apart from these celebrations the Plaza groups figure in the *Tep-Yarkwa*, one of the major festivals intercalated between the two phases of initiation. In the log-races characteristic of this ceremonial period the Plaza halves are regularly pitted against each other.

Finally, there is another dual division affecting only males, viz., the two pairs of age-classes that engage in competitive sport during the dry season. Once more there is a correlation with East and West —in fact, the pairs of active classes bear exactly the same designations as the two exogamous divisions. Notwithstanding this nomenclature, the two forms of dual grouping do not coincide at all, since each of the age-classes comprises members of both moieties.

The total number of age-classes, inactive and active in sport, is indefinite. The system is tied up with the initiation ceremonies, which thus require brief mention. All males undergo two phases of initiation, each being repeated at intervals of two or three years, so that the complete cycle occupies about ten years. All those jointly initiated form a fixed class for the rest of their lives, so that apart from the youngest boys the whole male population is grouped into age strata. Even the as yet uninitiated boys who look forward to initiation at the next celebration form an unofficial age-class and mimic the activities of the young men.

The active classes have each a definite position in the plaza. This, however, shifts whenever the unofficial boys' group receives formal admission to the plaza, which automatically promotes the oldest active class to the athletically inactive status of councilors. Its members move to the very center of the plaza, continuing, however, to preserve their identity with reference to any surviving predecessors. Thus, recently there were three councilor classes of eight, four, and two men, respectively, each occupying a distinctive position in the plaza center and representing the "graduates" of 1903, 1893, and 1883. . . .

If the Canella specialized in developing dual divisions wherever they could, the Apinaye,[35] a closely related tribe, specialized in age-classes and initiation rites for their boys.

All males are, among the latter, divided into four age-classes:

1. Boys prior to the warrior initiation; that is, until about fifteen.
2. The warriors, from the beginning of the second phase of their own initiation until the close of the second initiation phase of the next younger group; that is, until about the age of twenty-five. The first initiation phase forms the transition from boyhood to warrior's status.
3. The mature men. Entrance into this group follows almost automatically when the training of a new warrior group is completed with the close of the second initiation phase. Men leave this class without any accompanying ceremony at the age of fifty.
4. The elders. In older days they formed a council.

Yet important as is this division into age-classes, it pales into insignificance compared to the role played among the Apinaye by the intricate and elaborate ceremonies of initiation. Nowhere in the Americas does anything quite like it exist. Indeed we would have to turn to Australia for a parallel to this Ge ritual.

The Apinaye subjected all young males and a limited number of girls to an initiation, held at intervals of about ten years. This meant that considerable age differences divided the celebrants. There were two phases in this initiation, the second following immediately upon the first. Jointly they occupied more than a year.

The initiation rites begin when the elders and mature men find that a new generation is old enough for the ceremonies.

They secretly agree on its commencement and immediately appoint the two instructors, who are invariably the leaders of the immediately preceding initiation.

The two men assume direction of the ceremonial and order a plaza dance for the next morning before dawn. One warrior proceeds from house to house as their messenger and sees to it that all boys who can be considered for initiation shall appear. At the end of the dance, at daybreak, the instructors from either side seize by the arms the future *Kolti* leader of the initiates, make him stand in the plaza for a moment, then lead him, followed by all the warriors, to his mother's house. Before the door they halt and sing again. In the meantime the mother inside spreads a mat on the floor near the entrance, and on this the youth is laid, having to remain there for the time being. Then all again return to the plaza and proceed similarly with the *Kolre* leader of the initiates. Then after a while the two new leaders rise and likewise return to the plaza, where their mothers bring food for the warriors, though those two do not yet receive any part thereof. These leaders are invariably the instructors' sisters' sons.

The next morning at daybreak all the other initiates are similarly seized and led into their maternal homes, whereupon they with their leaders march into the *galeria* woods near the village in order to camp there. This signalizes the end of the preliminary rites and the beginning of the period of the boys' seclusion.

In the meantime their parents clean a round area on the east side of the village and only about 200 meters from the houses, this space sufficing for an assemblage of the initiates, who are to be arranged in a circle. Several days after the segregation of the initiates the instructors lead four virgins, two from each of the two divisions of the tribe, out of their maternal homes to the plaza where the initiates are assembled. They are bearers of the rather frequent "great" names *Amdyi* and *Koko*, which like all feminine names are transferred by a maternal aunt to her niece, so that this office of a girl auxiliary at festivals is also hereditary. The initiates are prohibited from any intimacy with these girls, each of whom is constantly accompanied by a particular lad who watches over her behavior.

The novices spend the day in their camp in the woods, where they erect a hut for rainy weather and are kept to themselves except for occasional visits from the instructors.

During this period their ear lobes and lower lips are perforated, for earplugs and labrets are the accepted signs that a man has attained social maturity. The boy sits on a mat laid on the ground before the operator's house, facing east. The hair about his temples has been clipped the day before. The operator sits himself directly in front of the boy, holding a wooden pin decorated with pendent arara feathers at the butt. Beside him is a bowl containing the little plugs prepared on the eve of the rite as well as some urucu pigment. First kneading the lobes between his fingertips, the operator wets the point of his pin in his mouth, dips it into the urucu, and marks a point on the lobe with it. After careful scrutiny he slowly pushes the pin through and leaves it sticking in the hole. He then looks about for one of the urucu-reddened plugs, licks it, pulls out the pin and substitutes the plug. The girls' lobes are similarly perforated.

The Apinaye earplug rarely exceeds 5 centimeters, the women's being barely 4 centimeters. Only the male sex has the lower lip perforated. The same operator performs this service. Here, too, the spot is first marked red, and on the pin or a little rod an equal distance is measured off from the corners of the mouth. None of the victims so much as move an eyelash. A little nail-shaped plug is inserted into the orifice immediately, and the wound is smeared with the scraped bark of a steppe tree called *piombeti*.

Every evening the initiates march in single file from the camp to their places of assembly. At the head walks the Kolti leader, followed, without fixed order, by the rank and file with the girls in their midst, the Kolre leader bringing up the rear. Arrived at their destination, they wait until dark, then silently move along their street to the circle of houses, and turn on to the outer path—the Kolti toward the right (north), the Kolre toward the left (south). As soon as each one reaches his maternal home, he signals to the inmates by throwing a bit of wood against the wall or roof. Thereupon his mother or sister hands out food for him.

Thus the two groups of novices circle round the village, cross each other at the western extremity, and reunite in the east, whence they jointly return to their place of assembly. There the food collected by all is put together, the instructors' shares being first segregated. This the latter dispatch to their wives through the errand boys. The residue is divided among the novices at their joint dinner, for which the girl auxiliaries fetch water to drink. The distribution of food devolves on the leaders.

After cleaning away all traces of their meal, the novices seat themselves in a circle, the Kolti on the north, the Kolre in the southern semicircle, but keeping a gap toward the opening of the path from the village. The Kolre leader sits to the right of the entrance, the Kolti leader at the eastern extremity.

Meanwhile, in the plaza the Kolre instructor blows his whistle. This is an interesting musical instrument, a slender cone made of a Lagenaria tip and provided with a lateral hole for blowing. Holding his instrument in one hand, he modulates the tones by rapidly thrusting in and withdrawing the middle finger of the other hand.

The player then goes to bring his Kolti colleague, and both proceed to the initiates, the Kolre walking behind the Kolti. At the entrance to the circle they stand still and the Kolti, in an undertone, addresses the initiates. They are asked how they are faring and told what they are to do on the following day. After an intermission the instructors depart, and some time after this the initiates depart for the plaza to take part in the customary evening dances. After these have closed, the novices once more form a circle round their instructors, singing their four songs while rhythmically beating time on the ground with their clubs. Then they scatter to their mothers' houses in order to sleep there. Before daybreak the leaders walk from house to house round the outside of the village, rousing and gathering together their followers. Usually they kindle a fire in the steppe somewhere beyond the village and wait till daylight, whereupon they march to their camp in the galeria woods.

The first task of the initiates in their camp consists in the manufacturing of their six group badges. These consist of:

1. A forehead band plaited in ribbon shape out of buriti bast, with two brushlike tassels extending upward obliquely across the forehead.
2. A necklace of a finger thickness, plaited out of envireira bast, with long bast streamers hanging down in the rear beyond the small of the back.
3. A girdle of the same black material, executed in the same technique.
4. A similar pair of wristlets.
5. A similar pair of kneebands.
6. A round club, one meter long, with laterally protruding roundish knob, this being a ceremonial weapon.

During the entire period of initiation the mature men, grouped into Kolti and Kolre, organize many races with ordinary buriti logs, which are piled up in the plaza. Almost daily at sunset the initiates with their girls, led by the instructors, take up the positions on this heap, facing east, and there chant their songs while beating time with their clubs.

There now follows the making of the spindle shafts by the initiates. This is tantamount to requesting their kinswomen to provide the cotton ornaments for the closing ceremony. It is very important and a detailed ceremonial always takes place in connection with it. Each novice makes as many shafts as he has kinswomen whom he assumes to be potentially interested in manufacturing a decorative outfit for him.

In the meantime each novice's mother constructs a passageway by the rear door through which her son enters her house at this period. Two rows of bacaba palm leaves are set into the ground and arched together at the top.

The next four or five days the novices, led by their instructors, go hunting. The game they capture is distributed among their maternal households. On the day after their hunt the initiates regather their spindle shafts and march to the creek under their masters' supervision. There they rub the shaft smooth with the rough leaves of the sambabyba and water. This procedure also follows a definite ceremony. The initiates sit down on both sides of the road near their spring, and their leaders, who sit opposite each other at the ends of the lines, nearest the water, twice exchange their shafts with them. Not before this do they begin with the smoothing, the rest following suit. When the work is done, the instructors are the first to rise and go. After a while the initiates follow them, waiting for the dark to resuspend their shafts from the transverse stick in the leafy tunnel behind their homes, whence their kinswomen remove them for use the following day.

The next day is devoted to the preparation of the novice's outfit for the closing and culminating ceremony. This outfit must be made of wholly white, spun cotton and consists of the following six parts:

1. A forehead cord, worn somewhat obliquely with reference to the hair furrow, and rearward. From the back of the head down to the middle of the back there is a fringe, and at the point of its attachment an arara feather is tied in.
2. A plaited necklace, an inch in width, with short, pendent arara feathers.
3. A girdle consisting of a thin rod not quite equal to the wearer's pelvic width; its cotton wrapping; and usually four— sometimes more—thick cords which at intervals extend down to the middle of the thigh.
4. A pair of forearm cords, wrapped round the upper third of the limb, with their ends hanging down as a thick fringe. Because of this ornament the novices constantly hold their forearms horizontally forward.
5. A pair of cords forming a wrapping of the width of a palm for the lower legs from the ankles up.
6. A pair of plaited anklets an inch wide with short pendent arara feathers or deer hoofs, according to the wearer's *kiye*.

But this does not complete the full outfit necessary for a ceremony so important in the lives of all these young men. In addition to the six articles just mentioned, the novices and their girl auxiliaries wear urucu-reddened earplugs terminating frontward in a curved tip, the base of which is sometimes decorated with an inlay of mother-of-pearl disks of mirror glass. The tip itself bears a feather rosette with an agouti tooth in the center, whence a parrot feather tassel is suspended by a thin cord down to the middle of the thigh.

At the closing performance the initiate must also carry in his hand a staff made of *pau-de-leite* wood, which may be as long as one meter and be the thickness of a finger. It is painted red with urucu and wrapped with leaves at the grip in the middle, for, because of their white cotton outfit, the novices must not soil their hands with urucu.

I have gone to such great length in describing what must seem to the reader rather unimportant, if not ridiculous, details, for two reasons. It seemed necessary, first, to point out how great the number of such details can actually become and what tremendous significance may be attached to them; and, secondly, in order to remind him that even the supposedly simplest tribes may, under certain circumstances, develop an elaborateness in regard to particular aspects of their life that is quite breathtaking and bewildering.

But let us now return to the rites again.

As soon as all persons engaged in preparing the requisite ornaments have finished, the closing ceremony is ready to begin. Three days are devoted to it, and it is ushered in by a race. The initiates' hair furrows are then cut and the novices are invested with the decorated set that has just been prepared. The really dramatic moment of the long and somewhat tedious ceremony is now at hand. The novices' Kolti leader and those inhabiting the same house as himself come marching out, all abreast and serious in mien and behavior. Singing in a low and muffled tone, they move slowly toward the front of the next house. From this the initiates living there emerge as soon as they approach and arrange themselves in a similar row beside one another. The two lines first sing facing each other, and then the second joins the first as a segment. Both now proceed to the next house, where a third segment is formed and added, and so forth, in turn.

During the first procession of these elaborately decorated initiates, their girls are supposed to play pranks of all kinds on them and indulge in general in all kinds of mischief. For instance, they take the gifts that have been donated, the bananas, the sweet potatoes, and the peanuts, and throw them at the donors' feet, in full view of the approaching marchers. Other people, particularly the women who have been following the novices' column, indulge in similar antics. They play, in short, the part of ceremonial buffoons and are given the appellation of "monkeys." The novices themselves must remain as deadly serious as ever, keep their heads bent, and their forearms in the prescribed horizontal position. When all have joined in, there is a second parade around the village, and then everyone again disperses to his respective maternal home. At noon all unite and again march from house to house, this time in single file, until they reach the plaza, where all fall out of line.

In the early afternoon they again march to the plaza, arrange themselves in a circle, and sing their initiate songs, in accelerated time, for the end of their trying ordeal is fast approaching.

They continue singing until nearly 5 P.M. Then the initiates severally go each to his girl's house to fetch a meat pie or a large bowlful of other food, which they set down on the mats that have in the meantime been deposited in the plaza. When this food collection is completed, the initiates form a circle around the mats and the Kolti leader slowly walks around the victuals, pausing for a moment after every step and mutely moving his lips. The Kolti instructor now steps forth from his dwelling, in all his festive regalia, and is followed by his colleague, also in ceremonial dress. Both enter the circle. The instructor looks at the food silently and grimly and then, facing about, returns with his companion to his house.

After sunset the novices, including the girl auxiliaries but without the youngest participants, take up places on the pile of logs in the plaza. Strictly speaking, they ought to maintain this position throughout the night, but only a small number are ever able to endure that, for after midnight it may become piercingly cold. They, too, finally sit down on the logs closely huddled together.

The next morning at dawn the novices go to their maternal homes to take off their decorations. At sunrise they go jointly to bathe and wash. Then they are painted red with urucu, their faces receiving stripes, and they are given red staves and a hair cord with the occipital feather, both important insignia. Assembling, they march in a zigzag from house to house, form a circle in the patio, and then go home, still divided into house groups.

After sunset the novices again take up positions on the pile of logs, where they spend the night in the same manner as the preceding one.

Early the next morning, at five, they come down from the logs, generally chilled to the bone, and go home. They now rest until sunrise. Then they march, the red staves in their hands, to the brook in order to bathe. The mother of one of the initiates then brings a meat pie, and all wait until the novices come. When they have arrived, they step up to an old woman who has been stationed beyond the village on the road to the creek and wipe off their red urucu paint against her body and hair, allegedly to guard against prematurely begetting children. When all have done this, one of them puts the pie on the woman's shoulder and sends her home with it, while the initiates proceed to the creek, where a sucupira tree—the *Timbira* symbol of strength and endurance—is stripped of its bark about to a man's height. Against this they once more rub themselves. Removing the bast from the stripped bark, they squeeze its sap with water into a small gourd bowl and drink this fluid in order to live long. Then they sing a chant referring to the red staves, bathe, rub themselves with the sucupira bast, and hide the staves in the water among the plants on the bank. Returning to the plaza, they form groups of four, march for a while back and forth, and then break their formation.

Thus this, the first phase of these long initiation rites, closes. Yet this first phase is really only preliminary to what, after all, constitutes the real purpose of this elaborate initiation: namely, the induction of these young men into the full status of warriors.

This takes place in the second phase of the initiation ceremonies, which we can summarize only briefly here.

The same leaders officiate during both phases. There is a long seclusion, during which instruction is given concerning a number of things. The novices are first taught how to prepare their respective ornaments. They are then strictly admonished about keeping their vow of chastity for as long as the period of seclusion lasts and about the necessity of obedience to their leaders. Finally the more serious of the problems that are soon to face them are brought up, particularly the care they must use in selecting a wife. They are cautioned against beating her and admonished at all times to pay proper consideration to her wishes. The length of the seclusion and the inculcation of these ethical teachings are really the only fundamental differences between the two phases of initiation.

At different periods in this second phase certain ceremonies are performed and games played which consume a considerable amount of time. At one time they obviously had some deep religious significance which has been lost today.

After the novices have come out of their seclusion for good, their hair is cut and a series of log races takes place to signify that they have now entered into the everyday world again.

And so, with this athletic let-up, are the young Apinaye ushered into full manhood. Thus do they attain to the warrior's estate.

Certainly we have, in the social structure just described, both complexity and detail. If the other aspects of their culture had anything comparable in complexity, anything even remotely so well integrated and formalized, it would clearly be utterly ridiculous to characterize these people as having, in any sense of the term, a simple culture. But we shall seek in vain for any evidences of such integration and formalization in anything but their social organization and their initiation rites. They are not to be found either in the material culture, in religion, or in mythology. It is true that we find detail there, but never true integration.

It is when we turn to their religion and mythology that the

archaic features of their culture clearly emerge. Let us begin
with the first.

Their religion seems to be centered around the sun and moon,
particularly the former. Particular emotional significance seems
to attach to the first of these deities. He appears to them in dreams
and visions that have a strange family resemblance to the puberty
and personal visionary experiences so common in most of North
America. Take, for example, the following impressive vision:[36]

I was hunting near the sources of the Botica creek. All along the
journey there I had been agitated and was constantly started without knowing why.

Suddenly I saw him standing under the drooping branches of a big
ateppe tree. He was standing there erect. His club was braced against
the ground beside him, his hand he held on the hilt. He was tall and
light-skinned, and his hair nearly descended to the ground behind
him. His whole body was painted, and on the outer side of his legs
were broad red stripes. His eyes were exactly like two stars. He was
very handsome.

I recognized at once that it was he. Then I lost all courage. My hair
stood on end, and my knees were trembling. I put my gun aside, for
I thought to myself that I should have to address him, but I could not
utter a sound because he was looking at me unwaveringly. Then I
lowered my head in order to get hold of myself and stood thus for a
long time. When I had grown somewhat calmer, I raised my head.
He was still standing and looking at me. Then I pulled myself together
and walked several steps toward him; then I could not go any further,
for my knees gave way. I again remembered standing for a long time,
then lowered my head, and tried again to regain composure. When
I raised my eyes again, he had already turned away and was slowly
walking through the steppe.

Then I grew very sad. I kept standing there for a long time after
he had vanished. Then I walked under the tree where he had stood.
I saw his footprints, painted red with urucu at the edges. Beside them
was the print of his club-head. I picked up my gun and returned to
the village. On the way I managed to kill two deer, which approached
me without the least shyness. At home I told my father everything.
Then all scolded me for not having had the courage to talk to him.

At night while I slept he reappeared to me. I addressed him, and he said he had been waiting for me in the steppe to talk to me, but since I had not approached he had gone away. He led me some distance behind the house and there showed me a spot on the ground where, he said, something was lying in storage for me. Then he vanished.

The next morning I immediately went there and touched the ground with the tip of my foot, perceiving something hard buried there. But others came to call me to go hunting. I was ashamed to stay behind and joined them. When we returned, I at once went back to the site he had shown me, but did not find anything any more.

Today I know that I was very stupid then. I should certainly have received from him great self-assurance if I had been able to talk to him. But I was still very young then; today I should act quite differently.

Vision-seeking in this fashion is, as I have just pointed out, a very old culture trait in North America and it is there, on the whole, more basically at home in the nonagricultural tribes. Since certain mythological themes and motifs as well as specific elements in the material culture also take us back to North American Indian tribes on the same economic level, there seems ample reason for assuming that here among these Ge tribes we actually are in the presence of much that belonged to an old, if indeed not the oldest, culture strata of aboriginal America. In this connection the presence, in the mythology, of the trickster-transformer cycle in which the hero only gradually succeeds in developing his function as a bringer of culture is of particular significance. Let us see what such a myth-cycle is like, for it can serve us in two manners: first, as a piece of folk literature, and, second, as an example of the persistence of themes and episodes that possibly belong to the oldest of all pan-American heritages. Episodes from the trickster sun-cycle follow:[37]

SUN AND MOON

I

First Sun came down to earth. Moon followed, but missed the spot. But when he went hunting the next morning, he saw Sun coming from afar. At once he stooped under a paty palm and crawled into the bush on all fours to hide. Sun followed his tracks and called to him to come out, asking whether by chance he was afraid of him. "No," answered Moon. He came out and excused himself, saying he had not known who it was.

2

Sun now told him he had already erected a hut by a brook and stored fruit there. He took Moon along, but made fun of him on the way for having hidden. Then Moon begged him not to speak of it any more; saying he had hidden from being ashamed of missing the place agreed upon.

3

Sun went ahead. When he came past a wasp nest hanging from a branch above the road, he passed it quickly, stopped at some distance, and said to Moon, "Do take the gourd-bottle there along!" But as soon as Moon touched the branch, the wasps pounced upon him and stung him all over his face. Wailing he ran to his comrade: "That was the gourd-bottle! Something has stung me." "What could it be?" asked Sun with a serious face, "perhaps a branch fell on you?" "No," lamented Moon, "it hurts very much!"

His eyes were all swollen from the wasps' stings so that he was unable to open them. Sun had to lead him like a blind man. But when they came to a tree lying transversely across the road, he jumped over it quickly, while Moon stumbled and fell. "Oh," said Sun, "I had not noticed the tree at all." Thus he acted three times; then Moon did not want to walk further. Sun had to carry him on his back, but he purposely pushed him against all the branches. Moon wailed, but Sun comforted him, saying he would get well sooner thereby. He pinched Moon's testicles, and when Moon cried out in alarm he soothed him, saying he had probably squeezed his testes against his back. At the hut he set Moon down precisely in a thorny shrub. Moon jumped aside, wailing he had been stung, but Sun said he had only stepped on some old dry twigs. At home Sun then pulled the wasp stings out of Moon's skin with his finger-nails and gave him medicine so that he was cured. He reserved one side of the house for him, inhabiting the other himself and leaving a space in the middle for dancing.

4

Sun went hunting. He heard the woodpeckers at work pecking honey out of the trees, went to the old woodpecker and begged for some honey. The woodpecker called him to come and gave him his share. He wore a brilliant red head-dress, which, however, was somewhat worn. A little farther on, however, Sun saw another woodpecker wearing a beautiful brand-new one. He went there and begged him, too, for honey, which he obtained. Then he further begged for the head-dress. The woodpecker at first refused, but was persuaded by the other woodpeckers. Thus he bade Sun step under the tree and warned him not to drop the head-ornament. Then he rolled it up and threw it down. As it dropped it was like real fire, but Sun caught it and threw it from one hand into the other till it had grown cold. At home he stored it in a lidded gourd, which he opened the next morning before going hunting, to make sure the ornament was still there.

Moon observed this, and when Sun was gone he opened the vessel, took out the head-dress, put it on, and danced with it in the house. Sun heard him dancing from afar as he came home and grew angry, scolding Moon, who excused himself, saying he liked the ornament so much.

The next morning he then begged Sun to help him get a similar ornament and importuned him until he finally took him along. They went together to the spot where the woodpeckers were at work on the bees' nests and asked first for honey. At first Sun got his share and ate it. Then when Moon, too, received his share, Sun murmured to himself, "Bee-bread! Bee-bread!" Then Moon's honeycomb had not a drop of honey, only bee-bread, about which he complained bitterly. Then Sun begged the woodpeckers for another head-dress, and at last one of them was willing to part with his. Sun prepared to catch it himself. Then Sun stepped aside, and Moon took his position under the tree. But when he saw the ornament dropping upon himself looking just like fire, he was afraid of grasping it and allowed it to drop to the ground. At once the entire grass of the steppe was aflame.

The two fled from the flames as fast as possible. Sun crawled into a fire-proof clay wasp nest, hiding there until the fire was over. Moon, seeing him, also hurriedly crawled into a wasp nest, but this was of pasteboard, so that the fire drove him out. He tried a second and a third nest with the same result, and only succeeded with a fourth in sheltering himself until the fire was over.

5

Sun went through the burnt steppe and called his comrade, who at last answered from afar. He came up and stood still at a distance, blackened by the smoke and with his hair singed off. Sun called him to come nearer and scolded him harshly. He struck him on the crown of his head with the palm of his hand so that he toppled over and remained seated on the ground. Weeping he declared he would never more take out the head-dress without permission.

Thereupon Sun proposed to search the burnt steppe for beasts that had perished in the fire. They found quantities of game and each put up a griddle for broiling it. All the slices on Sun's griddle, when opened, proved very fat. But when Moon cut *his* open, Sun murmured softly to himself, "Nothing but skin! Only skin!" And all were lean. Three times Moon came to his comrade's griddle to complain. Then the latter at last angrily took a slice of capybara from over the fire and threw it at Moon's belly, burning his skin so that he began to wail aloud. "Run to the creek," cried Sun, but when Moon got to the bank Sun murmured "Dry! Dry!" At once the creek dried up. Moon picked up mud in both hands and rubbed his scalded abdomen. Then he saw a turtle lying in the mud beside himself. In the meantime Sun said, "Water, return!" Soon the creek bed filled with water. But the turtle bit into Moon's scalded belly and clung fast. He wailed aloud and bitterly complained of his comrade's malice, but Sun answered it had happened merely by mistake.

At last they carried the game home and there each made a grate to spread out their slices of flesh anew. But Moon made no fire under his, so his flesh got full of maggots. When he had gone away, Sun went to his grate and inspected his damage. He took down a piece of wild hog and broke it into fragments on the ground. Then all the slices turned into all species of furry game. When Moon got home, he found nothing but the destroyed griddle and the tracks of game. Then he seized a slice of ostrich flesh from Sun's grate and knocked it against the ground; and forthwith the remaining slices turned into all species of game birds.

6

Sun went to the creek, where he found a burity palm with ripe fruits and ate his fill of them. Thus his faeces acquired a fine red color. When Moon noticed it, he immediately asked whence the red color came; he wanted his own faeces to be equally fine. Sun suggested that he eat the blossoms of the pau d'arco tree on an empty stomach. Moon did so, but his faeces got black. Then he sneaked after his comrade and caught him eating burity fruits. He went up and charged him with his lies, but Sun only answered he should come now and eat his fill, too. But as Moon was plucking the fruits, Sun murmured, "One side hard!" And all the fruits Moon tried were only somewhat ripe on one side, the other being hard and inedible. Then Moon, angered, hurled one fruit against the burity trunk, which then was still so low that standing up one could reach the fruits with one's hands. At once the trunk of the palm shot up to its present height, and similarly with the trunks of all other fruit-trees, which until then had still been as low as shrubs. In vain Sun cried, "Enough! Enough!" They all grew so high that henceforth no one could reach the fruits with his hands. Sun was very much annoyed, but Moon declared that was precisely the right way, for when thirsty a person could discover water from a distance by the tall burity palms.

7

Sun went hunting and found a nest with two young dwarf parrots, which he took along in order to raise them at home. He selected the one with more plumage, giving the other to his mate. They fed the little birds after returning from the chase, took them on their fingers, and taught them to speak.

8

One day, while both were out hunting, one of the dwarf parrots said to the other, "I pity our father. When he comes home tired from the chase, he must first prepare food for himself and us. We will help him." Then both parrots turned into girls and prepared the meal. While one was working, the other kept watching by the entrance. As Sun and Moon were returning, they heard the pounding of a mortar from afar, but then suddenly it ceased. As they entered, they found the meal ready, but the two dwarf parrots, as usual, were perched on their beam. They found human tracks, but to their amazement only in the house, not on the road. This continued for several days. At last Sun said to his comrade, "Let us hide on both sides of the house in the bush, and as soon as we hear the pounding in a mortar each of us shall run to one of the two doors."

They went each to his ambush and heard laughing and talking indoors. As soon as they heard pounding, they ran in and simultaneously entered by the two doors. The girls dropped their pestles, lowered their heads and sat down. They were very beautiful and of light skin, and their hair extended to their knees. Moon wanted to address them, but Sun prohibited it and himself first addressed one of them: "Is it you, then, who have been preparing our food?" The girl laughed, "We were sorry for you because you had to work when you came home from hunting. So we turned human and prepared your meals." Sun said, "Now you shall forever remain human!" The girl replied, "Settle between yourselves who is to marry whom!" At once Sun said, "You are mine!" And Moon said to the other, "You are mine!" They made platform beds for themselves and their wives and lived together with them.

9

Now Sun thought if they had women they ought to make a plantation. He staked out a bit of the woods and divided it into two sections, for himself and his comrade. Then he called the woodpecker Dya'i, the snail Duwu'dn and the quartz Klid, to start with the clearing. But Moon had slunk after him, and hearing the sound of work in the woods, he took a cudgel and hurled it in that direction. At once the three stopped work forever.

Sun and Moon planted bottle gourds in their cleared plots, and when they were ripe Sun chose a quiet, deep spot in the creek, and made a path thither. Moon did likewise a little further downstream. The next morning Sun went first to his plot; Moon, who was still sleeping, followed later. They got all gourds to the bank and then threw them into the water by pairs, and as soon as they came up they turned into a couple of human beings, who would sit down on the bridge crossing the creek. When Moon had made four human couples, Sun caused his next couple to be blind and lame. Moon went to his comrade and complained bitterly on seeing the handsome people Sun had made. But Sun said that was the way it should remain. Then Moon, too, uttered a magical formula, and several of

Sun's children also developed defects. Thus both continued till there were no gourds left.

10

Then Sun said, "Let us lay out a village for our children." They looked for a high site and laid out a circle, which Sun divided by an east-west line, saying, "I put my children on the north side!" "And I put mine on the south side!" answered Moon. Thus the two moieties arose, Kolti and Kolre. Then Sun asked, "Who shall rule the village?" Moon answered at once "Kolre!" But Sun said, "No, Kolti!" And so it was. That is why the Apinaye chiefs are still of the Kolti moiety. They married off their children and gave them good advice: "You must take pains to multiply! Fetch wasp larvae and let your wives smear them on their bodies, then you will have many children!"

Then Sun said to Moon: "Now our children are all married. Come, let us go!" "Yes," Moon agreed, "let us go! You shall light up for them by day, and I by night!" Then they assembled all the people in the plaza and Sun spoke: "My children! Now I am going off with my godchild!" And Moon replied, "Well, then, let us go, my god-father!" Then both rose to the sky.

Such myth-cycles belong to the very oldest cultures of aboriginal America. And if to the clear implications of this mythology we add the archaic features of their religious beliefs and the original simplicity of their methods of food production, the justification for regarding these tribes as having a simple culture seems warranted.

It is with the clear realization then that peoples like the Ge and their neighbors in the south, the Bororo of Matto Grosso, do represent this very early cultural layer of the two Americas that we must approach that one aspect of their culture, the presence of the dual organization and of clans, whose explanation and interpretation has caused so much controversy among scholars. Do these two traits belong together? Do they belong to the old layer? If they do not, when did they enter this region and to what other tribe or tribes do they owe their origin? Such are the questions that are quite legitimately asked. They are more easily asked than answered. And indeed up to the present no agreement has been reached among scholars as to how they are to be answered.

Clearly nothing final can be said today. Yet certain incontrovertible facts do stand out sharply. First let me point out that only a negligible number of tribes in North America exist where a clan organization is found without agriculture. The northwest coast of Canada is the one really great exception. In South America there are none at all, barring these Ge tribes. In marked contrast to this state of affairs is the distribution of the dual organization and its correlation with agriculture. This type of social structure is found among a significant number of non-agricultural peoples, the northwest coast of Canada, for instance, California, the Bororo, and many of the Ge tribes. Be it remembered that the Ge tribes who have agriculture at the present time, or who possibly had it at the time of the discovery of South America, must all have borrowed it from their Tupi-Guarani neighbors. However, the dual organization is also encountered in South America among the great Andean civilizations and a few of the simpler tribes in close contact with them, among the Tupi-Guarani tribes on the lower Madeira River and among one on the lower Tocantins and, finally, among two Arawak tribes, one north of the mouth of the Amazon and one along the western Amazon. In North America practically all the tribes with an agricultural economy possessed it. In this connection it might be well to point out that it prevailed in a form amazingly similar to that of the Ge, the two Arawak tribes mentioned, and the Bororo, in just that area most specifically connected with the Mound-Builders—the Southeast of the United States and the Mississippi-Ohio rivers. In both cases all the traits typical of the dual organization are present: exogamy; the halving of the village; symbolical designations for the two divisions either by cardinal points, by upper or lower, or by color; various forms of hostility and antagonism expressed particularly by games; reciprocal social functions; numerous ceremonial functions; special personal names and special facial decorations. In most instances, likewise, all these tribes possess clans that are allocated specifically to the two divisions.

The historical connection between the two is thus obvious. The only questions to be determined are again the fateful ones—

was the dual organization originally distinct from the clan organization and was it older? Are the two, clan and moiety, inextricably and inherently connected? How and, if possible, when, did they reach South America?

Some scholars have claimed that the dual organization as such spread to the Andean region and to the rest of South America from Mexico and Central America. Yet although the evidence for its existence among the Maya and Aztec is exceedingly poor —only one case has hitherto been found in Central America proper—it is safe to assume that both the Maya and Aztec-Toltec civilizations once had it. But whether it was through Mexico and Central America that it came to the Andeans, or the reverse, remains to be determined. If we assume the first, when did it take place? We know the Incas—that is, the Quechua—possessed both clans and the dual organization, and many scholars are of the belief that they took both over from the high cultures that had preceded them and that they conquered. If Mexico and Central America have passed it on to them, that must have been very early, certainly many hundred years before 1000 A.D.

But whether it came to Peru from Mexico or the reverse, as I am inclined very strongly to believe, is really immaterial to the specific question involved here, for it is extremely unlikely, not to say incredible, that it reached the Amazon Basin from the Andean civilizations. On what grounds some scholars make that assumption is not at all clear to me. It seems inherently unlikely that it was not already intimately associated with the clan organizations when it reached South America. We are thus, once more, thrown back for the route of entry upon the northern shores of the Gulf of Mexico, the delta of the Mississippi, and the Southeast. But that would really give us much more than a route. It would give us an approximate date: 1000 A.D. or later.

If both clan and dual organization came in this manner, only the Arawak could have brought them and only the Arawak could have been the disseminators. Indeed these same Arawak may have conceivably relayed them to Peru; that is, if there is any validity to the claim that the language of the *Uru* and *Chipaya* still spoken around Tiahuanaco is really a branch of the

Quechua linguistic stock, for the Uro-Chipaya have both the dual organization and clans.

The distribution of the two Arawak tribes that possess these telltale traits is highly suggestive in this connection. One, the *Palikur*, is north of the mouth of the Amazon; the other, the *Tukuna*, to the far west and on the Amazon. Thus they seem to stand at strategic points, pioneers and guardians at one and the same time.

Los de Abajo, the lowliest, the remnants of the original stock, apparently even they could hold their own only by compromise and readjustment and by withdrawing to the outer fringe of the continent. They too, like the Arawak, the Carib, the Amazon tribes, and the Tupi-Guarani, were touched and transformed by influences emanating from the great Mexican-Central American civilizations. Small wonder then that even a tribe like the Bororo, pushed into inhospitable Matto Grosso, should not only have myths that belong to the old basic structure but the bull-roarer and the dual organization as well.

CHAPTER VIII

Frontier and Refuge Place

THE TRIBES OF THE CHACO

"TO ENQUIRIES CONCERNING THEIR PLACE OF abode, they replied that it was at a great distance and could only be approached by crossing many marshes; a cunning answer dictated by their fears for themselves and their wives. . . . Lest their footsteps should betray their resorts, in returning home they practised the following artifice: if they went by a southern, they returned by a northern road, and contrariwise, so that the Spaniards could not form an idea of the place where they lurked." Thus wrote the celebrated Jesuit missionary Martin Dobritzhoffer[38] in 1784 about the peoples for whom he was searching far across the Paraná River, not far from Asunción.

Rain and still more rain poured down upon him as he made his first attempt, and it seemed to him as if the heavens had conspired to overwhelm him and to deter him from continuing. Bravely and stubbornly he began again after twenty days obstinate rains had forced a first return. Finally he was rewarded and came upon three large groups of Indians.

Their huts were built of palms interwoven with dry grass, so he tells us; each had eight openings and contained sixty inhabitants. Nets were scattered around in which they both sat and slept. Each family had its own fire. All, of whatever sex, wore triangular shells in their ears. The men shaved their heads, leaving only a circle of hair on the crown. At the age of seven their

lower lips were pierced and a thin reed inserted into the hole.
The men wore very little indeed, simply a narrow girdle around
their loins, but the women were covered from head to foot with
a white garment made from the bark of a certain tree. To add a
finishing touch to their attire, they wore crowns of long parrot
feathers on their heads. They maintained themselves by the
chase and used barbed arrows to shoot with. The good father,
who had come from the enchanting city of Graz, in Styria, to
this distant and inhospitable wilderness, continues as follows:[39]

They often lurk in thickets, for the purpose of shooting or ensnar-
ing antas, which they inveigle by a skilful imitation of their bray;
nor are they wholly averse to agriculture. In these woods there is an
amazing produce of maize and other fruits, as also of tobacco. On
going to bed they put their pots full of flesh or vegetables on the fire,
that their breakfast may be ready when they awake: for at earliest
dawn, the males, from seven years old and upwards, traverse the
woods with bundles of darts, in search of that game, on which they
must subsist for the day. The mothers put their babies in wicker
baskets, and carry them on their shoulders, when they travel in the
woods. From the hives with which the trees abound, they collect
quantities of most excellent honey, serving both for meat and drink.
Their name for God, in the Guarany tongue, is *Tupa*, but of that
God and his commandments, they care little to know. They are as
ignorant of the worship of idols, as they are of the Supreme Being.
The spirit of evil they call *Ananga*, but they pay him no adoration.
The magicians, or more properly impostors, who arrogate to themselves full power of warding and inflicting disease and death, of pre-
dicting future events, of raising floods and tempests, of transforming
themselves into tigers, and performing I know not what preter-
natural feats, they religiously·venerate. . . . Marriage with the most
distant relations they shun as highly criminal. They inclose their dead
in large vessels of clay, according to an old Guarany rite.
What their fate after this life may be, they never trouble themselves to enquire. They do not feed on human flesh, though the neighboring Indians reckon it a delicacy. Every stranger whatsoever,
Indian, Spaniard or Portuguese, they suspect of hostile intentions,
and receive in arms, believing every other race their enemies and
designers on their freedom.

The people whom Dobritzhoffer here describes bring us to one of the most interesting sections of the great southern continent, ethnologically speaking; to the famous Gran Chaco.

It is a sterile and unkind land for the most part, this Gran Chaco. The long river, the Pilcomayo, that bisects it, is navigable for only a short distance. Approximately where the Pilcomayo crosses the Capricorn extensive swamps open out in all directions. Its course is a most unsettled one and has changed many times. The soil around it consists of a fine earth transformed in the rainy season into mud; in the dry season into whirling dust. No stone is found anywhere. The moment you leave the Andes, stone in fact disappears. Nevertheless the river is of immense importance to the peoples around it because of the large number of fish it contains.

The nature of the landscape itself varies considerably. Woods alternate with grassy plains. The palms encountered, although considerable in number, are however of no use to the Indians, nor are there any trees from whose bark cloth can be made. For clothes and string rope they are dependent upon a spiny plant called *chakuar*. The arrow-grass, too, so important for other tribes, is absent here.

However, certain plants occur in an abundance quite unusual for South America, edible wild fruits—algarroba (*prosopis*), chanar (*gourliea decortitans*), tusca (*acacia aroma*) and mistol (*zizyphus mistol*). Without them life would be practically impossible in the Chaco, for game is poor, and the most the inhabitants can hope for are ostriches, small deer, and field voles, and these only are to be found in circumscribed sections. Added to all this is the weather, as a rule exceedingly hot, but bitterly cold when the south wind sweeps over the plains in May and June.

To such a land it cannot be assumed any people came willingly or of their free accord. Pressures of the most severe and continuous kind must have forced them into it. Nor can it be assumed that they would be likely to remain there without repeated attempts to emerge into more hospitable regions. We find these people consequently always pressing out from the

center, where the almost humanly impossible spots exist, to the
more kindly fringe, the northeast, the north, the east, and the
west. That fringe, quite naturally, they always found pre-
empted by other tribes. But more than that. They would have
found themselves, in every direction, in contact with complex
cultures. In eastern Bolivia—that is, to the north—they would
have encountered the Arawak tribe, the *Chané*, and the Tupi-
Guarani tribe, the Chiriguano; indeed influences from the great
Andean civilizations. Nordenskjöld, the well-known Swedish
anthropologist, in fact believed that all the Chaco tribes, even
those living in the central core, had been markedly affected by
the great Andean civilizations, an overstatement it seems to the
author. To the northeast they would again have come into contact with Arawak and Tupi-Guarani tribes. With the latter this
could not have been earlier than the beginning of the sixteenth
century, if that early, because the Tupi-Guarani did not reach
that area until then. The main contact, consequently, must have
been with the Arawak.

If, therefore, one of the Chaco tribes, the Mataco, have the
reputation of having had a definitely more complex culture than
the other Chaco tribes, that fact must be explained as due to their
proximity to and intimacy with a tribe like the Arawak Chané.

In contradistinction to practically all the other tribes of the
Argentinian Chaco, the Mataco are, and seem always to have
been, exceedingly peaceful. Whether the marginal agriculture
they did possess was old is doubtful, but this is not true of their
weaving and pottery nor of the use made by their medicine men
of narcotics. These possessions and the far more highly organized nature of their magical beliefs, their religion and their ceremonialism set them off from most of the typical Chaco tribes.
This superior organization of the nonmaterial aspects of their
life in no way, however, obscures the essential simplicity of their
lives. The Arawak and Tupi-Guarani impinged upon their life,
but no more. Essentially they remained as untouched as were
their Chaco neighbors, the *Toba-Pilaga*, the *Mbaya-Kadiueo*,
and the *Abipones*, or the dwellers in the northeastern Chaco, the
Chamacoco. That is, until the horse, in the seventeenth century,

had fundamentally transformed the civilization of the Mbaya-Kadiueo and the Abipones.

Stripped of its precolumbian and postcolumbian accretions the Mataco present us then with a picture of a culture of surprising simplicity. There is no dual organization and there are no clans. Magic and the medicine men rule supreme, just as they do among the nonagricultural tribes of North America. But how similar are these undifferentiated cultures of the two continents? Let us compare one trait, the concept of disease and its treatment.

Diseases, according to the Mataco, are invisible spirits with the appearance of human beings. They wear feathers like medicine men and are always exceedingly ugly. They leave their habitations to enter human beings, or steal their souls to make them sick. To expel them from one's body an individual must call in the aid of a medicine man, who finds out what they want. Their wishes are always for very concrete things. According to Métraux's informant they are satisfied with the essence of the food thus offered them, and human beings may eat it without danger to themselves if they have asked the disease spirits to partake first. Frequently one dances either to frighten the spirits away or exhaust them, for they seem compelled to participate and cannot refuse. It is when a medicine man feels that they are exhausted that he will speak to them. The disease will respond and ask whether he is angry, and when he answers, "No, I am just dancing," then he, the disease spirit, will beg him to desist, for he is scheduled to dance on the following day too.

Added to the belief that the disease spirit has either entered the body or taken away a man's soul is still another one; namely, that he has introduced small objects into the sick man's body to cause him great pain. The task of the medicine man is thus threefold: to expel the spirit, recover the soul, or extract the disease-injected objects. Presumably the proper diagnosis must be made first. One type of medicine man may be called in after another until the particular specialist arrives. There are specialists galore among all these Chaco tribes.

Two types of ceremonies for the expulsion of the disease spirit

exist: a general and a special one. The first must be performed
in the morning and in the open, far from all houses. All the
medicine men in the village participate, holding a rattle gourd
and a whistle in their hands. They are always dressed in ceremonial shirts, and the more famous ones have their faces painted
black and red.

Métraux thus describes a performance he witnessed:[40]

[It] consisted of a song without words. The singing was punctuated by the rattling of the gourds, and from time to time by the
clacking of hoof and rattle necklaces and the whistling of the flutes.
Each blowing of the whistle indicated a new phase in the traditional
sequence of events associated with the ceremony—new metamor-
phosis of the spirit of the medicine man, its arrival or departure from
a given place. The rattle gourd is sometimes brandished in a threatening manner, as though to scare away an invisible being. In turn,
without interrupting the ceremony, some of the performers took a
snuff of *hatax* powder. Those who had bunches of feathers stretched
them forward, making the same gesture which has already been described when speaking of the rattles. One of the performers was
running in front of and behind his colleagues, holding a bunch of
feathers in his hand and dusting them off from head to foot. He was
assisted by another who was holding bells and rattles which he
shook behind his companions. After they had taken a snuff of hatax
the performers went on singing, shaking the rattles, and performing
threatening gestures. Some of the medicine men sang the song of
their own spirits, ignoring the chants of their colleagues.

These preliminaries were succeeded by a direct attack against the
disease. Some individuals stepped out from the row, and with violent
gestures each one brandished his bunch of feathers or the rattle
gourds and then returned to their places in line. A man began kicking
the earth and was immediately imitated by others, who took up
handfuls of dust, which they threw in front of themselves. The
whole troop followed this example, and they rushed against the
disease. Some concentrated all their strength on a special spot, as
though they had driven the disease there, hitting the spot repeatedly
with their sabers or bunches of feathers, then stamping on the ground
as though they had buried their victim. The attack against the invisible enemy lasted for a long time. Others brandished bunches of
feathers which they had tied to the points of their spears.

After the disease has been expelled, following a pattern which we have now seen to be so common here in South America, a purification rite has to be performed. The medicine men first clean themselves, one wiping the other off. Then they blow on each other's heads and necks. All the participants are now called in, both men and women, and the directing medicine men and medicine women walk over to them, wipe their bodies with bunches of feathers, and blow on their heads. When this has been done with great care and circumspection, the medicine men rush outside to cut a piece of special earth that is covered with grass and then to bury the disease under it. The sounds of the whistles now follow each other at closer and closer intervals and the rattles tingle with greater energy and with more determination. When the particular disease has been a very severe one, repeated attempts have to be made before success can be achieved. The medicine men have first, for instance, to change themselves into ravens and subsequently into earth-bees.

When a disease spirit is to be expelled from a particular individual the procedure is not much different. Considerable distinctions in the length and the complexity of the treatment, however, exist, depending entirely upon the patient's ability to pay. Métraux has described the treatment for both a rich and a poor woman among the Mataco. That for the rich woman took place in an open space of about fifteen feet square that had been cleared not far from her habitation. A tentlike structure was set up in this square, and wooden posts as high as twenty feet erected, an old Argentinian flag being hoisted on one of them. Since the disease spirit had to be conciliated, certain objects that it was felt would please him were placed around the tent—a mosquito net, a weaving loom, an old suitcase, pieces of gaudily colored cloth, a saddle, a soldier's coat, a lamp, and a lance or a gun. A variegated assortment indeed, and one that should satisfy the most select of palates. At some distance from these objects fires had been started in order to prepare food both for the disease spirit and the participants.

The patient was seated in the middle of the tent, a pile of hay and many old rags around her. She had donned her best dress and was covered with ritual ornaments. As she sat there, five renowned medicine men, who had been called upon as consultants, approached her. They were old men decorated with feather belts, rattles, tropical helmets, and other valuable objects, and the lower part of their faces was painted black. Twenty other dancers now joined them, and the dancing and singing began, the patient always actively participating. A number of pauses occurred, during which the medicine men continually blew upon the patient. At one particular point the chief medicine man whistled on his bone flute and then suddenly came to an abrupt stop. It was now time for the patient to participate. The sick woman began dancing alone, lifting one foot and then the other a few inches from the ground, slowly and circumspectly, without moving from one particular spot. This she did to the accompaniment of rattles shaken rhythmically by two medicine men. After ten minutes all the medicine men joined her in the dancing, but only for a short time.

The final part of the treatment was now at hand. Two shaman approached the sick woman and began undressing her while still another shook his rattle down the whole length of her body. The ornaments were slowly moved, and as they fell to the ground the medicine men struck the place where they dropped and ran immediately to throw them away. They first shook them a number of times and then arranged them carefully in order. The sick woman now sat up in the middle of the tent and was given something to drink.

Such a ceremony may last a number of days. The one described above, for instance, lasted five hours a day for five days.

Contrasting with the pomp of this treatment was the one performed for a poor patient. "Another treatment of a more modest character," says Métraux, "was undertaken. In front of the woman's house a tent was stretched and she was placed in it. The offerings consisted only of some pieces of cloth and a few bags. When I arrived, the chief medicine man was speaking to the disease while an old woman, who was a magician, sang and blew on the patient. . . . After a pause, during which everybody drank some of the wine required of the disease, a singing man started to run around the patient, his body bent forward and his arms dangling. The chief medicine man spoke once more to the disease while the medicine woman continued blowing on the patient and another medicine man placed around her head the front pages of an illustrated novel. The man who was running stopped, and the chief medicine man. started talking with the others. Everybody sat down and drank some water, and two women began to walk rapidly around the others while they sang. One of them stopped, and after a short while the other one stopped too. Then all who were present started dancing."[41]

But it is not only a disease spirit who will enter a person's body and cause him to become ill. A man may also be entered by any of the innumerable evil spirits who infest the surroundings. The treatment is always essentially the same and always designed to achieve one end: expulsion.

Of the three theories of disease prevailing among the Mataco, two of them, soul loss and the introjection of injurious objects into the body, are of such world-wide distribution that they cannot be assigned to any particular culture or, for that matter, to any particular continent. The third one, however, the entrance of an evil spirit into a person's body and the whole phenomenon of possession, has a definitely circumscribed distribution in the new world and is fairly specifically associated with tribes who have a nonagricultural economy.

The same may be said of another phase of Chaco culture: dreams. Dreams are, we know, of extreme importance among all aboriginal peoples, but there are clear-cut gradations in the importance of the role they play. Among the nonagricultural *Algonquian* tribes of Canada, and of the plateau and basin regions of western United States as well as among the nonagricultural Californian Indians, dreams possess an immediate significance quite different from that which they enjoy in civilizations with an agricultural economy. These more sophisticated civilizations have frequently elaborated upon their dreams and "stylizised" them, as in the case of the well-known and widely distributed puberty dreams of North America; but they seem never to have meant to them what they did to the simpler peoples, and it is just this significance that we find so sharply defined among the Chaco Indians.

All South American investigators have commented upon this preoccupation with dreams, but no one has presented the pertinent information quite so clearly as the somewhat naïve and extroverted English missionary, W. B. Grubb. He is, I think, not overstating, at least, the Chaco theory of dreams when he says of the *Lengua*, whom he knew so well, that to them, "Dreaming is . . . an adventurous journeying of the soul attended by much danger. While the soul wanders, being ethereal, it is able to gratify the desires more freely than if it were in the body. The satisfaction which it derives in doing so, however, being incorporeal, is trifling in comparison with that which it enjoys in the body."[42] But the soul does not leave the body to embark on these dangerous adventures in response to a mere whim. On the contrary, concrete and important matters are involved.

To so wholly delightful and unregenerate an Englishman as the Reverend W. B. Grubb, the Lenguas were subjectivists, nay even philosophical idealists, of purest water. Does he not insist that they looked upon the body only as a house or, better, as an instrument in the hands of the soul? What they dreamt about was, in reality, a declaration of the will of the soul. So he insists the Lengua believed. It must be gratified, whenever possible, through the body. And the Indian not only takes seriously what his soul thus tells him, but he acts upon it. It was this aspect that so disconcerted the grim English missionary and almost upset all his values. He gives a number of examples of the practical consequences of bowing to the dictates of a dream, of which I will give two examples:[43]

In the early years of my sojourn in the Chaco I contracted with an Indian to remain with me and serve me for six consecutive months. In return for his services he was to receive a horse. He acted very well for six weeks, but one morning he was missing, and on inquiry I found that he had gone off at early dawn to his own village, four days' journey away. . . . Not only did I resent his leaving without the last warning, but I was also much disappointed at his breaking the contract at all.

A Mataco Indian from the Gran Chaco

Anxious to discuss whether I had unwittingly given him cause for offense . . . I closely questioned the other Indians. I was told in a matter-of-fact way that the man had gone off because his child was sick, and they seemed surprised at my resentment. On asking them why he had not spoken to me about it, they replied: "He knew very well you would not let him go." I thought over the matter carefully, and could not make out how he had come to know that his child was sick. No one had arrived who could possibly have brought such news so I concluded that his fellows had, in giving this excuse for him, tried to deceive me. Some two weeks afterwards, a visitor arrived from this man's village. I inquired of him about the child and he informed me that there was nothing wrong.

About a month afterwards, the man returned apparently in perfect good-humor, and proceeded quite as a matter of course to fulfill his duties. I challenged him about his late conduct. He had heard that I had been angry about his leaving, but his attitude was that of a man who had been unjustly accused. He told me that he did not want to leave me, that he had promised to work for me for six months, and that he never intended to break his word. When questioned about his child, he admitted that he left because he had thought the child was ill but it was not. . . . Apparently he did not in the least realize that he had done anything wrong. It was not until long after that I had learnt he had made this journey because he had dreamed that his child was sick.

Grubb, who thus remained so true an Englishman in spite of all temptation, goes on to give illustrations of the native belief that souls meet with each other in the land of dreams. He narrates how a man had arrived from a place one hundred and fifty miles away from where he was living and demanded compensation for some pumpkins which he, the Reverend Grubb, had stolen from his garden! One can imagine the surprise, not to say indignation, of the missionary and the tone of voice with which he told the Indian that he had not been near his village for a long time and could not consequently have stolen his pumpkins! He thought at first the whole matter was a joke, but soon perceived how serious it was. Finally, on expostulating strongly with him, the Indian admitted that the missionary had not taken the pumpkins. This bewildered the poor missionary all the more.

His first indignant reaction then gave way to curiosity concerning what really lay behind the accusation that had been made against him. Eventually he discovered that the man had dreamed that he had seen Grubb in his garden one night breaking off and carrying away three pumpkins and that it was for these three pumpkins that he wanted payment. "Yes," said the ever more amazed Englishman, "but you have just admitted that I did not take them!" Again the Indian assented, but immediately replied, "But if you had been there, you would surely have taken them." "In short," continues Grubb, "he regarded the act of my soul, which he supposes had met his in the garden, to be really my will, and what I should actually have done had I been there in the body."[44]

These two examples of Grubb refer, of course, to fairly unimportant matters, and it is extremely unlikely that the Lengua who, after all, have succeeded in maintaining themselves under unusually difficult physical conditions, would have long survived where the dream of a person bore on such fundamental questions as war or the obtaining of food. In spite, then, of Grubb's assertions, we can be certain that the area of practical life where the dream was all-determining was definitely circumscribed. The fact does remain, however, that in few regions of the American aboriginal world are dreams so important as in this nonagricultural, clanless Chaco.

Belonging as definitely to the old stratum of culture as the treatment of disease or the function of dreams is the mythology. The dominant figure in that mythology is the buffoon-hero, the trickster functioning at times as both unconscious and conscious transformer of the world out of an original chaos. The similarities between the episodes in such a trickster cycle as that of the Mataco and the trickster cycles of the North American Indians is almost unbelievable. It will also be well to compare this with that given on page 155 for the Apinaye and note both the similarities and the differences. I will select three episodes for illustration:[45]

1

TAWKXWAX AND THE MUD WASP

Nakwo is a kind of mud wasp which makes his nest with earth. Formerly this mud wasp was a man. When he had gone hunting and left his children at home, Tawkxwax, the trickster, happened to pass by and he ate all of Nakwo's children with the exception of one who managed to escape. When Nakwo came back he asked the boy: "Where are your brothers? Who ate them?" The child said, "I know; it was Tawkxwax."

Nakwo followed the trail of Tawkxwax and finally arrived at the place where he was lying asleep near a pool. Nakwo took some clay and stopped Tawkxwax' mouth, nose, eyes, and penis. He also smeared his fingers with mud. The *pitoi* bird, who was then a man, went fishing in the near-by pool. He saw Tawkxwax, whose stomach had swollen up. The bird went immediately in search of other birds who had become men too. They all came out with axes, but when they tried to cut off the mud, their axes broke off. A big bird whose head is very large tried in his turn, but his axe was not strong enough and broke off. The birds did not know what to do, for they no longer had any axes. Then came a very old bird who was armed with a tiny axe, but a solid.one. Just as he was opening the anus of Tawkxwax, all the accumulated excrement spouted on him and covered him with filth. Since that time this wasp is very bad-looking and his wings are gray.

2

TAWKXWAX AND THE JAGUAR

The jaguar, who had no more fire, decided to kill Tawkxwax, who had stolen it. He set out in pursuit of Tawkxwax, who did not know how to escape the wrath of the dangerous animal. He wanted to fly, but he had no feathers. He asked the *potsax* birds to lend him some feathers. Each potsax pulled out one feather and gave it to him. Tawkxwax smeared his body with wax in order to stick the feathers on. Thus he managed to fly through the air, escaping the jaguar, who stayed on the ground. Now Tawkxwax did not know how to fly, and he was very awkward. His clumsiness aroused the suspicions of the jaguar, who recognized him. He followed him, blowing as hard as he could in order to melt the wax on Tawkxwax's body. The wax melted, and the feathers on Tawkxwax's arms loosened and fell off. Tawkxwax could not remain in the air without feathers, and so he fell to earth. On touching the ground he became a man again and went to conceal himself in a hole. As the jaguar could not reach him in his hole, he removed a piece of his skin and covered the entrance of the hole where Tawkxwax was hiding. Tawkxwax became angry and thirsty, but he dared not leave his den for food, for he could see the jaguar at the entrance. After many days without food and water he became very thin and decided he would have to leave. Upon emerging from the den he found that the jaguar had been gone a long time, leaving only a piece of his skin at the entrance. Tawkxwax was very angry. He then went in search for food.

3

TAWKXWAX AND THE ARMADILLO'S CHILDREN

While walking along the bank of a river, Tawkxwax saw some children swimming. He decided to go swimming with them, and after going into the water three times he said, "Let us make a big fire to warm ourselves by." Tawkxwax made a snare with lianas and cut the nooses around the fire. He managed to have the playing children put their heads through the nooses. They came to the fire for a second time to warm themselves and play. As soon as their heads were in the nooses, Tawkxwax pulled the lianas and tightened the loops around the necks of the children. He removed one of the children, roasted, and ate him. When he finished his dinner he said, "What a wonderful meal, I want some more!" The children were the sons of the Armadillo. The armadillo had two caves, one under the ground and the second in the "other world." The children lived in the first. Tawkxwax dug into the second cave and fell into the "other world." In falling, he shouted, "Is there no root here to save me?" At that moment a root shot up under him and Tawkxwax did not fall, he remained hanging on the root above the precipice. He could not climb up or down. He thought that a bird could come and get him, and a bird did come. The bird said, "What are you doing here, Tawkxwax?" "I am hanging here and I want you to save me." The bird said, "Get on my shoulders, but close your eyes." The bird brought him back to the world, but instead of leaving him on the ground, he took him high into the sky, and then dropped him. In falling, Tawkxwax shouted, "May I change into a mortar?" When he touched the ground he was a mortar. He stood up and again became a man. . . .

Not all this simplicity and lack of integration and elaboration is primary. Some of it—how much it is impossible to say—is due to the impoverishment consequent upon the pressures that forced these central Chaco tribes into their inhospitable new home and the difficulties of eking out even a modest existence there. To succeed even in achieving that one new specialization was necessary: proficiency in war. And so we find this aspect of their culture unusually well developed and well organized. How well organized everything connected with warfare was, the description given by Grubb for the Lengua who were not even the most warlike of the Chaco tribes will indicate:[46]

When hostilities have been decided upon by the leaders of the people, the various "clans" are summoned by means of red arrows, signifying blood. These are carried from village to village by messengers, who tell the people to place the aged, the women, children, and the flocks in positions of safety, a certain number of men remaining to protect them. The rest hasten off to the appointed meeting-place. Once there, a war-chief is chosen, and then the plan of campaign is agreed upon.

The first step taken is to establish an excellent intelligence department. Their best men are sent out as spies, with the object of getting as close as possible to the enemy. At stated intervals messengers are posted, and through them communication is kept up between the spies and headquarters. When the favorable moment for attack has arrived, the men, divided into bands, are instructed to advance upon the enemy from certain positions. A supporting force is arranged for, and ambuscades are planned. The forces advance under cover of night, and the attack is invariably made at about the rising of the morning star, an hour or so before dawn. In case of defeat, a rallying-point is fixed upon; but should victory result, every man has his duty prearranged. Some guard the captives, others drive off the flocks, some attend to the plunder, while others are deputed to bury the dead and to care for the wounded.

The Indians, in their wars, exercise the greatest prudence, and never expose themselves in large numbers to be shot at. They are great strategists, and take every advantage of cover, a practice to which their hunting life so well accustoms them. As they procure their food as best as they can, obtaining roots from the forests, robbing gardens, and hunting what game they can find en route, they naturally form a very mobile force. Every man is supposed to look after himself; he knows the country as well by night as by day, and is therefore a complete unit in himself.

The Indians rarely fight in a body, as their one object is to overthrow their enemy with as little loss of life to themselves as possible. This method makes it extremely difficult for trained troops to fight successfully against them. Disciplined soldiers are dependent upon each other, and of necessity are compelled to form camps, and keep more or less together. They rarely succeed in surrounding a body of Indians, or in forcing them into the open, whereas the Indian sniper with his bow and arrow gains a decided advantage in spite of the inferiority of his weapons. His arrow makes no noise, and he is thus able to pick off sentinels without alarming the enemy's outposts; and as in such a country as this the invading force has to pasture its horses, the Indian frequently succeeds in capturing, or at least stampeding, them.

When attacking an Indian village, it is their custom first to discharge a flight or two of arrows, and then rush in with their clubs. They kill all grown men and women who do not succeed in escaping, and spare only the younger women and children. This is done for obvious reasons. The younger women they marry, and all soon settle down to the care of their families. The children readily amalgamate with the tribe, the more so as captives are generally well treated, and admitted to equal privileges with their conquerors. With the older people, however, the hostile feeling never dies out; they are constantly seeking to escape, and were they to save any number of grown men, they would revolt upon any favorable opportunity. Wounded men receive no quarter, but are killed on the spot, as the Indian asserts that, if spared, they would take the first opportunity to revenge themselves.

The reasons given for invariably selecting the hour before dawn for making the attack are, that the enemy, if unaware of the presence of an attacking force, sleep most heavily at that hour, and that the few who might happen to be awake, do not move far from the village fires owing to the chill of the morning.

Let us take an actual example of their tactics.

The village in question was situated on the southern side of a large forest. To the east and south flowed a sluggish swamp stream, and on the western bank nearest to the village there were some dug-out canoes, used by the *Kisapang* for crossing. To the south-west lay a stretch of open country covered with ant-hills, and to the north-west a number of small woods, with spaces between, leading out into the open country beyond.

The attacking force, having been previously informed of the location and surroundings of the village by the spies, advanced under cover of night and took up the following positions. The main body occupied the spaces on the north-west, while a reserve force remained some distance in the rear. In the open ant-hill plain, a small body of good marksmen were located, hiding themselves behind the ant-hills, and another body took up a position in a small wood opposite the place where the canoes lay. Swimming across the river, they brought them over to their own side. The main body, when the moment was considered favorable, made a rush upon the village, their shouts being the signal to the others. Those in the ant-hill plain remained under cover in order to cut off any fugitives who might attempt to escape that way, while half the force on the east crossed over in the canoes, and, just as the villagers were closing with the invaders from the north-west, rushed up and attacked from behind.

Taken unawares, and in the dim light, the villagers, after fighting stubbornly for a time in order to cover the retreat of their women and children, who had mostly escaped into the forest behind them, scattered in all directions. Some rushed for the plain, and were shot down by those in hiding behind the ant-hills; the others tried to escape by the canoes, but were intercepted by the other half of the force left on the east for that very purpose.

This marked preoccupation with warfare was unquestionably an old trait of these people. Without it no tribe could have survived long or, at least, maintained any degree of independence. And it must have been this long experience in attack and defense that laid the foundation for that amazing transformation of simple tribes like the Mbaya-Kadiueo and the Abipones, after they had once adopted the horse, into militant and efficient terrorists and, after a fashion, into "empire" builders. A similar type of transformation had taken place in the United States with tribes like the *Ute* and the *Apache*, although both of these remained essentially destroyers. To the Mbaya-Kadiueo and Abipones, those members of the Old Stock who succeeded in reorganizing and revivifying an impoverished culture, we shall accordingly turn.

CHAPTER IX

The Old Stock Reorganizes

THE HORSEMEN OF THE CHACO

IT WOULD HAVE REQUIRED NOT A LITTLE IMAGI-
nation, when the inhabitants of central and northern Chaco were
first discovered by the Spaniards, to picture any of these Indians,
then living in ignoble obscurity, as ever having the energy or
the creative ability to transform their simple culture into a terroristic force through the instrumentality of something they had
taken from the much-hated Spaniards. We know, of course,
that the *Sioux*, a far more advanced tribe than any of these
Chaco peoples, also reorganized their lives when they adopted
the horse, but they attempted no subjugation of their Indian
neighbors, and their raids upon the whites were always in the
nature of a defense.

That was quite different in the Chaco, particularly with one
tribe, the Mbaya-Kadiueo. Not only did the latter harass and
terrify the Spaniards, but they reduced other tribes to vassalage.
Such, for instance, was the fate that befell the highly organized
agricultural community in northwestern Chaco, the Arawak
tribe called the Chané. And all this they achieved after they
adopted the horse. To explain the strange phenomenon represented by their culture, more, however, was necessary than simple
hatred of the newcomers and the incorporation of the horse into
their way of life. Let us attempt to see what these factors may
have been.

As we have already pointed out, on the fringe of the Chaco—
the west, the north, and the east—life was comparatively easy.
The tribes living there all lived settled lives. Some of them, like
the *Araucanians* to the north and the *Calchaqui* to the west, had
been profoundly influenced by the great Andean civilizations
and had developed cultural subcenters of their own, especially
the latter. To a far more limited extent this was also true of the
Tupi-Guarani tribe: the Chiriguano, and the Arawak tribe: the
Chané. To the east and northeast sat the Tupi-Guarani tribes,
comparatively recent intruders. The only place of escape for
those tribes trapped against their will in the heart of this desolate
country was thus occupied by peoples who had ample means for
protecting themselves from attack under ordinary conditions.
And so the Mbaya-Kadiueo, the Abipones, the Toba were held
in a firm vise against which no amount of straining or of kicking
against the pricks availed them anything.

The whole situation changed with the advent of the Spaniards.
Although bitter fighting was necessary, the Calchaqui and the
Araucanians were eventually subjugated and their power
broken. The Tupi-Guarani and the Arawak Chané became converted to Christianity, or what passed for such, rather easily.
During the conflicts between the Spaniards and the Calchaqui,
the Chaco tribes withdrew more and more to their own difficult
country, there to protect themselves as long as they could against
the utterly wild and undisciplined Europeans, who even tried to
penetrate into the Chaco proper in their search for gold. These
tribes did not stay there long. But when they finally emerged
they came on horseback, and their new career began. Two things
seemed to be uppermost in their minds: first, how to obtain some
of the new things the Spaniards had introduced, and second,
how to maintain themselves. Like modern military strategists
they adopted the motto that attack was the best method of
defense.

When did they obtain their horses? As early as 1641, the Abipones, Dobritzhoffer says, had already become dexterous horsemen. The same writer tells us that according to an old Abipone
informant, his people originally stole horses in order to drive

off herds from the lands of the Spaniards and that in the space of fifty years, one hundred thousand horses were thus obtained. Dobritzhoffer insists that this number is not exaggerated, for he claims that as many as four thousand were carried off from the Spaniards in one assault. Whatever the case may be, by 1675, both Abipones and Mbaya-Kadiueo had become horsemen of great repute, with an affection for the horse that only a pastoral people can feel. "As many nations worship the crocodile, the snake and the ape as divinities, the Abipones would adore their horses if idolatry prevailed among them," so said the famous missionary and ethnologist. In spite of himself he admired these die-hards. "It is certainly difficult to understand by what means about a thousand savages (for the whole nation of the Abipones hardly contained more who were able to bear arms) had the power of disturbing an immense province. Unanimous hatred of the Spaniards, craft, tolerance of labor, and the alliance of the *Mocobies* stood them in the stead of numbers. Barreda, commander at St. Iago, repeatedly affirmed that were he to hear that all the Abipones had been slain, ten only surviving, he should still judge it necessary to have the watch continued in every part of Paraguay. He therefore thought one tally of Abipones sufficient to distress a whole province.

"There was no retreat so sequestered that they did not discover, and furiously overrun; no place so remote or well fortified by nature, that they thought impenetrable. They swam across those vast rivers, the Paraná and Paraguay, even where they are united in one channel, and pleasantly conversing at the same time. They rode over vast precipices, sometimes ascending, and sometimes, which was still more frightful, descending, till they reached the confines of Córdoba and St. Iago, and there, alas! what torrents of blood they caused to flow! Trackless woods full of rushes and thick trees, marshes and lakes rendered slippery with mud, they crossed with ease. That immense plain of a hundred and fifty leagues, which lies between the banks of the Paraná and the Salado, is sometimes flooded to such a degree, that it resembles a vast lake; this happens after long and incessant rain; when, as is often the case, no rain falls for many months, that immense tract of land is so parched by the burning sky, that the smallest bird would fail to find a drop of water there.

"Yet the Abipones, regardless of these impediments, arrived at the dwellings of the Spaniards, whom they intended to rob, by a journey of many days, sometimes having to pass through water, at others entirely destitute of it."[47]

What their mode of life was before they became horsemen we can determine fairly well, for it could not have been very different from that of the Toba-Pilaga or the Lengua. They were nonagricultural nomads, nomads like the other true Chaco tribes, from compulsion and not from desire. Chieftainship seems always to have been important in war and was inherited in the male line, but only if the heir was qualified; that is, if he had proved his capacity and valor. Whether the indications of a division into classes based on military attainment existed before the advent of the horse and the consequent change in their whole social organization appears more than doubtful. Yet it seems likely that the elaborate ceremony connected with a man's elevation to the rank of a chief is precolumbian even if much of the elaboration is secondary and postcolumbian. It would indeed be exceedingly difficult to explain how a tribe as simple from every point of view as the Abipones were, except for the technique of warfare, could possibly have developed true social classes. Nevertheless, when Dobritzhoffer was with them and, for at least a hundred years before, there seems to have been a definite division of the people into nonhereditary "nobles" and "non-nobles," adoption into the "noble" class being signalized by the adoption of a new name and a special language. Let us, however, see what the ceremony entailed. Many elements in it will recall the customs of peoples at the other end of the continent, as Dobritzhoffer himself has pointed out.

When it has been decided to elevate a man to the rank of *hocheri*, because of his valor and services in war, he must submit to a test of fortitude strangely reminiscent of the puberty ordeals of the Taulipang (cf. page 127) of the Amazon Basin. It consists of placing a black bead on his tongue which is to be kept there three days, during which time he may not speak, eat, or drink.

On the evening preceding his elevation there is a ceremonial lament by the women for the dead chiefs, and particularly for the one whom the new warrior is to succeed. They all flock to the entrance of his tent, disrobe to the waist, let down their hair, and, standing in a long row, intone their chant. Throughout the night this continues without let-up. At dawn the prospective chief comes out of his tent. He is dressed for the occasion and holds a spear in his hand. Immediately upon emerging he leaps upon a horse that has been made ready for him and that has also been decorated for the great event—laden with feathers, small bells, and various trappings. He gallops toward the north, followed by a great troop of fellow Abipones. Then he reverses his direction and turns home. In his tent he is greeted by an old medicine woman whose function it is to initiate the elevation rites proper. His spear is taken by a woman of "noble" birth while he dismounts, the other women attendants striking their lips and shouting. After he has dismounted, the old medicine woman delivers a long admonitory speech at the end of which he again mounts his horse and gallops to the south, returning to be once more harangued by the old woman. This procedure is repeated two more times, once for the east and once for the west. Then all betake themselves to the tent where the actual investiture takes place. It consists of three things: the cutting of the hair, "so that," as Dobritzhoffer quaintly remarks, "from the forehead to the back part of the head there is left a baldness or streak three inches wide"; the recital of the new chief's achievements by the initiating medicine women; and the change of name. The panegyric really consists of enumerating his right to chieftainship—his warlike disposition, his knowledge of arms, and, of course, of horses, the number of enemy he has slain, and the valor of his ancestors.

As soon as his new name is proclaimed by the group of initiating women, the rites are over, except for the spectators. "They," adds Dobritzhoffer, "do not like dry ceremonies to be protracted to a great length, but joyfully fly to skins full of honeyed liquor, and conclude the business with a famous drinking-match."

The importance of the chief is further evidenced by the ceremonies celebrating the birth of a male child to him. As soon as this is known, a large group of virgins repair to the house of the newly born child and run around the roof, shaking palm boughs to symbolize, first, that he will become famous in war, and, second, that he will become a scourge to his enemies. The real celebration, however, consists of a series of games played by virgins and young unmarried men that lasts eight days. On the first day an unusually strong woman, whose legs are encased in a wrapping made of ostrich feathers, visits all the huts of the encampment armed with a hide twisted in the form of a Hercules' club. With this she and her accompanying group of virgins whip and put to flight all the men encountered. On the second day there are two wrestling matches, one for the girls and the other for the boys. On the third day both groups again, independently, perform certain dances; and on the·fourth the leader of the girls goes through the town challenging the strongest woman in each house to a wrestling match. The last four days are of no great importance.

In marked contrast to the prestige the chief apparently possessed was the power he actually wielded. The cacique of the Abipones, Dobritzhoffer insists, had really no power. "It is more of a burden than an honor and often brings with it greater danger than profit. For they revere their cacique neither as a master nor pay him tribute or attendance as is usual with other nations. They invest him neither with the authority of a judge, an arbitrator, or an avenger. . . . If he were to rebuke [people] for their transgressions with a single harsh word, he would be punished in the next drinking party with the fists of intoxicated savages, and publicly loaded with insults, as a friend to the Spaniards, and a greater lover of ease than of his people."[48]

This contradiction between a chief's apparent status and his actual power and influence is significant. It clearly reflects an unintegrated culture, the existence of a new set of standards and customs not as yet thoroughly assimilated. We will not be wrong then in rejecting both the "classes" and the extreme riotous individualism as either old or original. If that is so, then we can regard the social-economic conditions and the attitudes toward the individual and the group existing among the Lengua as closely approximating to the older type of economic structure which once prevailed in the whole Chaco. According to Grubb, whose book on the latter tribe we have already mentioned so often, their social system represented socialism at its worst. This is what he says:[49]

The land belonged to the people generally, and no Indian, not even a chief, has any direct claim to any part of it over his fellows. No Indian is encouraged to have more possessions than his neighbor. Their flocks feed on the common pasture, and they only lay claim to their gardens while actually cultivating them.

The natural products of the country, such as game, honey, wild fruits, fish, and firewood, are the common property of all, and native law enjoins the widest hospitality.

Every man is supposed to hunt; there is no such thing as a leisured class, not even among the chiefs.

The aged must be kept at the expense of the community, as also the sick or disabled.

Competition in the way of one man trying to rise superior to his fellowmen, to rule over others, or to better himself at their expense, is strongly discouraged, and almost non-existent.

Those who have been traveling, and therefore not able to produce crops or those who for any other reason have no means of subsistence for the time being, have a claim on the community.

To account for a transformation so profound, more was necessary, I pointed out, than the simple adoption of the horse. On the other hand, it was something which the possession of the horse and that alone permitted; namely, an intimate and pro-tracted contact with the Araucanians and Calchaqui. It is in the social organization of these advanced peoples that the key to the new social structure of the Abipones is to be found.

That this transformation was accomplished by means of the horse does not make it any less an Indian achievement or lessen its importance for the study of historical transformations, as an example of how a crude, impoverished, non-agricultural tribe could, within five or six generations, change into an equestrian community and attempt a career of conquest and subjugation along the lines of Attila and Genghis Khan.

But we must now leave the Abipones and see how another of the Chaco tribes, the Mbaya-Kadiueo, started out on its career and the nature of the success it achieved. It was different from that of the Abipones and, on the whole, achieved more positive results.

Before they obtained horses, around 1672, the Mbaya-Kadiueo were a nonagricultural people who had already been sufficiently influenced by contact with the Spaniards to possess small herds of cattle and sheep, to learn the smelting of silver, and to use iron extensively. Within four generations they had become expert horsemen. Indeed, according to our best authority, the Jesuit priest Sanchez Labrador, the horse had by this time entered so completely into their life that, as he says, they knew more about the diseases of these animals than they did about their own.

In the case of the Abipones we can be fairly certain that their culture was of the simplest kind before the arrival of the Spaniards. This was not true of the Mbaya-Kadiueo, for they seem to have been already in contact with the highly organized and elaborate civilization of the Chané to the west of them before that time. But that they had already, at that time, subjugated them and reduced them to practical slavery—that is, to people on whose forced agriculture they subsisted—that is highly improbable. This type of economic system they certainly learned from the whites. Yet their contact with the Chané, in early times, must have been sufficiently intimate for them to have adopted the latter's stratified society. In short, they had actually achieved a complete reorganization of their social structure before the horse came to them.

It is the skill with which they utilized this new organization after the horse had been adopted, and the intelligent manner in which they imitated the terroristic methods of the whites, that excites our admiration. They were going to fight the hated stranger by taking over those methods of his that they judged had given him his strength. They realized early that an im-

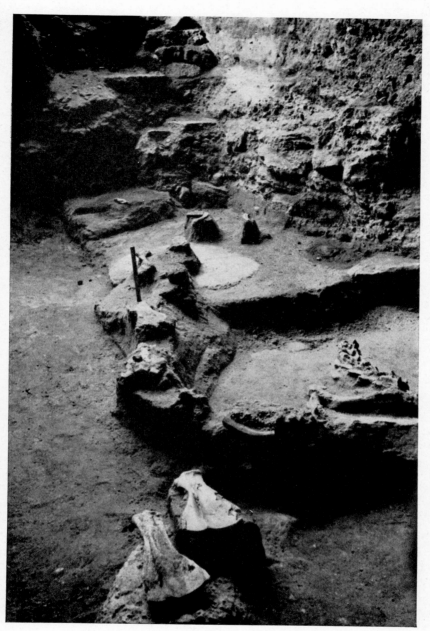

Remains of the Aboriginal Fuegian Horse

portant element in the ease with which the Spaniards and Portuguese spread over the country was the existence of a military class free from the necessity of procuring its own food. They went the Spaniard one better. Instead of having one portion of their own people subordinated to the task of raising food, they reduced their ancient host, the Chané, to whom they owed practically everything that was complicated in their old life, to that position. They themselves became exclusively a military class. This is a unique phenomenon in aboriginal American history, and the only example remotely comparable to it is the incorporation of other tribes into the Iroquois system and their partial reduction to a kind of vassalage. This too had been possible by the utilization of new elements introduced by the whites.

Four factors, then, were involved in the new culture that the Mbaya-Kadiueo possessed in the eighteenth century: first, an early taking over of a highly organized social structure based on stratified classes; second, the adoption, by 1600 or thereabouts, of a pastoral life; third, the adoption, around 1672, of the horse; and fourth, the introduction of agriculture and herding.

Since, as we have just pointed out, the reduction of the Chané to the position of virtual serfs was very late and is so unusual a phenomenon among aboriginal peoples of America, one is naturally inquisitive about the methods that were employed to bring it about. The explanation offered by Sanchez Labrador is interesting but hardly adequate. According to him, it somewhat resembled the well-known policy of dynastic intermarriages. "As far as can be determined," he writes, "[the Mbaya] reduced the Guana [Chané] to servitude not by arms but through marriage. Certain chiefs of the [Mbaya] married female chiefs of the Guana, and the descendants of these female chiefs became in perpetuity the vassals of the descendants of their husbands." This phraseology must, of course, not be taken too seriously. The Chané never had had "vassals." The Calchaqui, however, did have, and there is always the possibility that the Chané, who had been in some contact with them, did take over some of the political "theories" of the former.

But what type of vassalage did the Chané actually endure at

the hands of their conquerors? Our source tells us that the
Chané, of their own accord and without remuneration, subjected themselves to the Mbaya-Kadiueo and cultivated the soil
for them, but that they would frequently return to their own
homes without objections from their masters. Yet he is equally
insistent that their position was definitely that of slaves—slaves,
it is true, who were unusually well treated, but still slaves. And
we must concur. Let us then try to describe what the societal
structure of the Mbaya-Kadiueo was that enabled them to
achieve this.

"There are two types of chiefs [among the Mbaya-
Kadiueo]," states Sanchez Labrador.[50] "The first inherited by
blood, the second appointed. The first are called *niniotage,* but
this group adds the honorific, *great chief,* to their names. . . .
All children, male and female alike, of great chiefs, are regarded
as chiefs by blood. So, too, are the children, of the chiefs of any
band that attaches itself to these great chiefs. The second class
was composed of individuals who were given this status at the
birth of a chief's son. . . . The difference between the two lies in
the fact that among the great chiefs titles and honors are passed
on in perpetuity, whereas among the latter they become extinguished at the death of the holder. Another distinction lies
in the fact that the first group are the heads of their respective
families and soldiers. Each group lives apart and separated from
the other, for the pride of these great chiefs is such that equals
resent the slightest suggestion of subordination, the one to the
other. The second class of chiefs then remains, in spite of the
title bestowed on them, soldiers and subordinates."

Yet despite his apparently high status, the attitude toward
such a great chief was almost identical with that described before among the Abipones. He was only obeyed implicitly, if
even then, in war. The resemblance to the Abipones is further
strengthened by the importance attached to the birth of a son
to the great chief and the eight-day ceremony performed on
that occasion. There can be no question but that the class distinctions among the Mbaya-Kadiueo were far more profound
than among the Abipones. This must not, however, be regarded

as anything but a purely secondary elaboration of a system that had been borrowed, in probably late precolumbian times, from tribes like the Calchaqui, the Araucanians, and the Chané, who stood guard at the approaches to the Andes and to whom the great civilizations of the highlands were much more than a mere name.

CHAPTER X

Ultima Thule

THE FUEGIANS

IF THE GRAN CHACO REPRESENTED, TO ALL IN-
tents and purposes, both a refuge place and the last frontier
against the new forces that swept the aboriginal world of South
America, what shall we call the land that lay to the south? What
type of culture should we expect to find there? The answer has
always been exactly what explorers from Magellan on have
found. As late as 1929 we find an English-Chilean writer referring to one of the Fuegian tribes, the *Alakaluf* "as human
amphibians who are still living in a state of complete degradation and savagery, and have up to the present resisted all attempts to educate and civilize them."[51]

Nothing is farther from the truth, except the second half of
this statement, for the Alakaluf are very much like the *Yahgans*,
who are not the simplest of peoples, as we shall soon see. But
whether this is so or not, having now reached the antipodes,
can we say that what we encounter represents, by and large,
the earliest culture in the Americas? There is no agriculture.
But has there been change? Is there any indication of loss of old
elements or the addition of new ones? For many years the anthropologist would have scoffed at the notion of Fuegian culture
ever having been different from what it is now. Yet within the
last few years excavations among the northern group, the *Ona*,

have demonstrated that no less than five distinct strata exist there, set off definitely, the one from the other, by the nature of the implements encountered. The uppermost stratum has small arrow points of the modern Ona type, while the lowest has spear points and, wonder of wonders, the bones of extinct horses, which they apparently did not ride but ate. Change there has consequently been, at least, in the material world. Has there been a corresponding change in customs and beliefs? Let us see.

Lowie[52] has very well contrasted the differences between the Ona in the north and east of Tierra del Fuego and the Yahgan in the south and west. The former are completely ignorant of navigation and do not even know how to swim, gaining their subsistence entirely by chasing guanaco herds or digging rodents out of their burrows. The Yahgan, on the contrary, are adept on the water, spend most of their time in exceedingly fragile bark canoes, gathering mussels and harpooning seals and whales. One of these ways of obtaining food, the latter, may conceivably represent the persistence of an old economy. The second clearly does not.

The same contrast comes out in connection with the economic role of women. The Yahgan woman must do the paddling of the canoe, although her husband actually makes it. She must catch the fish, spit the crab, and pry loose the important food staple, the *Mytilus* shellfish. The Ona woman, on the other hand, has very little to do with the food supply, her husband shooting the guanacos and ferreting out the edible rodents. This difference in functioning is carried over into the ceremonial life of the two tribes, the Yahgan men and women passing through a complicated initiation rite, while the Ona woman is strictly barred from it. Indeed, one of the secondary purposes of the Ona initiation is to intimidate the women and keep them in proper subjection. A mild form of this terrorization of the women also exists among the Yahgan, but in quite another connection. As Lowie points out, however, the Yahgan must have borrowed this from the Ona, for "an antifeminist tendency is so foreign to the spirit of Yahgan culture that actually the bars are let down for a few "trustworthy" women who are allowed to view the performance of what is in principle a society for keeping their sex in place."[53]

The social organization of the Ona and Yahgan has probably undergone considerable transformations in the course of their journey from Alaska to Tierra del Fuego and from the conditions imposed by the land in which they live. At the present time the single family is the fundamental unit, descent is "patrilineal," marriage within the group strictly forbidden. The Ona groups have, in fact, many of the earmarks of the clan. If it really represents the remains of a true clan, its nearest neighbors who have the clan are the Chané to the northwest and the Ge tribes of southwest Brazil.

Before turning to the really salient trait of Yahgan and Ona culture, its ceremonialism, it might be well to point out a few more of its characteristics that it is important for us to bear in mind. It possesses the couvade, the taboo between a man and his father-in-law, the widespread South American theory of disease, and myths and tales that have an amazing resemblance to some of those of California and the western basin of the United States.

The outstanding events in the life of the Yahgan are: first, the long and arduous initiation through which all boys and girls pass; and second, the men's secret society. We have excellent descriptions of both by W. Koppers and M. Gusinde, and I shall lean heavily on them for the summary that follows.

The men's secret society is always under the direction of an older medicine man, and it is he who also narrates the sacred origin myth of the ceremony. For the Yahgan, that myth runs as follows: [54]

The *kina*, men's secret society, was first performed by women living far up to the north of the *isla grande* and beyond it to the pampa. In the beginning the women possessed all the power. They it was who gave commands to the men which the latter had to obey, just as today the reverse holds true. In those days, too, the women, not the men, sat at the prow of the canoe, while the men were relegated to the stern. They were completely subservient to the women and had to perform all those duties which now fall to the lot of

women—the work within the house, such as attending the infants,
caring for the fire, and cleaning the skins.

The women had destined this condition to remain unchangeable.
For that reason they created the great ceremonial lodge and all its
ritual. To the men they said, "We are seeking Tanowa wherever it is
she dwells, whether within the earth or elsewhere, so that she may be
induced to enter the great lodge." The men accepted as truth all that
the women told them, and they were perforce compelled to accompany them whenever they broke up camp.

But Tanowa was not to be found in the place where they were
looking. So they moved on along the north coast of the isla grande
as far as its northern point. Wherever they paused to rest they built
a kina and performed within it. Thus they wandered along the east
coast of the island, bearing toward the south. Wherever they played,
a broad, beautiful pampa sprang up. And thus they continued their
search for the great evil one Tanowa. . . . [Finally] they crossed the
Cordilleras and came to the Beagle Channel . . . and so to Boca del
Infierno, where they performed the kina for a long time. They
emerged from the great lodge painted and with masks and called
to the men saying, "Look, this is the spirit Suna-yaka, this is the spirit
Wuasenim-yaka," and so on. The men believed them, although, of
course, actually, these were the women themselves all painted up.
But because the masks hid their faces the men did not recognize them.

When they realized after much searching and repeated perform-
ances that Tanowa was nowhere to be found, they decided to stay in
Boca del Infierno. They were very much pleased with the place and
said, "Let us stay here and fool the men into believing that we have
at last found Tanowa, that we have induced her to come out of the
earth and enter our great lodge!" So they took a piece of skin and
rolled it into a thick bundle and struck the ground with it so heavily
that the earth shook and heaved. They themselves then began shouting and shrieking and yelling to attract the attention of the men.
The poor men ran into their huts, frightened and terrified, shouting,
"The women have finally found Tanowa! She has emerged from out
the earth!" And so they tarried at Boca del Infierno and the men
were kept in terror and submission, performing all the work the
women laid upon them.

Now one of these men was Lem, the Sun. He was an excellent
hunter and was repeatedly sent to bring food for the women while
they were performing the kina, for they were very fond of meat.

One day as he was packing a guanaco he had killed, he heard the voices of two girls near the encampment. Curiosity overpowered him, and he sneaked up upon them to see what they were doing. He then saw that they were washing off the paint which they had put upon their bodies in order to impersonate the spirits. At the same time, they were practicing themselves in imitating the voice of Lem's daughter, who played a leading part in the kina performance. "Let us practice well," they were saying, "so that we can imitate Lem's daughter perfectly and thus help her in her singing and in the deception we are playing on the men."

Thereupon Lem suddenly jumped out of the brush where he lay hidden and asked them sternly, "What are you doing here?" They were numb with fear. "Come, you must tell me all that you are doing here and all that takes place in the kina-lodge. I have been listening to you now for some time so that I already know plenty as it is." The poor girls stood there blushing with shame and perspiring with fear. But nothing availed them anything. So they told Lem this: "It is the women who paint themselves and wear masks. There are no spirits here. It is the women who do the shouting and the screaming and the yelling in order to instil fear into you men, not Tanowa." When they had finished, Lem spoke to them and said, "As recompense for what you have told me, I give you this advice. Stay right here where you are. Under no conditions must you return to the encampment or to the kina-lodge. If you do evil harm will surely befall you." So the two girls stayed there and were transformed later on, into small sweet-water ducks.

Angrily Lem then approached the encampment, planning all the time how he was going to revenge himself upon the women. Arrived at his own hut he threw the guanaco on the ground, muttering between his teeth, "So that's why I have to tote all these carcasses around all day! Just to have my daughter make a dupe of me and all the other men! They take this meat from me as if it was intended for Tanowa, whereas they eat it themselves in the kina-lodge!" And all those near him looked surprised and puzzled, and asked themselves, "What's happened? What is it Lem said? Why is he so angry?"

And so the story goes on to tell how the women tried in vain to again instill fear into the men. Through simple stratagems the men soon succeeded in identifying their wives and daughters. Finally it came to an open battle between the men and

the women, and the women were all transformed into different
kinds of animals. At the end Lem, the Sun, leaves the earth to
become fixed in the firmament, and with him go his brother,
the rainbow and his brother's wife, the moon.

What does such a myth mean? Are we to interpret the role
as originally assigned to women here as reflecting a time when
women had a much higher status among the Yahgan than they
do now? Are we dealing here simply with mythological phan-
tasy? Or must we deliver ourselves, bound hand and foot, to
the tender mercies of the psychoanalysts? Everything we know
about the Yahgan indicates that an historical fact is reflected
here. The contradiction between the actual status of women
there and what this ceremony implies can best be resolved by
regarding the kina as borrowed from the northern Ona, as
Lowie among others has suggested. We will best understand
the kina then if we turn to the parent Ona ceremony, the
kloketen.

Initiation into this men's secret society generally lasted two
years, of which most of the time was spent in fairly complete
seclusion and solitude. The diet was most meager, almost exclusively the lean meat of the adult male guanaco. During the
first few weeks the young men were brought frequently to the
initiation lodge, where they were terrorized and tormented by
the older members, painted and masked, who impersonated
various spirits. It was in this initiation lodge that they were also
taught to endure physical pain. Wooden splinters were thrust
in their arms, and they were to exhibit no pain as these worked
themselves out through the flesh. There too they were instructed
in the tribal lore and inculcated with the tribal ethical ideals.

The initiation lodge was a large and solid tent made of heavy
logs which were in part covered with sod. Every log was given
a name, such as "seal," "kelp-goose," "duck," "grass," "sea,"
etc., and to each individual a log was assigned.

Discipline throughout the trial period was rigorous. When
the candidate was brought to the great initiation lodge he must
sit there without moving his legs under him, supporting his head
on his arm. He was neither to talk nor to laugh. He was given

little time to sleep. Most of the time, both day and night, he spent out in the open, making his way through the woods, and across the hills, either hunting or practicing himself in shooting.

The novice was taught the true nature of the masks almost immediately after he had been brought, frightened and terrified, to the initiation lodge. As he stood there anxiously awaiting what was to happen, a masked figure impersonating a spirit rushed upon him and wrestled with him roughly. Only when he was completely exhausted by the struggle did the masked figures stop and let him uncover the face of one of the impersonators.

The spirits thus impersonated were intimately bound up with the landscape in which the Ona live. According to W. S. Barclay, they were the following:

Sh'ord, a malicious underground spirit with crooked legs. He was represented as covered all over with the feathers of birds, stuck on with grease.

Hach'i, the spirit of the moss and lichen-covered rocks. He was painted slate color, with daubs of red and yellow clay, and wore horns.

H'alpin was a woman, the spirit of the clouds and mists. She was dressed all in white, and had a very long head. This shape was given by binding twigs to the back of the head, which was then covered with skin and painted.

Tan'u was the spirit of the streams and lakes. She was the sister of H'alpin, and was adorned in the same way except that her color was red.

K'mantu was the spirit of the beech forests, and was clothed with tree bark and moss.

Hash'ai was very squat and had a claw on the forefinger of each hand. This spirit seems to have been an embodiment of that nervous fear which makes itself felt in the deep forests, when branches creep and twigs snap for no apparent reason.

The origin myth of the kloketen ceremony is practically identical with that of the kina given before. In it the official purpose of the rite is clearly stated, to teach the young men its secrets and to terrify and cow the women. But of course its

political and sociological import goes far beyond such comparatively trivial goals. Actually it is a combination of the very widespread puberty fasting and training and some old masked ceremonial performed only by men.

What significance are we to attach to the presence, at the end
of the great southern continent, of so complicated a ceremony,
with all the indications of its being composite in origin? Perhaps the archaeological evidence that within possibly the last
2,000 years Fuegian material culture has changed markedly has
some bearing here. Can we, for instance, find any elements in
the religious and ceremonial life of the Ona that would throw
some light on their probable relative age? Naturally our first
impulse is to look for cognates to the masks, the cowing of the
women, the themes and episodes of the strange origin myth.
The reader will probably have detected them already. There is
one region where they are all to be found; namely, in certain
parts of the Amazon. There we find the employment of tall
conical masks, the ceremonial lodges from which women are
barred, and the practice of terrorizing the women by making
them believe that the masked figures they see and the sounds
they hear exist, and, finally, a myth to the effect that formerly
it was the women who performed the ceremony and the men
who were cowed.

From these facts surely only one influence can be legitimately
drawn; namely, that these cultures somehow belong together.
But how? Even the southern part of the Araguaya River in
eastern Brazil, where dwells a tribe with a somewhat similar
ceremony, is many miles away, almost 3,000 to be specific.
Under these conditions, only one hypothesis is reasonable: that
we are dealing here with the survival of a culture that was once
fairly widespread throughout South America and is now only
to be encountered in certain rather isolated spots—the Rio
Negro, the southern Araguaya, and Tierra del Fuego. But
masked dances are the earmarks of a somewhat complicated
culture. In the overwhelming number of cases they are always
associated with agricultural economies. Certainly that is true
for South America. The Fuegians—Ona and Yahgan—assuredly

never had agriculture. But a trait like that of a secret men's society, where the members wear masks and impersonate spirits, can be disseminated as such without the rest of the traits of the civilization to which it belongs. This would, however, mean either that contact with the northern peoples as far as Matto Grosso once existed or that, at one time at least, part of the inhabitants now living in Tierra del Fuego lived farther north.

The picture we thus obtain of the Fuegians—that is, Ona and Yahgan—is quite different from the one customarily drawn. Contrary to the generally held belief, they are anything but simple. The natives of central California and of the western basin of the United States are far more so. Nor are the Fuegians overawed or overwhelmed by an inimical environment. To that they have in fact made an amazing adjustment without becoming either culturally impoverished or disrupted. And, above all, they have not entirely forgotten the ties that bind them to the other cultures of South America. Indeed, as we have just seen, echoes from the panpipes of the Rio Negro are still heard in this Ultima Thule.

CHAPTER XI

On the Fringe of the Great Civilizations

THE CHANÉ, CHIRIGUANO, JIVARO, AND ARAUCANIANS

IN CONTRAST TO THE INFLUENCE THE GREAT civilizations of Mexico had upon all the other Indians of the northern continent, that exercised by the great Andean civilizations upon the tribes to the east of them was comparatively small and late. Until the Inca ascendancy, apart from the Calchaqui area of northwestern Argentine, little indeed of it had drifted down into the Amazonian jungle or the Bolivian Chaco, except apparently to one tribe, the Chané. After the fourteenth century this was different. The Incas swept down to the south to overwhelm the Araucanians in northern Chile, made repeated attempts to attack the *Jivaro* in western Ecuador, and attacked the Chiriguano in the Bolivian Chaco.

Why this was so it is not difficult to understand. Of the three great civilizations of the Andes—the *Chimu, Nasca,* and *Tiahuanaco*—the first two stuck to the Pacific coast line and the third, a mountain culture, was compelled for a long time to limit its expansion to the region in its immediate vicinity. When finally it did spread, it was to the west. To these historical facts is to be added the nature of the terrain which separated the great civilizations from the simpler peoples to the east.

When eventually Andean influences did make themselves felt, the peoples they encountered in the lowlands were no longer simple in their culture. By 1100, certainly by 1200, A.D., the Arawak and Tupi-Guarani had spread agriculture and its associated superstructure throughout all of the Amazon region and northwestern Bolivia. We will not be going far wrong in assuming that the Chané, an Arawak tribe, had reached the Bolivian Chaco at least by 1200, if not earlier, and we know that the Chiriguano, a Tupi-Guarani tribe, had found their way to the same place by at least 1500. Before attempting to see what the nature of the Andean influence upon these two tribes was, let us then first briefly describe their culture.

The Chané have already been mentioned in a previous chapter (cf. page 190) as having been reduced to a condition of semi-servitude by the Mbaya-Kadiueo of the Chaco. But this was in the eighteenth century and was a postcolumbian political phenomenon. Nor was it the first time that the Chané had been conquered. The same fate had befallen them two centuries earlier, when the Chiriguano burst upon them from the east. Indeed, so thoroughly had the Chané been brought under the influence of these virile invaders that they, in part, gave up their own language and even incorporated some of the customs of the newcomers; and since, likewise, they must have incorporated a number of the traits belonging to the cultures that lay in the path of their long journey from the mouth of the Orinoco to the Bolivian Chaco, one would expect the Chané to possess a highly eclectic and unintegrated civilization. Yet we find nothing of the sort. It seems to have been just the contrary, and my surmise is that their life had, in fact, become redundantly well-integrated; that it had become rigid and incapable of change. Their social organization bears this out. They seem to have been divided into larger and smaller groups presided over respectively by major chiefs and minor chiefs. These major chiefs had great prestige and considerable power and saw to it that the minor chiefs were always related to them. Below them was a definite group of commoners, with whom intermarriage was prohibited.

Whence came this class division? We know the Arawak of the Antilles possessed it, yet no evidence exists for its presence in any other of the continental Arawak tribes except the *Ter-*

reno, and probably the Paressi, far to the east. These three Arawak tribes represent the farthest penetrations of this stock into these respective areas. They have lived there for many generations and have in all three places been culture givers par excellence. It is quite conceivable, therefore, that they have actually preserved the older division into stratified classes that was so characteristic of the Arawak of the West Indies and has disappeared everywhere else among the Arawak of South America. The other old Arawak trait they possessed was, of course, the extensive cultivation of maize.

Yet, although these two traits formed, as it were, the core of Chané civilization, associated with them was to be found a large number of elements belonging to the Amazon region. Of these, certainly the most interesting are the masks, the habit of erecting maize barns on piles, the hammock used as a bed, the seat, the panpipe, fish poison, and manioc.

It was thus a rich and well-knit culture which the Chané brought with them to the Bolivian Chaco. Now what, can it be claimed, did the great civiliations of the Andean add? Nordenskiöld[55] has listed these elements, and their enumeration will indicate clearly how secondary, in the main, they were. They were as follows: coca, poncho shirt, water pitchers, double pitchers, pitcher with a bulging neck, vessel provided with ears or handles, wooden hook, wooden spade, wooden spoon and bowl, sandal, woven girdle, Peruvian loom, bodkin of bone, drum, long and round wooden whistle, pincers, wooden comb, certain games, etc.

These are, after all, very minor elements, and the explanation for this meager influence lies not simply in the fact that the Andean influences were late and incidental but in the fact that Chané culture was a highly specialized and rich one to begin with.

But let us now turn to the Chiriguano. In spite of the fact that their own culture was by no means simple—they were, after all, a Tupi-Guarani tribe—and in spite of the great political influence they had upon the Chané, they had borrowed practically everything of cultural importance they possessed from the latter. Nordenskiöld could point to only two elements of their own culture that they introduced: urn-burial and the lipstick. But they have a significance of another and special kind for us, that of being a center for a number of postcolumbian religious and messianic movements similar in many respects to those that swept aboriginal North America from the eighteenth century on and which culminated in the famous Ghost Dance. As examples of the manner in which South American Indians reacted to the encroachments of the white intruders they are well worth studying.

Two myths had always had a particularly strong influence upon Tupi-Guarani thought: the one narrating the accomplishments of the culture-bringing god, and the other dealing with the search for the "land-where-there-was-no-evil." The second was to play an important role after the advent of the whites, because it became, in many instances, the official explanation for their wanderings.

As in North America, the progress of the European invaders divided the natives into three camps, the complete assimilationists, the compromisers, and the die-hards. It was among the latter two, but more particularly among the die-hards, that leaders arose who preached the doctrine that the invading terrorists must be resisted at all costs and preparations made to drive them out of the land. The leaders represented themselves as the reincarnations of the culture-hero, the god who had been reborn among them for the express purpose of leading his people out of their misery and degradation to a land where they could live their own lives, retain their old customs, where their ancestors would come to life again, and where there would be no evil. There was sufficient resemblance between these teachings and those of Christianity for such a movement to have a strong appeal even among Indians who had been superficially converted to Catholicism.

Such "prophets" were described as early as the sixteenth century among the Tupinamba. Their number and influence increased with great rapidity as the natives saw themselves threatened with annihilation. Among the Chiriguano these religious leaders naturally had greater influence than in the other Tupi-Guarani tribes, for the Chiriguano, after all, had but lately finished a stupendous and triumphant journey across the continent and had brought a highly civilized tribe under their control. They were not prepared to submit to having themselves and their culture easily destroyed. It is not surprising then that the two most important and most successful of these movements should have been found among them. The first occurred in 1778 and the last as late as 1892, almost contemporaneous with the last Sioux outbreak. An excellent contemporary account of that of 1778 exists, which we will here briefly summarize.

The movement was inaugurated, says the unknown author of the account, by the appearance of an Indian accompanied by many so-called "wild" Chiriguano. The leader claimed to be divine and told the Indians of the mission where he first appeared that the day of judgment would soon be upon them. He claimed to possess certain miraculous gifts, among them, for instance, the power of causing showers of fire to rain down upon them, of transforming men into stone, of destroying towns and cattle, and, above all, of completely exterminating all those individuals who did not believe in him and follow him. He preached in both Chiriguano and Spanish.

To give some idea of the wholly syncretistic nature of this new religion, it may be pointed out that accompanying this particular prophet were two other personages, one a woman to whom he gave the name Maria Chesu and who was supposed to be the Virgin Mary herself, and the other an individual supposed to be the reincarnation of the *Inca* (Rey Inga). The latter had been reborn and come among them again to regain his former possessions and reward all those who followed him and the prophet.

The excitement was tremendous, and Indians flocked to the prophet from all directions. But let me continue in the words of the manuscript itself:[56]

The claims and threats of this false prophet and pretended God caused great consternation and confusion among the people of

Mazabi and the pueblos adjoining it. Then God, in his wisdom, permitted one of the leaders of the pueblo of Abapo, who was then visiting relatives at Mazabi, to become cognizant of the preachings of this false prophet and of his threats both to the Indians in general and to those of the three missions in particular. Frightened and terrified, this man fled at night to his own people and told them under cover of secrecy what he had heard and seen in Mazabi. Such a secret could not, of course, be guarded, and the news spread like wildfire. Soon eight hundred foolish people, wild with excitement and fear, fled at night from the mission without telling the priests. Indeed so precipitous was their flight that they left their houses just as they were, abandoning everything—food, furniture, indeed even their own children and parents. Husbands deserted wives and wives husbands. Shouting and gesticulating, madly they made their way to the neighborhood of Rio Grande de Guaypay on their way to Mazabi, in search of the false god, hoping and believing that under his protection they would escape the destruction and the ruin he had prophesied was about to overtake everyone. Nothing that the priests of the mission could do when they found out what had happened was of much avail. A few returned, but the vast majority continued their intemperate scramble toward Mazabi, where the pretended prophet and god sat on his false and wicked throne. . . .

The excitement was, of course, soon put down with the use of soldiers, just as was our Ghost Dance.

The Chiriguano outbreak of 1892 was somewhat different in character, for it represented a determined attempt on the part of the Indians to reconquer their independence. As is well known, six hundred of the unfortunates were killed. The leader of the outbreak was a young man on whom the title of *Tunpa*, God, had been bestowed. Divine honors were paid him. He remained hidden and protected in a special hut, and all those who approached him had to kneel. Intercourse with him could only take place through intermediaries.

From the description of how these two relatively high cultures were able to resist the influence of the great Inca civilization, let us now turn to another tribe whose culture was much simpler: the Jivaro of eastern Ecuador. In contradistinction to both the Chané and the Chiriguano, they were not intruders into this territory. It had been their home from time immemorial, and they have successfully defended it now for more than five hundred years. As early as the middle of the fifteenth century, when the Inca Tupac-Yupangui undertook the conquest of the Kingdom of Quito, he attempted to conquer the Jivaro, but without success. His son, the Inca Huayna-Capac, tried again, but the military efficiency of the Jivaro, aided and abetted by the nature of the country in which they live and the climate, forced the Incas to withdraw in defeat after they had had some initial success. To a certain degree this same combination of climate and the natural difficulties of their terrain has protected them ever since from being profoundly influenced by alien cultures. For that reason their customs and social structure are all the more interesting. Undoubtedly they represent one of the earliest civilizations of the Amazon region and must at one time have possessed a nonagricultural economy, upon which has been superimposed an agricultural one.

For most laymen the Jivaro are associated with two things, warfare and the custom of shrinking the heads of their captured enemy. Both have become highly specialized among them and both are of more than usual significance because of their connections with other tribes and customs. Jivaro warfare is a combination of certain widely spread traits plus the complex of traits so typical of the blood feud, the kanaima, described in an earlier chapter as so characteristic of the Carib and Arawak. The head shrinking is a very special kind of head-trophy treatment that must go back very far, for it was apparently known to the *Chimu*, of the Nasca civilizations, which takes us back at least 1,000 years.

Since it is in their capacity of specialists that we shall describe the Jivaro, let us begin with the first of these, the blood feud. Here, as among practically all the jungle tribes of the western Amazon, it is always imperative to find out how a fellow member in times of peace has met his death. Particularly is this true in the case of an important man. To determine it, among the Jivaro, a medicine man must drink a special preparation that will enable him to discover whether death has been due to witchcraft and, if it has, to discover the murderer. The nearest male relative, just as among the Carib and Arawak, must then take it upon himself to avenge the murder. Many years may elapse before this can be accomplished, and the revenge may have to be passed on from father to son. Indeed, special provision is made for such a contingency. For instance, a father may and does exact such a promise on his deathbed.

To prepare for this revenge, the spirits must first be consulted, and for this purpose an individual will go into seclusion, retire to the forests, and fast there for three days and nights. The spirits will appear to him there, or at least manifest themselves to the faster in some fashion or other, favorably or unfavorably. Only then do the preparations for the revenge expedition properly begin.

Those readers acquainted with the fasting to obtain the help of a spirit so common to the North American Indians will be struck at once with the manifest similarity between the two. There, however, the specific resemblance between the ritualized feud complexes ceases.

As one might expect, the obligation to avenge a death may fall upon a whole group of individuals, and where the murderer belongs to another tribe, may take on the form of a tribal or village war party.

Let us assume it has taken on the latter form. About a week before the start, a chief is selected and the plans of attack carefully prepared. Part of these instructions are given during the *enema*, or war dance. This enema contains, among other things, a stereotyped dialogue, a stereotyped conversation between the warriors as they stand arranged in two rows facing each other. First one row and then the other speaks. And this is what they say:[57]

First row: Let us speak loudly!
Second row: Let us speak words!
First row: What are we going to say?
Second row: Let us quickly assemble!
First row: Let us avenge the blood-guilt!
Second row: Tomorrow, we will sleep far away.

First row: Let us quickly take our enemy!
Second row: Quickly, before he is told about it!
First row: So says the old one, the chief.
Second row: Let us go, to return quickly, youths!
First row: Quickly, quickly!
Second row: We have been fighting!
First row: We have killed!
Second row: We have revenged the blood!
First row: Let us cut off the head of the enemy!
Second row: Let us carry it with us.

In addition to this dialogue which, in a sense, is a type of magical formula to secure success, the Jivaro also sing a highly formalized war song the night before the expedition actually starts, which runs as follows:[58]

My brother, my brother,
Let us make war together!
To my son also I have said:
My son, my son,
Make you strong, make you brave!
Me they won't kill!
I will not die!
Myself I will kill my enemy!
I have dreamed and my dreams have been good.
I have seen "the Old Ones!"
I will take my enemy.
I have him already!
Presently I will be engaged in fighting!
All right, may my enemy come, may he come!
And may he take my life if he can.
If he kills me.
My sons will certainly see that it will be revenged.
May he kill someone else. . . .

Lack of space prevents us from following our warriors on the warpath itself, so let us picture their return and the ceremonies that then take place. As in the case of kanaima, so here too, the actual achievement of the goal is only one part of the strict ritual the avenger must observe. Upon the return of the warriors with their war trophies, the heads of their enemies, the victors must pass through a purification ceremony called "the washing off of the blood." The victor par excellence—that is, the first slayer—stays with his relatives until the trophy is prepared and ready. Only then can he make his solemn and triumphant entry into his own house. He is dressed like a penitent, his body without paint and ornaments, his hair untied. At his side stands an old warrior. Behind him stand other warriors arranged in a row.

The rites begin by presenting the first slayer with tobacco juice. After having drunk it, he proceeds to disengage the trophy from the cloth which envelops it. Then it is hung around his neck. Slowly and ceremoniously he now proceeds toward the house, continually smoothing the hair of the trophy. Behind him follow the warriors.

A few preliminary dances now take place, and then the actual washing off of the blood begins. He is placed on a small round bench close to a vessel which today contains the blood of a chicken. The women form a semicircle around him. Again he is given some tobacco juice to drink. Then the director of the ceremonies grasps his hand firmly and forces it down into the vessel with the chicken's blood. In this he must dip his index finger. He now draws a broad line with the blood along the front side of one of his legs. Then the slayer applies a similar stroke to his other leg. Throughout this proceeding the women dance around him singing, "They have painted you with blood so that you may start the fasting." This song completes the so-called blood-painting rite. Not only the slayer but his wife too must undergo the purification rites. Then when both have been purified, they go to the river, where they carefully wash their bodies.

Thus it is clear that among the Jivaro, as among practically all the western Amazon tribes, the one who avenges the death of a relative must be purified before he can again resume his normal relations with the world. The official theory is that otherwise the spirit of the person slain will, in his turn, kill the slayer. It is also clear that the blood-revenge ceremonial is here associated and secondarily merged with a whole series of distinct customs and rites that originally had no connection with it. In short, it is a conglomeration, like the ritualistic cannibalism that we have described before among the Tupinamba, and like the Plains' Sun Dance.

Following his re-entry into his house come a fairly large number of ceremonies. Two, in particular, deserve to be mentioned —the feast at which the slayer is painted with genipa and the rite called "the eating of the head." The first is given in order to bestow upon the victor added protection against the spirit of the victim, who, it is represented, is at all times revengeful and is craving for an opportunity to kill his slayer. It is also supposed to promote the victor's material wealth. The second rite has reference to a whole series of magical spells by means of which the spirit of the slain enemy is completely subjugated, mortified, and enslaved.

It but remains now to describe the thing for which the Jivaro are best known, the head shrinking. I am following very closely here the description as given by Up de Graff, the only white individual who has actually witnessed it.

A number of ceremonies naturally precede it. When these are over the head is placed upon a large leaf, and over it is placed another one.

The place of honor is reserved for the warrior who has actually cut off the head. As he sits there he is given some tobacco juice, and in recognition of his great achievement the chief of the tribe himself blows it through his nose.

The preparation of the head is then begun. It is a long and tedious process. The head is first peeled by carefully parting the hair straight down from the crown to the base of the skull and slitting the skin down the line formed by the parting, hard on to the bone of the skull. The skin is then turned back on both sides and peeled much as a stocking is drawn from the foot. Some cutting is almost always necessary at the eyes, ears, and nose, after which the flesh and muscles come off with the skin, leaving the skull clean and naked except for the eyes and teeth. The in-

cision from the crown to the base of the skull is then sewn together again. This is done with a bamboo needle and palm-leaf
fiber, the opening at the neck, for the time being, left untouched.
The lips are now skewered with three bamboo splinters, each
about two and a half inches long. To hold these tightly closed,
they are lashed together with strands of cotton fiber. Subsequently tassels are formed by the frayed ends of the fiber. The
next step concerns the eyes, nose, and ears. The eye holes are
closed by drawing down the upper eyelashes, and the eyebrows
prevented from falling by means of small pegs of bamboo, vertically set between the outer rim of the eyelashes and the shoulders of the corresponding eyebrows. The holes of the nose and
ears are temporarily plugged with cotton.

Up de Graff, upon whom I have relied entirely for the details
given above, describes the further proceedings as follows: [59]

The purpose of these several operations was to hold the features
of the face in position and to seal the openings, so that the head
could again be expanded to its normal proportions by filling it with
hot sand and thus permit an even contraction of the whole in the
further process of curing. The meat at the base of the neck was
"basted" with *chambira*, to prevent its wearing and wasting away by
handling in the succeeding operations.

The crocks which are used on these occasions have been made with
the utmost care by the medicine-men in person, far removed from all
human eyes and under auspicious lunar conditions; they are brought
carefully wrapped in palm-leaves to ensure the impossibility of their
being touched or seen by any unauthorized person until the moment
for the ceremony arrives. For every head there is one of these red,
baked clay, conical pots, some eighteen inches in diameter by eighteen inches deep; the apex of the cone rests on the earth, the sides
being supported by stones; in this way the fire has ample access to
the greatest possible surface.

The pots were filled with cold water, straight from the river, and
the boneless heads, filled with sand, placed in them. Within half an
hour, the water had been brought to a boiling-point. This was the
critical moment. The heads must be removed before the water
actually boils, to prevent the softening of the flesh and the scalding
of the roots of the hair, which would cause it to drop out. The heads,

on being removed, were found to have shrunk to about one-third of their original size.

The pots were cast away into the river, too holy to be put to any further use, and the fires were heaped up with fresh logs, to heat the sand on which they stood. For henceforth the sand played an important part in the proceedings. . . .

By now hot sand had been prepared in large quantities. This was poured into the heads at the neck-opening, and while thus filled they were ironed with hot stones picked up with the aid of palm-leaves. This process, which began that day on the sand bar, is continued in the ordinary way for some forty-eight hours until the skin is smooth and hard and as tough as tanned leather, the whole head gradually shrinking to the size of a large orange. The resemblance to the living man is extraordinary. Indeed, the reduced heads, when skillfully made, are exact miniatures of their former selves. Every feature, hair, and scar is retained intact, and even the expression is not always lost. When perfected, they are hung in the smoke of a fire to preserve them from the depredations of the multitudinous insects which would attack and demolish them.

Into late afternoon, the careful preparation of the heads continued. By this time, all were working with a will to cure them, so that a start downstream could be made that evening. Time and again the cool greasy sand was poured from the half-dried heads, giving out the odor of an evening meal, only to be refilled with a fresh hot supply. Flat stones were always in the fires, being heated for the constant ironing to which the faces were subjected; they slid easily over the skin, like a flat-iron on linen, due to the natural oil which exuded from the contracting pores.

Hot coarse pebbles were substituted for sand in the final process, the heads being constantly tilted from side to side to prevent them from burning the meat, as dice are shaken in a box. The small amount of oil still exuding on the face was now wiped away with fresh cotton as fast as it appeared and the operation continued until all the fat and grease was "fried out" of the head, when it was considered "cured" or mummified; shrunk to the last diminutive size attainable.

What the scalp is to the North American Indian, the battle-standard to the civilized warrior, the heads are to the Jivaro. But the comparison is only true up to a point. For whereas the glory of the battle-standard and the scalp is undying, that of the Jivara heads endures only to the end of the great Festival of Rejoicing with which

they are honored on the return of the war party to their homes. . . .
Afterwards the heads are shorn of their hair, which is converted
into permanent trophies in the form of belts to be worn round the
loin-cloths of their distinguished owners in battle or at the feast. The
possession of such a trophy singles a man out for special regard. But
the heads themselves have now lost their value, as surely as pearls
which have died. It is curious that the fanatical jealousy with which
they are guarded up to the time of the festival should give place to
that complete indifference which allows them to be thrown to the
children as playthings and finally lost in river or swamp. . . .

From these head-trophy specialists living within the shadow
of the great Andean civilizations from time immemorial, who
resisted both the Peruvian influence and that of their successors,
the Europeans, so valiantly and successfully, let us now turn to
another group whose struggle to maintain themselves against
both these terrorists was just as glorious if not so successful, the
Araucanians. The Araucanians, or the *Mapuche*, to give them
their rightful name, inhabited northern Chile from Aconcagua
to the Chacao Channel and the Gulf of Reloncavi. We know a
good deal about them not only from explorers and ethnologists
but from imaginative writers as well, for they became the subject
matter of two famous Spanish works of literature. Their struggle
against the Spaniards was immortalized in the famous narrative
poem *La Araucana,* by Alonso de Ercilla, and their valor and
virtues by a Spaniard who was captured by them and not killed,
Francisco Nuñez de Pineda y Bascuñan, in the almost equally
famous *Cautiverio feliz (Happy Captivity),* written in 1629.
The Inca Tupac-Yupangui had attempted to conquer the
Araucanians around the middle of the fifteenth century, and his
legions, although encountering stubborn resistance, did actually
push them as far south as the Maule River. But there he was effectively stopped. Nevertheless, culturally the Inca influence
was considerable. How much, it is impossible to say, but probably enough to have markedly transformed their political life
and, to a lesser degree, their religious and magical beliefs and
customs. It does not, however, seem to have had any appreciable
influence upon their war customs. To form any idea of what

their original life was like before the Inca conquest, we must therefore turn to these three last-mentioned elements in their civilization. Let us begin with the war customs.[60]

The torture of prisoners captured in war was quite common and had a somewhat elaborate ritual connected with it. The prisoner was brought to the field on a horse whose ears and tail had been cut off. He was then received by the warriors and chiefs, each forming a circle of their own, and as soon as he arrived, insults and shouts of contempt were hurled at him. His horse was now led around and made to face the direction of the unfortunate man's home, in order to further humiliate and torment him by reminding him of his loved ones at home, whom he would see no more. Finally it was impressed upon him that even after death the humiliation would continue, that flutes would be made out of his bones, and his memory made a jest. After he was killed, the corpse was cut into pieces, and after being placed at the end of their spears, the warriors would dash madly around hurling imprecations on unseen enemies and threatening them with dire vengeance. In addition, they would frequently cut open the breast of a captured enemy, in particular one who was famous for his valor. His heart would then be torn out and presented to their chief. He was supposed to bite into it in order thus to acquire the valor of the slain man.

Rites of this kind remind one definitely of the war customs of many peoples of the Amazon. They certainly do not belong in this region. And the same holds true for their religious ceremonies, particularly for their most famous one, the *ngillatun*. Even today the ngillatun retains much of its former function of propitiating the spirits in times of bad crops, when disease afflicts the cattle, or in order to end a drought. Whatever it may have been originally, today it is obviously a thoroughly hybrid creation containing many Christian and doubtless Inca elements and implications. The participants assemble in an open field so that a ritually prepared tree trunk can be visible to all. This tree trunk has a ladder cut into it and is called *rewe*. It is always decorated with branches of the cinnamon tree. It is the most sacred object in the ceremony, and guests and participants accompanied by the priests and flute players surround and dance about it unceasingly.

This constitutes the first part of the ritual. The second part varies somewhat, depending upon the particular purpose for which the ngillatun is being performed. Generally a lamb whose ears have previously been cut off is sacrificed and its blood gathered in wooden vessels. With this blood the worshipers moisten their ears, and then offer up a prayer to one whom they call *Ngenechen,* the master of mankind, asking him for help and aid. The invocation generally used is the following:[61]

We kneel before thee today, Father. We pray thee to forgive us; that our children may not die, but live.

We pray to thee for rain, that the fields may be fruitful and that we may have cattle. O great, Gold-headed Man, and you Great Woman, say "Let there be rain"; we pray to the two Great and Ancient Ones.

May they aid us in all things. May they defend us against all harm!

We are gazing upwards; twice will we kneel. O Golden Knife, say, "Let not the children fall sick!"

You are in the midst of heaven. All things were made by you. In you is life.

After the invocation has been offered up, the leader of the ceremony pours the blood of the animal into a small hole dug beforehand at the foot of the rewe. "This is the moment," so says our informant,[62] "at which the *machi* (medicine-men), who up to that time have been exclusively engaged in fumigating the rewe with the tobacco smoke from their pipes, have to commence their activities. To the round of the music made by their flutes . . . as well as of their own drums, the medicine-men and flute-players dance, moving their heads from side to side. Some of the spectators also dance in a line facing towards the cinnamon tree. In the midst of this tumult the chief medicine-man intones the invocation suitable for the occasion which the other medicine-men go on repeating. And they gyrate and dance and move their heads with such energy that they are soon overcome by giddiness. Before succumbing, a medicine-woman drops her drum and quickly climbs up the rewe. There she remains in a trance, supported by the branches, and receives from above the inspiration of Ngenechen. The *dumgumachife*, who has up to this moment played no part in the ceremony, approaches the medicine-woman in order to ask her whether 'Ngenechen' has come and she invariably replies in the affirmative, mentioning some mountains known in the neighborhood famed for their height or some other unusual peculiarity.

"The medium (that is, this medicine-woman) sets forth the desires of the family to the spirit incorporated in the machi. The latter causes some little bells to ring automatically and replies, granting what is asked and reproaching the Mapuches for neglecting the celebration of the *ngillatuns*. The Indians believe that it is the spirit that is speaking to them by the mouth of the machi. She then falls, as if fainting, into the arms of the flute-player or into a blanket which is held in readiness. She recovers herself for a moment, drinks some water or *chicha* and again gyrates to the sound of drum. . . ."

The same elaborateness and sophistication evident above is also found in their oral literature and can again be best explained as due to the profound influence exercised by the Incas in precolumbian times and the Spaniards later on. Take, for instance, the following two songs:[63]

1

He wears on his body
his large well worked blanket
and his chiripa
And his wonderful sash.
Like the rising sun
is the gold trarilonco
he wears on his forehead.
In his proudly held head
like a lion in bearing
he has always strength.
His countenance is clean
and beardless
And his sleek hair

is black.
Such is the aspect
of a great chief,
Mamita, mamita.

2

Who is this,
like the tiger,
riding the wind
with his phantom-like body?
When the oaks see him,
When the peoples see him
they speak with hushed voices
Saying to one another:
"Lo brother, there is
Caupolican's specter."

Their strange social organization gives the same impression; namely, that tremendous transformations must have taken place in their original mode of life, transformations that must have long antedated even the Inca conquest of the fifteenth century. We do not have to go far afield to find out to whom to ascribe them, for to the north of the Araucanians there existed civilizations of a very high order, civilizations that had reached their maturity long before the Incas were a power to be reckoned with; namely, the Calchaqui (*Diaguite*) and the Atacamana.

The Araucanians, in short, have probably fundamentally reorganized their original civilization three times, twice during the precolumbian period and once since. It is this amazing capacity for adjusting the old to the new, for making the old function as long as possible, and this ability to intelligently weld the new with the old, that has kept them a vigorous and virile minority in Chile and which holds a definite promise that within the near future they will once more come into their own.

And thus we see, skirting the eastern slopes of the mighty Cordillera, peoples of different stock and in different stages of culture impinging in various degrees upon the great civilizations that clung so persistently to the mountains and the shores of the Pacific. Their contact with them was, in the main, but passing and late. For the peoples still further east, the peoples of the Amazon and of Matto Grosso, these great civilizations meant nothing, nor did they know that far to the west rose a temple to the Sun God in which an amazing prayer, altogether foreign to them, was intoned every August:

> *O Creator! O Conquering, ever-present Uiracocha!*
> *Thou who art in the ends of the earth without equal!*
> *Thou who gavest life and valor to man saying*
> *Let this be a man;*
> *And to woman, saying,*
> *Let this be a woman.*
> *Thou who madest them and gave them being!*
> *Thou who art in the high heavens*
> *And among the clouds of the tempest,*
> *Grant this with long life*
> *And accept this sacrifice,*
> *O Creator!*

PART III

The Great Civilizations

CHAPTER XII

Peruvian Itineraries

CIEZA DE LEON AND ADOLPH BANDELIER

IN THE YEAR 1532 THERE EMBARKED AT SEVILLE
for South America a youth named Pedro de Cieza de Leon. He
was fourteen years old and he received his baptism of blood and
his introduction to the inhabitants of the New World as soon
as he landed. That was at a place where afterwards the city of
Cartagena was built. This young man was destined to be much
more than a mere soldier and adventurer. "As I noted the many
great and strange things that are to be seen in this new world
of the Indies," so he wrote later on, "there came upon me a
strong desire to write an account of some of them." The account he wrote is one of the most famous and fascinating travel
narratives in the world, *The Chronicle of Peru*, published at
Antwerp in 1554.

As we listen to him enumerate the mighty things of Peru,
the lofty mountains and profound valleys, the numerous rivers
small and large, deep and shallow, over which he traveled,
"conquering and discovering," as he quaintly says, there must
come back to all those who knew him and who have read his
works the memory of that other traveler and explorer who in
1840 left his native home when barely eight years old, Adolph
Bandelier, of Berne, the true founder of American archaeology.
He too has left us an account, a journal of his stay in Peru. This

unfortunately is unpublished and still unavailable. But there is a letter which the author possesses that gives in some detail his itinerary for the first year and a half after his arrival at Lima in 1892.

I cannot think of anything more enlightening or more suitable as an introduction to the great civilizations we are now to describe than the juxtaposition of these two itineraries separated three hundred and fifty years, the one from the other. And so we shall let the two men speak, each in his own words and each with his own idiosyncracies.

I

PEDRO DE CIEZA DE LEON TO THE MOST PUISSANT
LORD DON PHILIP, THE PRINCE OF THE SPAINS,
OUR LORD[64]

What I have written here is concerning true and important things, both pleasant and useful, which happened in our time and I dedicate it to your Highness. The attempt savors of temerity in so unlearned a man, but others of more learning are too much occupied in the wars to write. Oftentimes, when the other soldiers were reposing, I was tiring myself by writing. Neither fatigue nor the ruggedness of the country, nor the mountains and rivers, nor intolerable hunger and suffering, have ever been sufficient to obstruct my two duties; namely, writing and following my flag and my captain without fault. . . .

The city of San Miguel is the first that was founded in this kingdom, by the marquis Don Francisco Pizarro; and here the first temple was raised in honor of God our Lord. To describe the coast valleys, I must begin with the valley of Tumbez, through which flows a river which rises (as I have before said) in the province of Paltas, and falls into the South Sea. The land of this valley of Tumbez is naturally very dry and sterile, but it sometimes rains, and showers even extend to near the city of San Miguel. But these showers take place in the parts nearest to the mountains, and it never rains in the vicinity of the sea coast.

The valley of Tumbez was formerly thickly peopled and well cultivated, full of beautiful fresh watercourses drawn from the river to irrigate the land, and yielded maize and other things necessary for the support of man, besides plenty of delicious fruit. The ancient chiefs of the valley, before they were subjugated by the Yncas, were dreaded and obeyed by their subjects in a greater degree than any other chiefs of whom I have yet written, as is notorious to all, and they were served with much ceremony. They dressed in mantles and shirts, and wore an ornament on their heads, consisting of a circlet of wool adorned with pieces of gold and silver, and very small beads, called *chaquira*. These Indians were addicted to their religion, and were great sacrificers, as is stated at large in my account of the founding of the cities of Puerto Viejo and Guayaquil. They are very industrious laborers in the fields, and carry heavy burdens. They till the ground in concert, with beautiful regularity, and raise maize and many kinds of well-tasted roots. The maize yields a harvest twice in the year, and the beans and peas also come up abundantly when they are sown. Their clothes are made of cotton, which they grow in the valley, according to the quantity they require. These natives of Tumbez also have a great fishery, from which they derive no small profit, for with it, and their trade to the mountains, they have always been rich.

From the valley of Tumbez a journey of two days brings the traveler to the valley of Solana, which was thickly peopled in former days, and contained edifices and store-houses. The royal road of the Yncas passes through these valleys, with pleasant shady trees on either side. Leaving Solana, the road next comes to Pocheos, on a river called Pocheos, though some call it the Maycahuilca, because there is a chief or lord of that name in the valley. This valley was once very thickly populated indeed, as we are led to suppose from the numerous remains of great buildings. These buildings, though now in ruins, prove that the valley was as populous as the natives describe, and they also show the great estimation in which the Kings Yncas held this place, for here there were royal palaces and other buildings. Time and wars have so entirely obliterated them that nothing can be seen now but vast numbers of great tombs of those dead who once cultivated all the fields in this valley.

Two more days' journey beyond Pocheos brings us to the great and wide valley of Piura, where two or three rivers unite, which is the reason why this valley is so broad. In it is built the city of San Miguel. Although this city is now held in little estimation, the repartimientos being small and poor, it is just to remember that it deserves privileges and honor, because it was the beginning of all the cities that have since been built, and is on the site selected by the brave Spaniards, before the great lord Atahualpa was seized by them. At first the city was founded on the site called Tangarara, which was abandoned on account of its unhealthiness. It is now built between two very pleasant level valleys, full of trees. It is said to be rather unhealthy, and the people suffer in their eyes from the wind and dust of summer and the dampness of winter. They say that it never rains in this district, but some dew falls from heaven, and, at intervals of a few years, a heavy shower of rain comes down. The valley is like that of Tumbez, and there are many vines, figs, and other trees of Spain growing in it . . .

Before going any further, it seems well that I should say what I have learned in the matter of there being no rain. In the mountains summer commences in April, and lasts during May, June, July, August, and September. In October winter begins, and lasts during November, December, January, February, and March, so that there is little difference in the seasons between this land and our Spain. The fields are ploughed in the proper seasons, and the days and nights are almost equal. The time when the days increase a little and are longest, is during the month of November. But in the coast valleys bordering on the South Sea, the seasons are opposite to what I have here described; for when it is summer in the mountains it is winter on the coast, where we begin the summer in October, lasting till April, and then the winter commences.

It is truly a strange thing to consider this great difference in the same country. What is still more worthy of note is, that you may start in the morning from a country where it is raining, and, before vespers, you will find yourself in another where it never rains. From the beginning of October it never rains in any of the coast valleys, except in such small showers as scarcely to lay the dust. For this reason the inhabitants are dependent upon irrigation, and do not cultivate more land than what the rivers can irrigate, for everywhere else (by reason of the sterility) not even a blade of grass will grow, but all is an intensely dry, stony, or sandy waste, where nothing is seen but a tree with few leaves and no fruit. In some parts there are thorn bushes and cacti, in others nothing but sand.

What they call winter on the coast is nothing more than the season when clouds arise, which look as if they were charged with plenty of rain, but nothing comes of it save a drizzle so light that it barely damps the ground. It is a strange thing that though, as I have said, the heavens are well charged with clouds, yet it does not rain more than these slight showers. At the same time, some days pass during which the sun is not seen, being concealed by the thickness of the clouds. As the mountains are so high, and the coast valleys so low, it would appear that the former attract the clouds to themselves without allowing them to abide in the low lands. And when it is the natural time for rain, it falls in the mountains, while there is none in the plains, but, on the contrary, great heat. On the other hand, the light showers fall on the coast when the region of the mountains is clear and rainless.

There is another curious thing, which is that there is only one wind on this coast, and that is from the south; and although the wind from that quarter is moist and attracts rain in other countries, it is not so here, and this wind prevails continually along the coast as far as Tumbez. Further up the coast, as there are other winds, it rains, and the winds are accompanied by heavy showers. I do not know the natural reason for these things, but it is clear that this sterile rainless region extends from 4° south of the equinoctial line to beyond the tropic of capricorn.

Another thing, very worthy of note, is, that on the equinoctial line in some parts it is hot and moist, and in others cold and dry; but this land of the coast of Peru is hot and dry, while on either side it rains. I have gathered all this from what I have myself seen, and he who can assign natural reasons for these things, let him do so. As for me, I have said what I saw, and can do no more. . . .

In this place I will give an account of the grand road which the Yncas ordered to be made along the coast valleys, which, although now it is in ruins in many places, still shows how grand a work it once was, and how great was the power of those who ordered it to be made.

Huayna Ccapac, and Tupac Ynca Yupanqui, his father, were those who, according to the Indians, descended to the coast and visited all the valleys and provinces of the Yuncas, although some say that Ynca Yupanqui, the grandfather of Huayna Ccapac and father of Tupac Ynca, was the first who saw the coast and traversed its deserts. The Caciques and officers, by order of the Yncas, made a road fifteen feet wide through these coast valleys, with a strong wall on each side. The whole space of this road was smooth and shaded by trees. These trees, in many places, spread their branches laden with fruit over the road, and many birds fluttered amongst the leaves. In every valley there was a principal station for the Yncas, with depots of provisions for the troops. If anything was not ready, a severe punishment was inflicted, and if any of those whose duty it was to traverse the road, entered the fields or dwellings of the Indians, although the damage they did was small, they were ordered to be put to death. The walls on each side extended from one place to another, except where the sand drifted so high that the Indians could not pave the road with cement, when huge posts, like beams, were driven in at regular intervals to point out the way. Care was taken to keep the road clean, to renew any part of the walls that was out of repair, and to replace any of the posts which might be displaced by the wind in the deserts. This coast road was certainly a great work, though not so difficult as that over the mountains. . . .

All those who live in these mountains are called Serranos, and those who inhabit the coast are called Yuncas; and in many parts of the mountains where the rivers flow, as the mountains are very high, the plains are sheltered and warm, and in some of them there is as much heat as there is on the coast. The inhabitants who live in these warm valleys and plains, although they are strictly in the mountains, are also called Yuncas. Throughout Peru, when they speak of these warm and sheltered places between the mountains, they call them Yuncas, and the inhabitants have no other name, though they may have in their own districts. Thus, those who live in the parts already mentioned, and all who live in the coast valleys of Peru, are called Yuncas, because they live in a warm land. . . .

On setting out from San Miguel there is a distance of twenty-two leagues over a sandy waste before reaching the valley of Motupe. The road is very wearisome, especially by the route which is now used. There are certain little ravines on this road, but, although some streams descend from the mountains, they do not reach these ravines, but are lost in the sand, in such sort that no use can be made of the water. To go over these twenty-two leagues it is necessary to set out in the afternoon, and, traveling all night, some springs are reached early in the morning, where the traveler can drink, and go on without feeling the heat of the sun. It is usual for travelers to carry calabashes of water and bottles of wine with them.

In the valley of Motupe the royal road of the Yncas is seen, broad and constructed in the manner described in a former chapter. This valley is broad and very fertile, and although a good sized river flows down into it from the mountains, all the water is lost before reaching

the sea. The algarobas and other trees grow well, on account of the
moisture which they find under their roots. In the lower part of the
valley there are villages of Indians, who are supported by water
which they obtain from deep wells. They get all that they require
by exchanging one thing for another amongst themselves, for they
do not use money, nor is any die for coining to be found in these
parts. They say that there were great buildings for the Yncas in this
valley; and the people had, and still have, their huacas, or burial-
places in the barren heights and stony places leading to the Sierra.
The late wars have reduced the numbers of the Indians, and the buildings have fallen into ruins, the present inhabitants living in small huts,
built in the same way as those described in a former chapter. At
certain seasons they trade with the people of the Sierra; and in the
valley there are great fields of cotton, with which they make their
clothes.

Four leagues from Motupe is the fresh and beautiful valley of
Xayanca, which is nearly four leagues broad. A pleasant river flows
through it, whence they lead channels which serve to irrigate all the
land that the Indians choose to sow. In former times this valley was
thickly peopled, like all the others, and it contained great buildings
and storehouses belonging to the principal chiefs, where their officers were stationed. The native chiefs of these valleys were reverenced by their subjects, and those who survive still are so. They go
about with a retinue of servants and women, and have their porters
and guards.

From this valley the road leads to that of Tuqueme, which is also
large, pleasant, and full of trees and bushes. It contains vestiges of
edifices, which are now ruined and abandoned. A short journey further on brings us to another very beautiful valley called Cinto. And
the reader is to understand that from valley to valley the way is over
sandy and parched-up stony wastes, where no living thing is to be
seen, neither grass nor tree; nothing but a few birds that may be seen
flying. Those who travel over the broad sandy deserts, and catch
sight of the valley (although still far off) are much cheered, especially
if they are on foot, under a hot sun, and suffering from thirst. Men
who are new to the country should not travel over these wastes,
except with good guides who know the way.

Further on is the valley of Collique, through which flows a river
of the same name, so broad that it cannot be forded except in the

season when it is summer in the Sierra, and winter on the coast. Nevertheless the natives are so well practiced in the management of irrigation channels that, even when it is winter in the Sierra, they sometimes leave the main stream dry. This valley, like the others, is broad and full of trees, but there is a want of inhabitants, for most of them have been carried off by the wars with the Spaniards, and by the evils which these wars brought with them.

Beyond the valley of Collique there is another valley called Sana, which resembles the others. Further on is the valley of Pacasmayu, which is the most fertile and populous of any that I have yet mentioned. The natives of this valley, before they were conquered by the Yncas, were powerful, and respected by their neighbors, and they had great temples where they offered sacrifices to their gods. They are all now in ruins. In the rocks and hills of the surrounding desert there are a great quantity of huacas, which are the burial-places of these Indians. In all these valleys there are clergymen or friars who look after the conversion and teaching of the Indians, not permitting them to practice their ancient religious customs or usages.

A very fine river flows through this valley of Pacasmayu, whence they lead many large channels, sufficient to irrigate all the fields that are cultivated by the Indians, and they raise the fruits and roots already enumerated. The royal road of the Yncas passes through this valley, as it does through all the others, and here there were great buildings for the Yncas' use. The natives tell some ancient traditions of their fathers, which, being fables, I shall not write down. The lieutenants of the Yncas collected the tribute, and stored it in the buildings which were made to receive it, whence it was taken to the chief station in the province, the place selected for the residence of the captain-general, and where the temple of the sun was erected.

In this valley of Pacasmayu they make a great quantity of cotton cloth; the land is suited for breeding cows, still better for pigs and goats, and the climate is healthy. I passed through this valley in the month of September, in the year 1548, to join the other soldiers who had come from the government of Popayan to reinforce the royal camp, and chastise the late rebellion. It then appeared to me to be extremely pleasant, and I praised God on seeing its freshness, with so many trees and flowers, and branches full of a thousand kinds of birds.

Further on is the valley of Chacma, not less fertile and abundant than that of Pascamayu, and in addition it contains great quantities of sweet cane, of which they make much excellent sugar, and other conserves. There is here a Dominican monastery, which the reverend father Friar Domingo de Santo Tomas founded.

Four leagues further on is the valley of Chimu, which is broad and very large, and here the city of Truxillo is built. Some Indians relate that, in ancient times, before the Yncas extended their sway so far, there was a powerful lord in this valley, who was called Chimu, as the valley is now. He did great things, was victorious in many battles, and built certain edifices which even now, though so ancient, clearly appear to have been very grand. When the Kings Yncas made themselves lords of these coast valleys, they held that of Chimu in great estimation, and ordered large buildings and pleasure-houses to be erected in it. The royal road, built with its walls, also passes through the valley. The native chiefs of this valley were always esteemed and held to be rich. This is known to be true, for in the tombs of the principal men much gold and silver have been found. But at present there are few Indians in the valley, most of the land being divided amongst Spaniards who are citizens of the new city of Truxillo, to form their estates. The sea port, called the roadstead of Truxillo, is not very far from the valley, and all along the coast they kill much fish for the supply of the city and of the Indians themselves. . . .

The distance from the city of Truxillo to that of the Kings is eighty leagues, over sandy deserts and intervening valleys. After leaving Truxillo the first village is Guanape, being seven leagues on the road. This valley was no less noted among the natives in times past for the chicha which was brewed there, than Madrigal or San Martin in Castille are for the good wine that they yield. In ancient times the valley of Guanape was very populous, and was the residence of chiefs, who were honorably and well treated by the Yncas after they submitted to their rule. The Indians who have survived the wars and troubles are skillful in their labor, drawing channels of water from the river to irrigate their fields. The remains may be clearly seen of the buildings and store-houses erected by the Kings Yncas. There is a useful port at this valley, where many of the ships which sail on the South Sea, from Panama to Peru, call for supplies.

From Guanape the road leads to the valley of Santa, but before reaching it there is a valley with no river, but a small well at which travelers quench their thirst. This well may be caused by some river which flows through the bowels of the earth. In former days the valley of Santa was very populous, and there were great chiefs who, at first, even defied the Yncas. They say of them that it was more by intrigue and a display of friendship than by force of arms, that they were induced to acknowledge the Yncas as their lords. Afterwards the Yncas honored them, and held them in great esteem, and the chiefs erected grand edifices by order of the Yncas. This valley is one of the largest of any we have passed. A great and rapid river flows through it, which is much swollen when the season in the Sierra is winter, so that some Spaniards have been drowned in crossing from one side to the other. There are now balsas for crossing it. The valley contained many thousands of Indians in former times, but now there are only four hundred; and this is a lamentable thing to contemplate.

That which I most admired, in passing through this valley, was the great number of burial-places, and that in all parts of the barren hills above the valley there were quantities of tombs made according to the custom of the Indians, and full of the bones of the dead. Thus the things that are most worthy of notice in the valley are the tombs of the dead and the fields which they cultivated when alive. They used to take great channels of water from the river, with which they irrigated the land. But now there are few Indians, and most of the fields which were once cultivated, are converted into woods, ground overgrown with brambles, and such dense thickets that, in some places, it is difficult to make a way through them. The natives go dressed in shirts and mantles, and the women also. They wear a head-dress on their heads to distinguish them from other tribes. All the fruits I have already mentioned grow well in this valley, and the pulses of Spain; and the Indians kill much fish. The ships sailing along the coast always take in water at the river of Santa. And as there are many thickets and few inhabitants, the mosquitoes swarm in such numbers as to be grievous to those who pass through or sleep in this valley.

Two days' journey further on is the valley of Huambacho, of which I shall say no more than that it resembles those already described, that there were buildings in it erected by its chiefs, and that the inhabitants drew channels of water from the river which flows through it, to irrigate their crops.

I went in a day and a-half from this valley to that of Guarmay, which was likewise very populous in former days. At present they breed great quantities of cattle, horses, and pigs in it.

From Guarmay the road leads to Parmonga, which is no less pleasant than the other valleys, but I believe that it contains no Indians at all who avail themselves of its fertility. . . .

Two leagues from this valley is the river Huaman, a word which, in our language, means "falcon," but it is usually called "the ravine." When it rains much in the Sierra, this river is dangerous, and some people have been drowned in crossing it. One day's journey further on brings us to the valley of Huara, whence we pass to that of Lima.

The valley of Lima is the largest and broadest of all those of which I have written between it and Tumbez; and, as it was large, so it was very populous. But now there are few native Indians, for, as the city was built on their land, and as their fields and water-courses were taken from them, some have now gone to one valley and some to another. If by chance some have remained, they continue to irrigate their fields. . . .

Four leagues from the City of the Kings, traveling down the coast, is the valley of Pachacamac, which is very famous among these Indians. This valley is fruitful and pleasant, and in it there was one of the grandest temples that is to be seen in these parts. They say of it that, although the Kings Yncas built many temples besides the temple of Cuzco, and enriched them greatly, yet none were equal to this temple of Pachacamac. It was built on the top of a small hill, entirely made of earth and adobes (bricks baked in the sun). The edifice had many doors, and the doors and walls were painted over with wild beasts. Within the temple, where they placed the idol, were the priests, who feigned no small amount of sanctity. When they performed sacrifices before the people, they went with their faces towards the doors and their backs to the idols, with their eyes to the ground, and they were filled with a mighty trembling. Indeed, their perturbation was so great, according to the accounts of those Indians who are still living, that it may almost be compared with that of which we read concerning the priests of Apollo when the gentiles sought for their vain replies. The Indians further relate that they sacrificed animals, and some human blood of persons whom they had killed, before the figure of this devil, which, at their most solemn festivals, gave replies, and when the people heard them, they believed them to be true. In the terraces and lower parts of this temple a great sum in gold and silver was buried.

The priests were much reverenced, and the chiefs obeyed them in many of the things which they ordered. Near the temple many great buildings were erected for the use of those who came on pilgrimage, and no one was considered worthy to be buried in the vicinity of the temple except the chiefs, or those who came as pilgrims bringing offerings to the temple. When the annual festivals of the year were celebrated, a great concourse of people assembled, rejoicing to the sound of such instruments of music as they use.

When the Lords Yncas, in extending their sway, came to this valley of Pachacamac, and saw the grandeur and great antiquity of the temple, and the reverence paid to it by all the people in the neighbourhood, they knew that it would be very difficult to put aside this feeling, although it was their general practice to order temples to the sun to be built in all the countries they conquered. They, therefore, agreed with the native chiefs and with the ministers of this god or devil, that the temple of Pachacamac should continue with the authority and reverence it formerly possessed, and that the loftiest part should be set aside as a temple of the sun. This order of the Yncas having been obeyed, the temple of the sun became very rich, and many virgins were placed in it. The devil Pachacamac was delighted with this agreement, and they affirm that he showed great satisfaction in his replies, seeing that his ends were served both by the one party and the other, while the souls of the unfortunate simpletons remained in his power. . . .

From this temple of Pachacamac, where the temple is, the road leads to Chilca, and at that place there is a thing well worthy of note, for it is very strange. It is this—that neither rain falls from heaven, nor does any river or spring flow through the land, and yet the greater part of the valley is full of crops of Indian corn, of roots, and of fruit trees. It is a marvelous thing to hear what the Indians do in this valley. In order to secure the necessary moisture, they make broad and very deep holes where they sow their crops, and God is served by their growing with the aid of dew alone; but by no means could they make the maize grow if they did not put two heads of sardines to each grain, these sardines being small fish which they catch with nets in the sea. At the time of sowing, these fishes heads are put with the maize in the same hole that is made for the grain, and in this manner the grain grows and yields abundantly. It is certainly a notable thing that in a land where it does not rain, and where nothing but a very fine dew falls, people should be able to live at their ease. The water which the natives of this village drink is taken from very deep wells, and they catch so many sardines in the sea, that the supply is sufficient to maintain all the inhabitants, besides using many for manuring the crops. There were buildings and store-houses of the Yncas in this valley, for their reception when they visited the provinces of their kingdom. . . .

A little more than five leagues beyond the valley of Mala is that of Guarco, which is highly spoken of in this kingdom, being large, broad, and full of fruit trees. Especially there are many guayavas, which are very delicious and fragrant, and still more guavas. The wheat and maize yield plentifully, and all other things that are sown, as well those of the country as the trees of Spain. There are also pigeons, doves, and other kinds of birds. The thickets of bushes in this valley are very shady, and irrigating channels flow through them. The inhabitants say that, in times past, the valley was very populous, and that the people contended with their neighbours, and with those of the Sierra.

When the Yncas advanced their conquests and extended their sway over all the provinces they came in contact with, the natives of this valley had no wish to become vassals, seeing that their fathers had left them free. They showed great valor, and maintained the war with no less spirit than virtue for more than four years, during which time many notable things fell out between the combatants. It was a protracted war, and although the Ynca himself retired to Cuzco in the summer, on account of the heat, his troops continued fighting. On account of the length of the war, which the Ynca desired to bring to a close, he came down with his nobles to build a new city which he called Cuzco, after his principal seat of government. The Indians relate that he ordered that the different divisions of the new city should have the same names as those of Cuzco. Finally, but not until they had fought to the last extremity, the natives of the valley of Guarco were subdued, and subjected to the yoke of the tyrant king, who had no other right to be their lord than that which the fortune of war had given him. Having brought the enterprise to a successful conclusion, the Ynca returned with his troops to Cuzco, and the name of the new city was lost. Nevertheless he ordered the most handsome and imposing fortress in the whole kingdom to be erected on a high hill commanding the valley, to commemorate his victory. It is built on great square slabs, the portals are very well made, and the halls and courts are very large. From the upper part of this royal house a stone flight of steps leads down to the sea, and the waves dash with such force against the base of the edifice, that it causes wonder to think how it could have been built with such strength and solidity. In its time this fortress was richly adorned with paintings, and it contained great treasure in the days of the Kings Yncas. Although the building is so strong, and the stones so large, there does not appear to be any mortar or other cement by which they were joined together. When the edifice was built they say that, on reaching the interior of the rock, they made holes with their picks and other tools, and filled them with great slabs and stones, and thus it is that the building is so strong. Considering that it is built by these Indians, the building is worthy of praise, and must cause admiration to those who see it, although now it is ruined and deserted. It may still be seen to have been a great work in times past. It seems to me that both Spaniards and Indians should be forbidden, under heavy penalties, from doing further injury either to this building or to the remains of the fortress at Cuzco; for these two edifices are those which should cause most admiration in all Peru, and, as time rolls on, they may even be made use of for some good purpose. . . .

About two leagues beyond the fortress of Guarco is a rather large river called Lunahuana, and the valley which it forms is like all the rest. Six miles further on is the large and beautiful valley of Chincha, so far famed throughout Peru, as well as feared in former days by the other natives. When the Marquis Don Francisco Pizarro, with his thirteen companions, discovered the coast of this kingdom, it was said on all sides that Chincha was the fairest and best part of it. Thus it was that, by reason of the fame borne by the place, and without knowing the secrets of the soil, he sought from his Majesty the government of a territory extending from the river of Santiago or Tempulla to this valley of Chincha.

As to the origin of the Indians of Chincha, they say that, in time past, a quantity of them set out under the banner of a valiant captain of their own tribe and arrived at this valley of Chincha, where they found many inhabitants, but all of such small stature that the tallest was barely two cubits high. The new comers being valiant, and the natives cowardly and timid, the former gained possession. They also affirm that all the natives perished, and that the fathers of the grandfathers of men now alive saw their bones in certain tombs which were as small as has been described.

These Indians thus became lords of the valley; they flourished and multiplied, and built their villages close together. They say that they heard a certain oracle near a rock, and that they all hold the place to be sacred. They call it Chincha and Camay. They constantly made sacrifices, and the devil held converse with the older

men, and deceived them as he did all the other Indians. The principal
chiefs of the valley, and many other Indians, have now become
Christians, and a monastery of the glorious Saint Dominic has been
founded in the valley. . . .

This valley is one of the largest in all Peru, and it is a beautiful
thing to see its channels of water and groves of trees, and the great
abundance of fruit, more especially the luscious and fragrant pepinos,
not like those of Spain, although they bear some resemblance. These
are yellow when the peel is taken off, and so delicious that it is
necessary to eat many of them before a man is satisfied. In the
thickets there are the same birds as have already been mentioned.
There are scarcely any sheep of the country, because the wars
between the Christians have caused their destruction. This valley
yields plenty of wheat, and they cultivate vines which they have
planted. The valley yields all the other things which have been
planted by the Spaniards.

There were an immense quantity of burial-places made on the
surrounding arid heights. The Spaniards opened many of them, and
obtained a great quantity of gold. The native Indians were fond of
dancing, and the chiefs went about with much ceremony and parade,
and were reverenced by their vassals. After the Yncas established
their rule, the natives copied many customs from them, adopted
their dress, and imitated them in all other things as their sole lords. . . .

After leaving the beautiful provinces of Chincha, and traveling
over sandy wastes, the traveler reaches the refreshing valley of Yca,
which was not less rich and populous than the others. A river flows
through it, which, during some months in the year when the season
is summer in the Sierra, has so little water that the inhabitants of
the valley feel the want of it. In the days of their prosperity, before
they were subdued by the Spaniards, and when they enjoyed the
government of the Yncas, besides the channels with which they
irrigated the valley, they had one much larger than the rest, brought
with great skill from the mountains in such wise that it flowed without reducing the quantity of water in the river. Now that this great
channel is destroyed, they make deep holes in the bed of the river
when it is dry, and thus they obtain water to drink, and for watering
their crops. In this valley of Yca there were great lords in former
times who were much feared and reverenced. The Yncas ordered
palaces and other buildings to be made in the valley. The inhabitants

had the same customs as the other Indians, burying live women and great treasure with their dead.

In this valley there are very large woods of algaroba trees, and many fruit trees of the kinds already described; besides deer, pigeons, doves, and other game. The people breed much cattle.

From this valley of Yca the road leads to the beautiful rivers and valleys of Nasca, which were also very populous in times past, and the streams were made to irrigate the fields. The late wars destroyed by their cruelty (as is well known) all these poor Indians. Some Spaniards of credit told me that the greatest harm to the Indians was done during the dispute of the two governors Pizarro and Almagro, respecting the boundaries of their jurisdictions, which cost so dear, as the reader will see in the proper place. . . .

Now that I have finished all I have to say concerning the coast valleys, I shall return to the mountains. I have already written an account of the villages and edifices from Quito to Loxa, and of the province of Huancabamba, where I halted, in order to treat of the foundation of San Miguel and of other subjects. Returning now to the former route, it seems to me that the distance from Huancabamba to the province of Caxamarca is fifty leagues, a little more or less. This province is famous as the scene of Atahualpa's imprisonment, and is noted throughout the kingdom for its riches. The natives of Caxamarca state that they were much esteemed by their neighbours before the Yncas subdued them, and that they had their temples and places of worship in the loftier parts of the mountains. Some of them say that they were first subdued by the Ynca Yupanqui, others that it was not so, but that his son Tupac Ynca Yupanqui first conquered them. Whoever it may have been, it is stated positively that before he became lord of Caxamarca, they killed the greater part of his troops, and that they were brought under his yoke more by intrigues and by soft and winning speeches than by force. The native chiefs of this province were much respected by their Indians, and they had many women. One of the wives was the principal, and her son, if she had one, succeeded in the lordship. When the chiefs died the same customs were observed as have already been described. Their wives and riches were buried with them, and there was much and long-continued lamentation. Their temples and places of worship were much venerated, and the blood of sheep and lambs was offered up as sacrifice. They say that the ministers of these temples conversed with the devil; and when they celebrated their festivals, they assembled a vast concourse of people in a clear open space, and performed dances, during which they consumed no small quantity of wine made from maize. They all go dressed in mantles and rich tunics, and wear a peculiar head-dress as a distinguishing mark, being narrow cords in the manner of a fillet. . . .

This province of Caxamarca is very fertile, and yields wheat like another Sicily. They also breed stock, and raise abundance of maize and of edible roots, and of all the fruits which I have mentioned as growing in other parts. Besides these, there are falcons, many partridges, doves, pigeons, and other game. The natives are well-mannered, peaceful, and amongst themselves they have some good customs, so as to pass through this life without care. They think little of honor, and are not ambitious of having any, but they are hospitable to Christians who pass through their province, and give them good food, without doing them any evil turn, even when the traveler is solitary. For these and other things the Spaniards praise the Indians of Caxamarca. They are very ingenious in forming irrigating channels, building houses, cultivating the land, breeding stock, and in working gold and silver. They also make, with their hands, as good tapestry from the wool of their sheep as is to be found in Flanders, and so fine that the threads of it look like silk, although they are only wool. The women are amorous, and some of them are beautiful. They go dressed in the same way as the Pallas, or ladies of Cuzco. The temples and huacas are now in ruins, and the idols are broken, many of the Indians having become Christians. . . .

This land of (lake) Bombon (Chinchaycocha) is level and very cold, and the mountains are some distance from the lake. The Indians have their villages round the lake, with large dykes. These natives of Bombon had great numbers of sheep, and, although most of them have been destroyed in the late wars, yet some still remain, and in the desert heights there are quantities of the wild kinds. There is little maize in this country on account of the cold, but there is no want of other provision by which the people are sustained. There are some islands and rocks in the lake, where the Indians form garrisons in time of war, and are thus safe from their enemies. Concerning the water which flows from this lake, it is held for certain that it forms the source of the famous river of La Plata, because it becomes a powerful river in the valley of Xauxa, and further on it is joined by the rivers of Parcos, Vilcas, Abancay, Apurimac, and Yucay. Thence it flows to the west, traversing many lands, where it receives other rivers which are still unknown to us, until it finally reaches Paraguay, the country discovered by those Christian Spaniards who first came to the river of La Plata. I myself believe, from what I have heard of this great river, that it owes its origin to two or three branches, or perhaps more; like the rivers Maranon, Santa Martha, Darien, and others in those parts. However this may be, in this kingdom of Peru, we believe that it owes its source to the lake of Bombon, which receives the water caused by the melting of the snow from the heat of the sun on the desert heights, and of this there cannot be little.

II

ADOLPH F. BANDELIER TO HIS FRIEND, THOMAS JANVIER[65]

It is today just eighteen months since I reached Lima for the first time, and so many memories come back to me on this occasion that I must spend a few moments with you recalling the pleasant weeks . . . in the city of Mexico and remembering the sphere of activity in which I was then engaged in comparison with the one which has occupied me and my time during the past two years. The change is a great one, the scene very different. . . .

Summer has set in with us, and a summer of which the "oldest inhabitant" of course says that it is truly exceptional. That oldest inhabitant seems to be found everywhere, and his sayings here are probably as trustworthy as in other parts of the world. Last winter was cool on the coast, and it left behind stragglers in the shape of dark and gloomy days, foggy nights, as late as December. Now, sunshine is everywhere; the days are sometimes warm, and always the heat is damp. In this respect the climate of Lima is less agreeable than that of Truxillo. The latter town lies on a rather dry stretch, and there are no heights rising along its outskirts; as for instance here at Lima the Cerro de San Cristóbal and others, the steep slopes of which arrest the sea fogs in their drift to the interior, compelling them to hover over the city. In winter, these fogs therefore enshroud the whole town and its vicinity; in summer the sun dispels the cloud, distributing its moisture through the surrounding atmosphere and creating the dampness that oppresses and increases the disagreeable effect of an otherwise moderately warm temperature.

Although the Peruvian coast, as far as I have seen it until now, everywhere presents the same type of aridity; rising in particular places to sheer repulsiveness, there is still a variety of climatological features, or rather, there are very marked variations in degree of unhealthiness. Thus Lima and its immediate vicinity are not reputed for malignant fevers. Two *leguas* towards the interior, the deeply cut valleys must be avoided, in March and April at least, by him who is not thoroughly acclimatized. The immediate beach is nowhere dangerous to the incipient traveler in Peru through intermittent fevers but, as for instance, at Chimbote, Chicama, Truxillo, etc., very few leguas inland suffice to transport one into regions where pernicious intermittence becomes an actual danger. This is the result of watercourses descending from the high Sierra, gradually sinking into the sand that forms the soil of the whole coast, and dwindling down to sluggish fillets ere they reach the shore line. If, in addition to these peculiarities, the gorges are narrow and deep, so as to permit the rugged and dry slopes to intercept wholesome currents of air, the conditions are given for malarial sites where only long residence may harden human nature to a degree sufficient to resist the effects of endemic diseases.

In the Sierra, as far as I have been able to observe in northeastern Peru, conditions are substantially distinct. A great variety of local climates appear. Generally speaking, the Sierra, at least in the North, is overwhelmingly humid. Only during four or five months in the year may the traveler circulate in the departments of Cajamarca and Amazonas with impunity from daily and drenching showers. From the end of May till the middle of September lasts the period favorable for exploration and travel. Afterwards, there occur daily interruptions in the form of thunderstorms, and after December, the department of Amazonas for instance, becomes almost intransitable [this is Bandelier's strange word!]. It then rains sometimes for weeks incessantly, electric discharges are violent, and on the high and bleak "Jalcas," as the *Puna* is called in those sections, hailstorms and thunder last from sunrise till sunset, one cloud chasing the other without intermission.

The Jalca lacks the imposing scenery of the lower alpine regions of Switzerland. It is simply bleak; a rolling succession of hills overgrown by short grass. To him who crosses the Cordillera at Cajamarca, the sight of snowy peaks is denied. The Cordillera there is lowest in elevation above sea level, and as soon as he has gone beyond Cajamarca, he is amazed at the enormous depths of the gorges, at the gigantic and abrupt rises and interminable descents. From Celendin to the eastward he rises first 2,000 feet in two hours, then descends 5,400 feet in five hours, to the banks of the Marañon, rises again 8,400 feet in ten hours to an altitude of 13,000 feet on the crest of Calla-Calla, thence to follow a series of similar and colossal undulations. The whole of the department of Amazonas not covered by the virgin forest of the Rio Huallaga does not afford more than a mile of truly level ground. Even the paths that hug the banks of streams are ups and downs, rising and falling along slopes that ascend on either side thousands of feet, and from a climate in which coffee, cocoa, bananas, and sugar cane grow easily, to one in which the barley, the wheat, and the potatoes of temperate zones form almost the only cultivated plants. At one glance the rider embraces the vegetable products of the tropics as well as those of northern Europe and of New England.

The basin or valley of Cajamarca is charged with being quite feverish or feverful. The deep cleft in which the Marañon runs at Balsas is much drier. In general, with few exceptions, what lies west of that stream is more devoid of vegetation than what lies east of it. When I approached the last slopes of the Marañon cleft I thought to be on the bank of the upper Rio Yaqui in Sonora. So completely did the prevailing types of vegetation resemble, without being identical, the gaunt forms of the cacti of northern Mexico. Further to the east, however, appeared the vanguard of the flora of the Amazon Basin. Every aboriginal ruin there is covered with an almost impenetrable thicket or low timber, every step must be achieved by means of the hacking-knife (*punal*) or of the machete. During the rainy season, the ruins of Malca, of Macro, of Tshu-shin, or Pucara and all the other numerous small clusters of aboriginal vestiges so abundant about Chachapoyas, become as good as closed to the student. I had made a number of surveys after the rains had already commenced and only succeeded by dint of persistence and with the aid of a troop of Indians, cutting and cleaning before me, opening vistas for the theodolite, and preventing dangerous falls over roots and creepers, into chasms and thickets of thorns, by careful attendance to every step taken by the surveyor.

Mexico presents, also, great contrasts within the scope of its limits, but they do hardly equal, in suddenness and in shortness of distances, those presented by the Peruvian landscape. Travel in the interior, where the few railroads have not penetrated, is of course made on animals, and progress is slow owing to the extreme asperity of the trails. Nevertheless, after three days spent from Pacasmayo on the coast on a very gradual rise in a long and picturesque cleft, one rises at once thousands of feet almost suddenly; and from the groves of oranges, bananas, and other tropical fruit to the heights of San Pablo, where the steep slopes are covered with yellow patches of ripening wheat hedged in by the maguey plants so characteristic of Mexican landscape. I am told, but have not seen it yet, that further south ascent to the uppermost plateau is much more on an inclined plane. Those southern regions of the Cordillera I have attempted to reach three times in vain: first death, then sickness and relapses, drove me back to the coast, until last winter, when against the advice of medical science I crossed the Cordillera back and forth to investigate the hardly known surroundings of Chachapoyas and to determine the eastern limit of ruins in that direction. Previous to that time I had worked on the coast, only penetrating from Pisco to Huaya Grande, a distance of not over forty miles in a direct line from the seashore. . . .

It was not my intention to begin in Peru but a circumstance which I could not change at the time compelled me to remain at Lima. I soon saw that the Rimac Valley presented a fertile field for archaeological studies, provided they were performed systematically. . . .

I, therefore, turned my attention to the ruins around Lima. To my surprise, not one of the works that treated of Peruvian ruins presented the two essential points required in American archaeology as far as architecture was concerned: namely, detailed study of construction and complete surveys of entire clusters, like villages, towns, and well-defined groups of mounds. I know of only two attempts of complete ground plans of entire clusters, the one of the ruins called Pachacamac in what is now the Lurin Valley south of Lima, by Rivero and Tschudi in their magnificently illustrated *Antiguedades Peruanas,* and the one by Charles Wiener in his well-known work, of the enormous ruins of Chan-chan or Chimu near Truxillo. Both, I regret to say, are utterly inadequate. . . . You know it is not my habit to blame any predecessor of mine, but I felt the necessity of going over the ground again, as not a single building is indicated with that clearness that (alone) makes a ground plan of practical value for science.

Hence, seeing that, I felt that the ground was virgin almost everywhere in Peru from the standpoint of thorough research, and thus began at the nearest points at once. The surveys of the groups of artificial mounds at the hacienda of Lince at the very doors of Lima furnished me with the detail of construction of these edifices showing that although one of them had been raised to an altitude of fifty feet and occupied a base of several hundreds of feet in length and width, the mode of construction did not in the least correspond to the impression of stupendous workmanship conveyed by more superficial examination. I found that these extensive lumps had been formed by a gratework of adobe, the interstices of which had been filled in by rubble and sandy soil, so that the fabric did not require either a very great number of hands or a long time for its construction.

I also found that while every mound showed traces of buildings on its slopes or on the summit, these buildings were small, with disproportionally thick walls and, in many cases, without permanent roofs. The latter feature becomes explained by the absence of rain on the coast, except at very long intervals. I also noticed that all these constructions stood in some relation to vestiges of long walls of considerable width serving formerly as pathways as well as for enclosures, and it became clear to me, from the condition of the ground and positive traditions of former times, that these elevated pathways were necessary to secure transit over the Rimac Valley during the aboriginal period when agriculture was much more limited, a fact amply proven by contemporaneous documents in my possession.

Having thus secured a study of the mound groups, I then proceeded to investigate the largest ancient settlement of the lower Rimac Valley, the ruins of ancient Surco near Chorrillos. Here I found the mound structure only as an exceptional feature, limited to three specimens, whereas the remainder of the ruins standing on high and sloping ground and overlooking the formerly marshy fields of the hacienda of Villa consisted of buildings similar to those on the summit of the Lince group but on natural bases. The complete ground plan of Surco furnished me also, not with the absolute number of people that inhabited it, which would be an impossibility, but with a maximum figure—indicating the greatest possible number of inhabitants. For Surco that maximum is six thousand souls, a figure very respectable indeed, but still far below usual estimates.

Thence I proceeded to the celebrated site of Pachacamac. I have documentary evidence to the effect that the proper ancient name of this settlement and of Lurin was Irma—in the language of its inhabitants—and that Pachacamac was an appellative of recent origin at the time of the Spanish conquest. There I obtained also the complete ground plan and identified easily, by means of it, the various buildings noticed in the reports of the first Spaniards who visited the place. The maximum number of souls that Irma can have contained was twelve thousand, and this represented, with the exception of two more insignificant clusters, the entire population of that fertile valley previous to the coming of the Spaniards. In architecture Irma hardly varies from the remains in the Rimac Valley, at least the variations are purely incidental and local, not generic, and find their explanation in varied topographical features. At Irma, or Pachacamac, the artificial mound is only represented by few specimens lying on the lowest levels and where traces of former marshes are still visible. The highest eminence on which stood the house of the Sun is still encased by a frame of adobe walls. A high spur running out from that hill has its slopes solidified by thick adobe framings and many of the buildings standing on lower levels, but still above the formerly swampy sites, rest on prismatic masses of adobe, thus artificially raised, as the sandy basis would not have afforded sufficient security, not even for the modest structures which the artificial substructure supported.

On my way to Cuzco I was induced to examine the ruins between Pisco and Huaya Grande. At Tambo Colorado I found an exceedingly well-preserved specimen of a small ancient pueblo, and there I saw the edifice of stone for the first time, alongside of the adobe buildings but without any noticeable difference in architectural type. There also I had an opportunity of studying the *andenes* or artificial garden beds raised on arid slopes and in the beds of so-called *yapanas*, or mountain torrents, and noticed with surprise the great similarity of the Peruvian *anden* with the *banquitos* of the Sierra Madre in Sonora and the enclosed garden plots among the ruins at Ojo Caliente and Rito Colorado in northern New Mexico as well as of central Arizona. . . .

After surveying, in May last, the extensive group of mounds at the Magdalena Del Mar near Lima, and after an unsuccessful attempt to obtain the plan of Cajamarquilla, where I had to abandon the work on account of congestion caused by the excessive heat, I turned to the most extensive aboriginal ruins in America, the great cluster at Chan-chan, near Truxillo. There I found myself face to face with a labyrinth of courts, mounds, and thousands of small houses scattered all together over a fortunately level area, the perimeter of which is about eight and one-half English miles. To give you any idea of these ruins I will say that one of the outer walls is over fourteen thousand feet long and that in some places the walls of single courts stand to the height of 35 feet. Forty thousand is the maximum of people which this enormous cluster can have sheltered, for not three-fourths of the whole area were occupied by buildings. The rest were garden plots, still admirably preserved in many places with their corresponding irrigation channels. Chan-chan is prevailingly of adobe and the type of architecture resembles closely both Irma and Cajamarquilla with slight differences. Here I found the explanation of a peculiarity that had already struck me in Peruvian ruins of large size. Not one of them bears the character of a compact town or city. The abodes are scattered in separate clusters. This is specially marked in Chan-chan. The feature of localized ayllus or clans explains this, and I afterwards found that it still prevails in some places in the Sierra. Thus all these large settlements were simply the homes of an entire tribe. At Chan-chan this becomes still clearer from the fact that with the exception of few outlying ruins of isolated buildings or mounds and the enormous artificial hill of Moche which guarded approach to the river from that side, there are no settlements of ancient date in the Truxillo Valley, so that Chan-chan sheltered, up to a few hundred, the entire population of that section.

At Chan-chan, also, I met a singular feature already observed by the late E. G. Squier but which he could not explain. A number of structures stand on artificial platforms constructed after the manner of the mounds at the Lince and many of them excavated. In one of them stands intact, in others only the traces of, an altar of adobe. Coupled with documentary and reliable oral information and with the innumerable traditions and legends current in Peru of "treasure" contained in the center of such aboriginal edifices, this altar becomes an important feature. There is no doubt that idols of gold, of silver, copper, wood, stone, or clay are met with in almost every one of the raised bases or pyramidal fabrics in Peru. It establishes the ethnological fact that the Peruvians followed the same custom still prevailing among the New Mexican and other aborigines of giving to each thing inanimate, but used by them for any purpose, a heart or fetish which served as a protective charm. . . .

On my way to the Marañon country I visited the sculptured

monoliths at San Pablo near Cajamarca and expect daily photographs of these vestiges. They are generally six feet high and rudely carved. Similar monoliths stand in the vicinity of Hualgayoc, and I have the photograph of a carved face from the ruins of Malca on the hacienda of Kue-la-pe near Chachapoyas.

Lastly, in the Marañon district, I secured, the incessant rains notwithstanding, the ground plans of nine ruins. The type of architecture there is different from that on the coast and around Cajamarca. The dwellings—all of stone—are mere round huts with one narrow doorway. On the Marañon proper, however, the rectangular stone house reappears. The collections from that region are meager, I regret to say. Only six intact specimens of pottery could be obtained, but a number of potsherds from at least ten different sites. Not a single complete body was saved. Even in natural recesses the "mummy" fell to pieces at the first touch. So I had to be content with seven skulls, pottery and fragments, some shreds of cloth, and stone implements. Not a single specimen of copper was to be obtained, although I heard of their existence.

During all the time I have been in Peru I have seen only three implements of flint. The most diligent inquiries, the promises of ample reward, were powerless to secure anything of obsidian or flint. In copper implements, the collections are especially rich and the finds at Chan-chan will still further increase their number, adding many pieces so far not represented anywhere.

At Cajamarca, the complete modification of the town by the Spaniards has obliterated nearly every trace of the ancient settlement. But in addition to photographs of what little there remains, I secured the plans of the interesting graves at Yerba Buena and of the burial caves at Ventanillas. On the journey to and from Cajamarca several ruins were examined, but they offered nothing of special interest.

But all this is only a beginning. To explore Peru alone, not speaking of Ecuador and Bolivia, requires many years yet. Every place of some size requires a month or months of close investigation, and of such places there are many, many more. Distances are great and the ways of communication highly primitive. It is also difficult to obtain solid information about the sites and the way thither in the country itself. As soon as one penetrates into the interior he must select carefully the period of the year, for if he selects the season of rains, rare are the days on which he can work outdoors satisfactorily.

Along the coast, winter is excessively hot; that is, the present season. Last January, at Pisco, I was unable to obtain men for excavations owing to the scorching heat and the fetid exhalations from the graves to which nobody wanted to expose himself by opening them.

Numberless are the difficulties to be encountered and it requires first of all—*patience, patience,* and *perseverance.* But the field is probably the richest in all America.

CHAPTER XIII

The Empire Builders

THE QUECHUA[66]

THERE ARE TWO WAYS OF APPROACHING THE great civilizations that Cieza de Leon chartered in the sixteenth century and whose ruins Adolph Bandelier surveyed in the late nineteenth. We can either assess them in terms of their artistic accomplishments or in terms of the social-political structure they reared. We shall attempt the latter. This means, however, that we are describing only the last phase of Peruvian-Bolivian aboriginal history, and it also means that we are limiting ourselves to one type of society, that of the *Quechua* people, the Incas. Many other peoples, we know, formed part and parcel of the Inca civilization, and their customs and social organization often clashed with it. But in the sixteenth century, when the Spanish chroniclers made their surveys, the impress of the Inca system on all these nations was so profound and had transformed the fundamental features of these cultures so completely that little remained of the older ways of life, at least politically.

It is with the Incas then we shall deal, and here again we shall limit ourselves to them as the constructors of a new type of state, the builders of an amazing empire. We know this was a late achievement in Peruvian-Bolivian history and of fairly short duration. It was beginning to crumble visibly when the great gangster, Pizarro, arrived. To understand it, a few words on the earlier history of this area are necessary.

We can assume that there were nowhere in South America any high civilizations much before the Christian era, and we can further assume that when they did arise, their development was rapid, localized, and discontinuous; that simple tribes continued to exist not only on their margins but practically in their very midst. The Quechua had once been such a simple fishing-hunting community, and that was only one among a number. Assuredly, that was long before 1000 A.D. Just as the Quechua played havoc with the old civilizations after 1200 A.D., so other peoples who had once been fishing-hunting communities must have played havoc with them before and thus added to the clash and turmoil that is the especial earmark of the Andean civilizations, as it was of the great civilizations of Yucatan and Mexico. It stands to reason that you cannot have one civilization developing along the northern coast of Peru, another along the southern, and still another in the Bolivian highlands, all within five hundred years of each other, without upheavals, crises, and depressions. Each one of them naturally sought to expand, and each one of them, in expanding, collided with the other.

Yet the periods of peace were long enough to permit distinctive elaborations to arise. We know a good deal about the industries, arts, and economic developments and specializations of these peoples, but we naturally know very little about their social organization. It has generally been assumed that the Incas (Quechua) took over an old social organization when they took over practically everything else from the peoples they had conquered and displaced. But this is a pure assumption. There is no reason whatsoever for believing, for instance, that the clan organization, the division in two halves or moieties and matrilineal descent were not characteristic of the Inca before they began their career of conquest. Nor is there any real evidence for believing that the earlier civilizations at Chimu and Nasca possessed them. The justified reaction against the extravagant claims first made for the Incas by scholars who ascribed far too much to them has now gone to the other extreme, so that today the tendency is to credit them with bringing nothing with them from their original home near Cuzco. Yet they must have been in contact with the *Aymara* there and the Aymara did have both clans and dual organization.

However, we cannot enter into a discussion of these historical questions here and must content ourselves with what we find to be characteristic of the Inca society when first encountered. We shall begin with the description of the administration and the administrators, both in practice and theory and then proceed to a description of the older basic units.

At the head of the Inca state stood the ruler, bearing the title of the Only Inca and looked upon as divine. An impassable distance separated him from his subjects. Formally and theoretically this government was a pure despotism. Actually the Inca never possessed the arbitrary power which we are accustomed to associate with European and Asiatic despots. Being at the same time civil, religious, and military head of the state, and credited with a divine lineage, his power in theory was unlimited and all authority thought of as completely centralized in his hands. Certainly from the fifteenth century on he raised armies and often commanded them in person, imposed taxes, made laws, and appointed the judges who executed them; that is, if we take the early chroniclers literally. But even if we do not, and we must guard against doing just this, his power was great, and the power of the caste to which he belonged incalculable, especially after the fifteenth century.

The distance between the Inca and the commoners was symbolized by the special garments worn by himself and his court and by the fact that he communicated with these commoners only by means of official "state progresses."

When he visited the provinces of the empire in time of peace, he traveled in great majesty, seated in rich litters fitted with loose poles of excellent wood and covered with gold and silver work. Over the litter there rose two high arches of gold set with precious stones, and long mantles fell around all sides of the litter so as to cover it completely. If the Inca did not wish to be seen, the mantles remained down, to be raised when he got

in or came out. In order that he might see the road and have
fresh air, holes were made in the curtains. The mantles and
curtains were covered with rich ornamentation. On some were
embroidered the sun and the moon, on others great curving
serpents and what appeared to be sticks passing across them.
These were borne as insignia or arms. The litters were raised
on the shoulders of the greatest and most important lords of
the kingdom, and he who was employed most frequently on
this duty was held to be most honored and in highest favor.

Around the litter marched the king's guard with the archers
and halberdiers, and in front went five thousand slingers, while
in the rear there were lancers with their leaders. On the flanks
of the road, and on the road itself, there were faithful runners
who kept a lookout and announced the approach of the lord.
So many people came out to see him pass that the hillsides were
covered, and they all blessed their sovereign, raising a great
cry and shouting their accustomed saying: "Very great and
powerful lord, son of the Sun, thou only art Lord! All the
world in truth hears thee."

Thus did the Spanish chroniclers describe the pomp with
which he traveled.

Because of the feeling that the Inca stood so high above all
others, noblemen and commons alike, the theory was developed,
very late probably, that his official wife had to be his half
sister. But this is manifestly a secondary explanation for an old
custom, part of an official credo. This *credo* is given by Garcilasso in the following words:[67]

"Know," a kinsman once told him, "that in ancient times all this
region was covered with forests and thickets and the people lived like
brute beasts without religion nor government, nor towns, nor houses;
without cultivating the land nor covering their bodies, for they knew
how to weave neither cotton nor wool to make garments. . . . Our
father, the Sun, seeing the human race in this poor condition, had
compassion upon them and from heaven sent down to earth a son
and a daughter to instruct them, so that they might adopt them as
their god; and also to give them precepts and laws by which to live
as reasonable and civilized men, as well as to teach them to dwell in

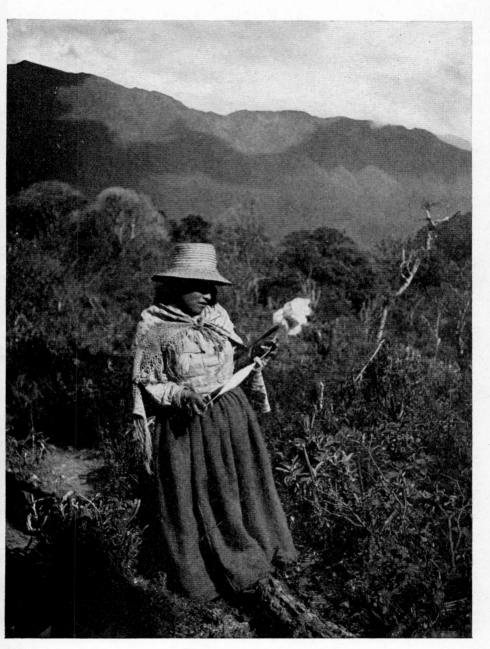

A Native Spinner from Ecuador

houses and towns, to cultivate maize and other crops, to breed flocks and to use the fruits of the earth as rational beings do, instead of existing like beasts. With these commands and attentions our father, the Sun, placed his two children in the lake of Titicaca saying to them that they might go where they pleased and that at every place that they stopped in order to eat or sleep, they were to thrust into the ground a scepter of gold which was half a yard long and two fingers in thickness. This staff he gave them as a sign and a token that in the place where, by one blow on the earth it should sink down and disappear, it was the desire of our father, the Sun they should remain and establish their court. Finally he said to them: 'When you have reduced these people to our service, you shall maintain them in habits of reason and justice by the practice of piety, clemency and meekness, assuming in all things the office of a pious father toward his beloved and tender children. For thus you will form a likeness and a reflection of me. I do good to the whole world, giving light that men may see and do their business, making them warm when they are cold, cherishing their pastures and crops, brightening their fruits and increasing their flocks, watering their land with dew and bringing fine weather and proper season. I take care to go around the earth each day that I may see what is necessary in the world and act as sustainer and benefactor. I desire that you shall imitate this example as I have sent you, my children, to the earth solely for instruction and benefit of those men who live like beasts. And from this time I constitute and name you as kings and lords over all the tribes, so that you may instruct them in rational works and government.' "

Yet, despite external appearances to the contrary, the power of the Inca was not absolute. Like most true bureaucracies, the state was governed by its officials and in virtue of the well-organized and skillfully adjusted hierarchy of its departments. What gave the sovereign his extensive influence and power was the simple fact that all the important offices in the realm, particularly all the high positions connected with the temples and their administration, were in the hands of his immediate family, over whom he naturally exercised considerable control. He did not, as some maintained, appoint them to these positions, however. These positions were the prerogatives of their class.

Though theoretically the sovereign was at the head of the

"church," his powers were always delegated to specially selected individuals. The presiding priest was generally his own brother. He in turn filled all the subordinate positions under him. Since the chief priests of all the temples had likewise to belong to the royal family, it is evident that in all ultimate matters pertaining to ritual and religion the Inca and his immediate family ruled supreme. The power of the priests, however, was greatly circumscribed and narrow in its scope. It was confined entirely to matters connected with ritual. The control of the "church," therefore, gave the royal family little political power, however important it may have been in adding to its prestige, its revenues, and the reverence in which it was held.

Inca society was thus based on a rigorous and clear-cut caste system consisting of nobles and commoners between whom marriage was prohibited. Cutting across this caste system, as we shall see later on, was the old dual organization and the clans. But before discussing them, let us first complete our description of the caste society of the Inca as it existed at the time of the Spaniards.

The nobles fell into two very distinct subdivisions: the members of the royal family, and the deposed chiefs of conquered nations with all their descendants. The extreme centralization, which was one of the astounding and marvelous features of Inca government, was due to the fortunate circumstances that all positions of importance, the command of the armies and of distant garrisons, and the control over the provinces, were bestowed upon members of the royal family, and that wherever possible they were required to live at the court.

To the nobles of the second class only minor posts were assigned. Their authority was local and confined to the districts in which they and their ancestors had been raised, a very wise arrangement, indeed, for in this way whatever local autonomy the central government permitted was in the hands of those who knew most about it and whose authority and decisions would be most acceptable to the conquered peoples. To keep their hold even on these minor officials, they were from time to time required to visit the capital.

For purposes of administration a fourfold division of the tribe was utilized that had the reputation of considerable antiquity. The whole kingdom was divided into four provinces, just as was the city of Cuzco, and four main roads radiated from the capital of the whole kingdom to the capital of each of the four provinces. Over each province ruled a governor who belonged to the immediate household of the Inca. These provinces were further subdivided into four sections, each having a population of ten thousand and over whom presided a subgovernor, also taken from the nobility. Finally there was a still more minute subdivision of the people into population units of one thousand, five hundred, one hundred, and fifty, respectively, with a graded hierarchy of officials presiding over them. Assuredly bureaucracy could go no further.

In the division of the land the same highly bureaucratic organization was evident. The whole kingdom was divided into three parts, the revenues of the first going to defray the expenses of the very costly ritual of the Sun and its enormous officialdom; those of the second to the maintenance of the royal family, i.e., the whole caste of the nobility; and those of the third being used for the people. The land assigned to the people was broken up into small allotments, the size dependent upon the needs of each individual family. Then came the famous regulations pertaining to individuals. Every Peruvian had to marry at a prescribed age, and he was at marriage provided with a dwelling and a piece of land sufficient for his own maintenance and that of his wife. As children were born to him the land allotment was increased, the amount for a son being double that for a daughter. In order to carry out such a regulation efficiently a redistribution of the soil was made every year and a tenant's possessions were increased or diminished according to the size of his family.

The land itself was of course cultivated wholly by the people, and the soil was tilled in a definitely prescribed rotation; for example, that belonging to the Sun—in other words, to the church—coming first; that belonging to the old, the sick, widows, orphans, and soldiers engaged in actual service coming second; that belonging to the individual tenant third; and that belonging to the Incas, last.

Similar regulations prevailed in all the other industries in the empire, such as the taking care of the flocks of llamas, the manufacture of cloth, the working of the mines, the execution of the great public works, etc. The care and breeding of the flocks of llamas, for instance, was attended to with the greatest minuteness. Those in charge of these flocks lived a life of considerably greater freedom than that which prevailed in the more temperate parts of the variegated Inca empire. One of the earliest Spanish chroniclers, Ondegardo, has left us an excellent description of many of the details connected with this matter.[68]

With regard to the flocks, they made many rules, some of which were so conducive to their preservation that it would be well if they were still observed. It may be said that in a great part of the kingdom the people are maintained by the flocks. They flourish in the coldest regions, and there also the Indians are settled, as in all parts of the Collao, and on the sides towards Arequipa and the coast, as well as throughout Carancas, Aullagas, Quilluas, and Collahuas. All those districts, if it were not for the flocks, might be looked upon as uninhabitable; for though they yield various crops, it is a usual thing for three out of five years to be without harvests, and there is no other kind of produce. But, by reason of the flocks, they are richer and can dress better than those who live in fertile districts. They are very healthy, and their villages are more populous than those in the warm lands, and the latter are even more frequently without their own products than those who possess flocks. The flocks are sent down with wool, and return laden with maize.

After the llamas were sheared, the wool was deposited in public magazines and then distributed to each family according to its wants. The spinning and the weaving now began. Both the quantity and quality of the fabric manufactured was determined upon at the capital, and the work was then. apportioned among the different provinces. As it was quite important to see that all the multifarious details connected with the manufacture of the different articles were entrusted to the most competent hands, special officers were appointed to superintend all operations. These officials entered the various households to see that each family employed the materials furnished for its own use in the manner that was intended, so that no one should be unprovided with the necessary apparel.

To carry out carefully supervised undertakings of this kind, wherein each individual had a prescribed place and prescribed work to perform, exact statistics of population were necessary, and these were obtained by keeping a register of all the births and deaths throughout the country. A general survey of the country was likewise made, in order to gain a correct idea of the character of the soil, its fertility, and the nature of its product. Only thus could the central government be in a position to determine the amount of requisitions so that the work could be apportioned among the respective provinces best qualified to execute it.

Ondegardo states that nothing was left to chance. The task of apportioning the labor, for instance, was assigned to the local authorities, and great care was taken that it should be done in such a manner that while the most competent hands were selected, no labor should fall disproportionately on any particular individual.

Not a detail was neglected. Every person had to work to the best of his ability at the thing he could do most efficiently. Most Peruvians of the lower class were husbandmen, but those whose work was of such a kind that they could not be expected to till the soil at the same time—miners, mechanics, and artisans, for instance—were exempted.

But if everyone had to work, no one, on the other hand, was overworked. No one was required to give more than a stipulated portion of his time to the public service. His place was then taken by another. Nor did any one have to worry about this public service interfering with his ordinary pursuits or the welfare of his family. Just as those engaged in public undertakings were maintained at the state's expense, so were their families.

To hold together such an empire, communications had to be as nearly perfect as possible, and we must not be too surprised to find good roads, good aqueducts, good bridges, and advan-

tageously placed fortresses everywhere. Nothing impressed the
Spanish conquerors more than these public roads. The most
famous and the one that must have presented the greatest difficulties in its construction was that which extended from
Quito to Cuzco and from Cuzco to Chile. We know from a
vivid description of this great highway given by the Spanish
viceroy what these roads were like. I shall summarize what he
says.

Every half league the Spaniards found small houses, well
roofed with wood and straw. Among the mountains they were
constructed against the rocks. The roads were lined with these
small houses at regular intervals. In each house two Indians were
stationed with provisions, furnished by the neighboring villages.
They were not left there permanently, but were relieved by
others from time to time. The system of government was so
efficient that it was only necessary to give the order to be certain that these men would always be at their designated stations.

Each province took charge of the posts within its boundaries,
including those which were on the coast deserts or in the region
of the snow. When it was necessary to give notice to the rulers
in Cuzco, or in any other part, of any event that had taken
place or which was connected with their service, the men at
the posts set out from Quito or Tomebamba, or from Chile or
Caranqui, or from whatever other part of the empire, whether
along the coast or in the mountains. They ran with great speed,
without stopping, each one covering over a half a league, for
the Indians who were stationed at the posts were chosen from
among the most active and swiftest of all their countrymen.
When one approached the next post he would call out to the
men who were in it and say: "Start at once and go to the next
post with the news that such and such has happened." And
thus news was relayed to the Inca or the governor of the
province. When the other runner heard what was shouted at
him, he started with the utmost speed, while the runner who
arrived went into the house to rest, and to eat and drink of what
was always kept in store there.

So well was this running performed that in a short time

people at distances of 300, 500, and even 800 leagues knew what had passed or what was needed or required.

One of these roads passed over the grand plateau, and the other along the lowlands on the borders of the ocean. The former, from the character of the country, was much the more difficult achievement. It was conducted over pathless sierras buried in snow; galleries had to be cut for leagues through the living rock; rivers to be crossed by means of bridges that swung suspended in the air; precipices to be scaled by stairways hewn out of the native bed; ravines of portentous depth to be filled up with solid masonry; in short, all the difficulties that beset a wild and mountainous region and which might appall the most courageous engineer of modern times were encountered and successfully overcome. The length of the road, of which only scattered fragments remain, is variously estimated from fifteen hundred to two thousand miles, and stone pillars, in the manner of European milestones, were erected at stated intervals of somewhat more than a league, all along the route. Its breadth scarcely exceeded twenty feet. It was built of heavy flags of freestone, and in some parts, at least, covered with a bituminous cement, which time has made harder than the stone itself.

The other great road lay through the level country between the Andes and the ocean. It was constructed in a different manner, as demanded by the nature of the ground, which was for the most part low, and in large part sandy. The causeway was raised on a high embankment of earth, and defended on either side by a parapet or wall of clay; and trees and odoriferous shrubs were planted along the margin in order to regale the sense of the traveler with their perfumes, and refresh him by their shades. In the strips of sandy waste which occasionally intervened, where the light and volatile soil was incapable of sustaining a road, huge piles were driven into the ground, to indicate the route to the traveler.

All along these highways, inns, or *tambos*, as they were called, were erected, at a distance of ten or twelve miles from each other, for the accommodation, more particularly, of the Inca and his suite, and for those who journeyed on the public business.

There were, in fact, few other travelers in Peru. Some of these buildings were on an extensive scale, consisting of a fortress, barracks, and other military works, surrounded by a parapet of stone, and covering a large tract of ground. These were evidently destined for the accommodation of the imperial armies when on their march across the country. The care of the great roads was committed to the districts through which they passed, and a large number of hands was constantly employed to keep them in repair. This was the more easily done in a country where the mode of traveling was altogether on foot.

The suspension bridges were often extraordinarily audacious. They were made of the tough fibers of the maguey or of osier. The osiers were then woven into cables of the thickness of a man's body and stretched across the water, being conducted through rings or holes cut in buttresses of stone raised on the opposite banks of the river and there bound securely to heavy pieces of timber. A number of these enormous cables bound together formed a bridge which, covered with planks, well secured and defended by a railing of osier, afforded a safe passage for a traveler.

We have so far discussed the organization of the empire and the methods used in administrating it. To make the picture complete it is now necessary to describe the manner in which, after the reduction of an enemy, its country was incorporated into the empire of the conqueror. The order of the steps taken as given by the Spanish chroniclers is probably just the reverse of what actually took place, but we will adhere to it here. The first step was a religious one. The worship of the sun was introduced, and temples which would take care of the numerous priesthood were erected. It was the duty of the priests to expound the new faith to the conquered people. The second step was also a religious one. The images of the gods of the conquered were removed to Cuzco and placed in temples where they could be worshiped by everybody as inferior deities. Then the census of the people and an economic survey of the country was taken. The land was divided according to certain principles well recognized throughout the whole kingdom. Whatever changes were introduced were always of such a nature that the estates remained in the hands of their former proprietors. On the whole the ancient customs and laws of the conquered people were left intact.

In the case of the common people of a conquered country, a far more obnoxious system of assimilation was adopted, particularly where there was the least suspicion of disaffection. Thousands would be transported to some distant quarter of the kingdom, where they were complete strangers and where mutual jealousies and hatreds would effectually check mutiny or rebellion. These conquered colonists played a great role in the Inca society. There were three classes of them. The first was employed in agriculture and industry and had more particularly to take care of the flocks belonging to the Inca and the Sun, as agriculturists, as cloth spinners, as silversmiths, sculptors, idol makers, quarrymen, and laborers. The second class was used in the various garrisons scattered throughout the kingdom. The third class were the colonists, and due care was taken to select them properly and not to impose upon them unnecessary burdens. They were always settled in valleys that seemed fertile and which had previously been uninhabited. The rulers were careful that the individual colonists selected from among the conquered population were always settled in climates similar to their own. The new land would be divided among these new settlers, and flocks and provisions given them until such time as they would be in a position to reap their own harvests. Finally, to make their lot as light as possible, no tributes were exacted of them for a stated number of years.

As a last measure, in order to take no chances that their plans for assimilation should go astray, the Incas removed all the deposed rulers and their relatives to Cuzco, where they were compelled to learn the language of the capital and the customs of the new lords in addition to basking in the sunshine of the splendors and privileges of the royal court itself. Indeed, the official language was systematically imposed upon the conquered people, and with this object in view all towns and villages in the conquered country were provided with teachers.

Arranged in their nine ranks, the hierarchy looked as follows:[69]

1. *Sapa Inca.* The Inca.
2. *Apu-cuna.* Four officials, each of whom was in charge of one of the four quarters.
3. *Tucuiricuc-cuna* (they-who-see-all). Officials having jurisdiction over forty thousand householders, called *guaman.*
4. *Hunu-camayu-cuna.* Officials in charge of ten thousand households.
5. *Huaranca-camayu-cuna.* Officials in charge of one thousand households.
6. *Pichca-pa chaca-camayu-cuna.* Officials in charge of five hundred households.
7. *Pachaca-camayu-cuna.* Officials in charge of one hundred households.
8. *Pichca-chunca-camayu-cuna.* Officials in charge of fifty households.
9. *Chunca-camayu-cuna.* Officials in charge of ten households.

To this it might be well to add the very detailed classification of individuals according to age and their economic value to the state:

1. *Mosoc-caparic.* Babe newly born and still in arms.
2. *Saya-huamrac.* Child able to stand, about one year old.
3. *Macta-puric.* Child between one and six.
4. *Ttanta-raquizic.* Bread-receiver. Child, six to eight.
5. *Pucllac-huamrac.* Boy playing about. Child, eight to sixteen.
6. *Cuca-pallac.* Coca-picker. Does light manual labor. Man, sixteen to twenty.
7. *Ima-huayna.* Almost a youth. Aids elders. Man, twenty to twenty-five.
8. *Puric.* Able bodied man; head of a household; payer of tribute. Man, twenty-five to fifty.
9. *Chaupi-rucu.* Half-old. Does only light work. Man, fifty to sixty.
10. *Puñuc-rucu.* Old-man-sleeping. Man, sixty and upwards.

Bearing this bureaucratic superstructure clearly in mind, let us now turn to what all scholars seem now to be agreed upon was the old basis of Inca social structure, the clan and the dual organization.

Although not frequently mentioned by the early chroniclers, and then misunderstood because it did not stand out as clearly as did the clans, the importance of the dual organization must not be underestimated. Garcilasso mentions it in his famous *Commentaries*. According to his manifestly mythical-historical account, the first Inca, when he founded Cuzco, divided it into two parts, *Hanan Cuzco*—that is, Upper Cuzco—and *Hurin Cuzco*—that is, Lower Cuzco—the followers of the "king" settling in the first and those of the "queen" in the second.

We have a much more authentic account in an old source, published in 1910, to the following effect:

In every district there are two divisions, one of which is known as *anansaya* and the other as *urinsaya*. Each of these divisions has a head chief who gives orders to the subchiefs of his own division but who has no authority over those of the other division, except that the head chief of anansaya is the real head chief for the whole province and is obeyed by the head chief of urinsaya, and holds a higher place than the other. Those of the anansaya division are seated on the right side in ceremonials and those of urinsaya on the left hand, in lower seats, which are called *duos*. Each head chief of a division is head of eight ayllus, and each ayllu has its head, all being seated in proper order, those of the urinsaya on the left hand behind their head chief, and those of *anansaya* on the right.

Whatever functions these moieties may once have had, at the time of the conquest, they were purely ceremonial. That they were once exogamous marriage groups is, however, more than likely.

Our evidence for the existence of the clan or ayllu is quite different. It is both clear and extensive. Bandelier, in his *Islands of Titicaca and Koati* quotes an ordinance which proves this beyond question and makes it more than likely that descent was originally in the female line. All the reorganizations of the later Incas did not seriously interfere with the clan's old and primary significance and functions. It remained what it had always been, an exogamus kin-group with a chief enjoying considerable powers on all those occasions where the group was endangered, particularly in war. The members of a clan regarded themselves as descended from a common animal ancestor—condor, puma, snake, etc.—or as connected together and mystically bound in some fashion with natural phenomena—a mountain, a river, the sun, the moon, etc. The typical village consisted, as a rule, roughly of one hundred houses, and was, theoretically, inhabited only by members of the same clan, each house containing one family. Near each house were grouped the few belongings the family as such was allowed to have—a garden plot, a small stable, and a storehouse. Adjacent to the ordinary village there was almost always to be found a fortified place of refuge.

It is with some such type of organization, somewhat simpler probably, that the Inca started. Let us attempt to reconstruct the various stages by which they transformed it into the great theocratic-socialist state and empire that we know.

In what exactly did their strength lie? They must have possessed some marked advantage over their highly cultured adversaries to have, within three hundred years, conquered all of modern Peru and Bolivia and part of Chile and to have brought considerable sections of Ecuador and portions of northwestern Argentine under their control. We will not go far wrong in assuming that this superiority lay in two facts: an efficient military "machine," and a compact and unified clan organization. They had, in short, unity and cohesiveness where, we know, their adversaries, the heirs to the great Tiahuanaco, the Chimu and the Nasca civilizations, had disunity and anarchy or, at least, extreme sectionalism. When they came to grips with a unified and centralized group like the *Chancas* to the west of them, the struggle was difficult and prolonged, as it also was in northern Chile.

After they made their first comparatively easy conquests of the region around Lake Titicaca, the old simple clan and dual organization must have been somewhat inadequate for handling the new problems. Changes must have been made then. But the real transformation apparently did not take place until the Incas had defeated and completely subdued the indomitable Chancas toward the middle of the fourteenth century under the reign of their greatest ruler, Viracocha. By that time a number of things had happened. They must have absorbed not only the artistic, architectural, technical, and agricultural-pastoral features of the people they had conquered but also certain of the social-political traits they possessed, such as the division into hereditary classes. That, of course, was utterly foreign to a clan organization. Of the different ways of solving so difficult and intricate a problem as that of adjusting a graded society to the inherently egalitarian society implied by the clan, the Incas attempted the rather unusual one of adding the hereditary classes as a kind of superstructure around the clan. Upon the conquered peoples it was easy enough to impose such a system, because they had no status except by sufferance. But how could such a system, which so flagrantly contradicted the whole essence of the clan structure, be imposed successfully upon the Inca peoples themselves? The answer must be only by force if at all. The attempt certainly was made. The bureau-cratic-socialist state of the Inca is the best proof of it.

To an amazing extent the attempt was successful. Yet two factors militated against its effectiveness—the persistence of the clan organization and its implications and the absence of a gov-ernmental machinery necessary for its proper enforcement. On paper it looked perfect, as if indeed a real compromise had been attained between the basic rights "guaranteed" by a normal func-tioning clan and the demands of the new ruling class. The famous laws governing labor and tribute that Fray Blas Valera has preserved for us provide, among other things, that the fol-lowing individuals be exempted from making any contribution of merchandise or of work: all males under twenty-five years of age, all men over fifty, all women, all sick persons, all persons incapable (the blind, the lame, or the maimed).

Five other egalitarian laws are mentioned:[70]

1. Tribute was to consist solely of labor, time, or skill as a work-man or artisan, or as a soldier. All men were equal in this respect, he being held to be rich who had children to aid him in making up his

appointed amount of tribute, and he who had none being considered to be poor.

2. Except for work as a husbandman or as a soldier, for which any *puric* might be called upon, no man was compelled to work at any craft save his own.

3. If tribute took the form of merchandise produced by the payer's labor, only the produce of his own region could be demanded of him, it being held to be unjust to demand from him fruits that his own land did not yield.

4. Every craftsman who labored in the service of the Inca or of his *curaca* must be provided with all the raw materials for his labor, so that his contribution consisted only of his time, work, or dexterity. His employment in this way was not to be more than two or three months in the year.

5. A craftsman was to be supplied with food, clothes, and medicine at need while he was working, and if his wife and children were aiding him, they were to be supplied with those things also. In this sort of work, not time but a special stint of accomplishment was required of the tribute payer, so that if he had help from his family, he could finish his task sooner than by himself, and could not be called upon again that year.

Perhaps it might be well, however, to give likewise those "laws" mentioned by Blas Valera that were concerned entirely with the collection of revenues with which to enrich the Inca ruling class. They were the following:[71]

The law on the subject of collecting the tribute was [the following]. At a certain time the collectors and accountants assembled in the chief village of each province with the knot-record keepers, and by means of the quipus and also of little pebbles, the accounts and reckonings were cast up with perfect accuracy in the presence of the official in charge. These officials saw by the knots the amount of labor that the Indians had performed, the crafts they had worked at, the roads they had traveled over by order of their superiors, and other tasks on which they had been employed. All this was deducted from the tribute that was due. Then they showed the collectors and the governor each thing by itself that was stored in the royal depots, such as the provisions, pepper, clothes, shoes, arms, and all other things that the Indians gave as tribute, down to the gold, silver, precious stones, and copper belonging to the king and the Sun, each item being recorded separately. They also reported what was in store in the depots of each village. The law ordained that the Inca governor of the province should have a duplicate of the accounts in his own custody, to check any error on the part either of the collectors or of the payers of tribute.

The surplus of the tribute, after the royal wants had been satisfied, were placed on deposit and drawn upon for the good of the people as required. Certain specially prized goods such as gold, silver, copper, precious stones, feathers, paints, and dyestuffs were restricted to the use of the imperial caste and to such favored curacas as might be honored with permission to use them.

In special cases tribute was paid in the form of work upon the roads, upon the temples, palaces, aqueducts, bridges, storehouses, or other public works. In other cases the tribute payers were called upon to serve as post runners or as litter bearers or as miners.

As is so often the case with a conquering caste, an ethical code was promulgated, couched in a combination of idealistic phraseology and sententious proverbs disguised to hide the fact that one was dealing with commands that had to be scrupulously obeyed. Such, for instance, are the apothegms ascribed to the famous Inca Pacha-cutec, to whom the Inca empire owed so much of its power. Garcilasso has recorded them:[72]

When subjects, captains, and curacas cordially obey the king, then the kingdom enjoys perfect peace and quiet.

Envy is a worm that gnaws and consumes the entrails of the envious.

He that envies another, injures himself.

He that kills another without authority or just cause condemns himself to death.

It is very just that he who is a thief should be put to death.

Adulterers, who destroy the peace and happiness of others, ought to be declared thieves, and condemned to death without mercy.

The noble and generous man is known by the patience he shows in adversity.

Judges who secretly receive gifts from suitors ought to be looked upon as thieves and punished with death as such.

The physician herbalist who is ignorant of the virtues of herbs or who, knowing the uses of some, has not attained to a knowledge of all, understands little or nothing. He ought to work until he knows all, as well the useful as the injurious plants, in order to deserve the name to which he pretends.

He who attempts to count the stars, not even knowing how to count the marks and knots of the quipus, ought to be held in derision.

Drunkenness, anger, and madness go together; but the first two are voluntary and to be removed, whereas the last is perpetual.

It would be quite ridiculous to imagine that these provisions were dictated by the ruling class out of the goodness of their hearts or because of some God-given sense of justice which it possessed. They were compromises with the egalitarian demands of the clan. They had to be fitted into one bureaucratic super-structure as best they could.

Thus we see that the Inca state structure was not, as so many have described it, the perfect plan of a perfect lawgiver to distribute justice equally, but an enforced compromise between two contradictory social-political systems. The purpose was not to create a "socialist" state but to secure the complete ascendancy of what had, in the course of time, become a military caste. All the provisions of that state had but one purpose: to serve that caste, keep it inviolable, and strengthen its power. Because of the basic clan structure of Inca society, its power over the Inca people proper was always limited. Its power was complete, however, over those tribes the Inca had subdued, and as their number became increasingly larger and larger, the Inca commoners were lost in it and were practically on the point of becoming merged with these conquered people when the Spanish Conquest intervened.

Almost as significant and as interesting as the Inca state was the wealth it accumulated. All of this belonged to the ruling class and was used exclusively for its benefit and pleasure and for the enhancement of its power. And we cannot more fittingly close this chapter than by giving some idea of its nature and extent.

Wealth has always been primarily a way of symbolizing position, of indicating the social distance separating one group from another. For that reason its ostentatious display has generally been a trait of those who have but recently acquired prestige and power. This is beautifully illustrated by the uses to which wealth was put among the Inca. If the official theory of the priestly adulators gave to gold and silver a mystical interpretation and identified the two precious metals with the tears and sweat of the primary Gods, the Sun and the Moon, that is but the means protected sycophants have always adopted to gloss over the weaknesses of their masters by giving them a religious significance. But the religious significance here was secondary. The possession of gold and silver meant prestige, was the insignia of office, the mark of social superiority and the symbol of power.

Gold and silver were regarded as belonging to the supreme ruler by right of birth. When his subjects were doing nothing else they were supposed to be collecting gold and silver and precious stones to be brought to the divine ruler as presents, on the innumerable occasions when officials paid their prescribed homage to him. That a considerable part of these metals went to the decorations of the temples and shrines we know. But since the administration of these shrines was exclusively in the hands of the rulers' relatives, it was still flowing into his hands and that of his class.

How much did a ruler collect in one year? Estimates differ, but Cieza de Leon figured they were approximately 15,000 arrobas of gold and 50,000 arrobas of silver; that is, about 6,000,000 and 20,500,000 ounces respectively. A natural query arises now: what was done with it? The answer will reveal how definitely it was regarded as a symbol of power and prestige.

So fixated were these parvenu rulers on the question of gold and silver that their claim to it extended beyond their death. When a ruler died, for instance, his bedroom, with all its precious possessions and furnishings, was permanently sealed. A portrait statue of gold was made and deposited in the great Sun Temple in Cuzco. His successor, the new ruler, then repeats the same procedure. He must erect a new palace and furnish it completely with precious furnishings. In short, the prestige a particular accumulation of wealth brings with it is not inherited. Every leader-ruler must accumulate his own treasure. This it is important to remember, for this accumulation then has all the appearance of being part of the investiture of power. The nonchalance with which it is treated thus takes on the form of a ritualistically determined and sanctioned conspicuous waste. That this conspicuous waste was not always ceremonial and had self-imposed material compensations goes without saying. The chroniclers reported that in the palace of the Inca Huayna Capac there were stored, to be used for the subsequent decoration of his palace, three chambers with gold furnishings, five with silver and 100,000 ingots of gold, each weighing five pounds.[73]

But it was not only the precious nature of the wealth that was important. Just as significant was its extent. Thus the Inca had at least 200 palaces. According to Cieza de Leon these were palaces and temples of the Sun every ten or twenty leagues, and lodges and depots at the disposal of the ruler every three or four leagues, along the great roads. The fact that they were new conquerors, who had to keep themselves entrenched, and were heads of a "jealous" nobility of their own where insubordination was quite frequent, explains this overdevelopment of dwellings only in part. More important was its display value.

These palaces were at times very large, with rooms measuring from 60 to 200 paces. One hall was credited with being able to hold 4,000 individuals. Garcilasso has devoted a whole chapter to these palaces in his *Commentaries*. Instead of tapestry, he tells us, the walls were covered with gold and silver and studded with jewels as well as hung with the figures of birds and other animals wrought in precious metals. There were even silver imitations of lichens. The baths were made of gold and silver supplied with running water from gold and silver spigots.

Lavishness was expressed in every conceivable manner. No object with which the ruler came in contact was made of any but precious material. In the magnificent gardens attached to the principal palaces were to be found artificial plants, made of gold and silver. These, according to Garcilasso, often represented the plants "with their leaves, flowers, and fruit; some just beginning to sprout, others half grown, others having reached maturity. They made fields of maize, with their leaves, *mazorcal*, canes, roots, and flowers, all exactly imitated. The beard of the *mazorca* was gold, and all the rest of silver, the parts being soldered together. They did the same thing with other plants, making the flowers, or any other part that became yellow, of gold, and the rest of silver."

Much of this precious wealth went into the symbols connected with the religious worship specifically connected with the Inca as a descendant of the Sun, as the incorporation of the Sun and as the mythical founder of the clan. There were the statues of the human founder of the clan, the representations of the mythical founder of the clan, and the mummies of the deceased Incas. The images of the personal founders of the clan had long been identified with the Incas themselves, and a fiction had grown up according to which each Inca founded a separate lineage. This was perpetuated and symbolized by the figures called *huauqui*. To all intents and purposes they were personal household gods and deified ancestors. These figures were often life-size. The huauqui of the Inca Manco Capac was in the form of a hawk and probably had two containers in it, each large enough, as it is said, to hold a cow cut in pieces.

Finally there was the "throne" itself. This was a stool of gold measuring a foot in height, the upper surface concave. It stood on a great board covered with gold that could easily be converted into a litter by attaching long poles to it. Naturally these poles were made of gold and silver.

The crowning symbol of the Inca's power were the temples to the Sun. The most magnificent of these was the one in Cuzco called the *Coricancha*, the Court of Gold. It consisted of six major buildings, arranged to form a court and linked together by an encircling wall. They were respectively: the Sanctuary of the Sun, the Chapel of the Moon, the Chapel of the Stars, the Chapel of the Lightning, the Chapel of the Rainbow, and the Sacristy. The chief sanctuary was that to the Sun, and it stood on a rounded apse. The altar itself was at the east end. "The roof was very lofty and of wood," says Garcilasso. "All four walls of the temple were covered, from roof to floor, with plates and slabs of gold. In the side where we should look for the high altar, they placed the figure of the Sun, made of a plate of gold of a thickness double that of the other plates which covered the walls. . . . On either side of the image of the Sun were the bodies of the dead kings, arranged according to priority as Children of the Sun, and embalmed so as to appear as if they were alive. They were seated on chairs of gold, placed upon the golden slabs on which they had been used to sit."

Naturally Pizarro and his fellow gangsters and looters melted down as rapidly as possible all the treasures of the Coricancha they could get their hands upon, but we have some incomplete records of what the nature of the great loot was. A summary of the inventory of the articles sent to Charles V contained the following:[74]

Thirty-four jars of gold, of varying standards and weights; the largest one weighed 58 pounds and 14 ounces; the smallest, 23 pounds and 8 ounces. Three of them were provided with covers also of gold.

Two bags, small, as they weighed between them two pounds and ten ounces.

A stalk of maize, of gold, with three leaves and two ears.

Two kettle drums (*atabales*) or drums (*tambores*) of 4 pounds, 4 ounces.

A panel of gold and silver, which enclosed the figures of an Indian man and woman, both of medium size.

Two platters which weighed 17 pounds, 5 ounces.

A sack, of 33 pounds and 15 ounces.

An idol with the figure of a man, of 11 pounds, 11 ounces.

A vase like a pitcher of 27 pounds weight.

Of silver objects, 100 jars were enumerated, the largest weighing 161 pounds and 12 ounces; and the smallest of 45 pounds and 4 ounces.

Another account of the booty connected with the ransom for Atahualpa speaks of five hundred old plates weighed four or five pounds apiece; other larger ones weighed ten or twelve pounds and with plates of this sort the walls of that temple were covered. They also brought a seat of very fine gold, worked into the form of a footstool, which weighed eighteen thousand pesos. Likewise they brought a fountain all of gold and very subtly worked, which was very fair to see as much for the skill of the work as for the shape which it had been given; and there were many other pieces such as vases, jars and plates which they also brought.

All that this human backwash of the great *Siglo d'Oro* could see here in Peru was plunder, and all that their descendants until the nineteenth century saw here was plunder, sanctified and rationalized. In this, of course, they were but continuing the policy of the Inca rulers, for, stripped of the restraining influence of the clan, their policy likewise had been terror and plunder.

It is somewhat refreshing to know that even within that ruling caste one man, one Inca, could arise who protested, who was willing to permanently bury the dead Incas. "He was going to take away from them all that they possessed; there were to be no more dead but only living." So spoke the Inca Huascar, and he was accordingly assassinated by the representative of these dead, Atahualpa, even although at that time he, Atahualpa, was a prisoner in the hands of another assassin, Pizarro.

Had Huascar's ideal been triumphant there might have been a new significance to the famous hymn to Uiracocha that has come down to us:

O Uiracocha! lord of the universe . . .
Might I behold thee,
Might I know thee,
Might I consider thee,
Might I understand thee!
O look down upon me,
For thou knowest me.
The Sun—the Moon,
The day—the night—
Spring—winter,
Are not ordained in vain
By thee
O Uiracocha!

They all arrive
At their destined ends,
Withersoever thou pleasest . . .
O hear me!
O choose me!
Let it not be
That I should tire,
That I should die.

The descendants of the Incas and of those they subjected have not been allowed either to tire or to die. The living death to which the Spaniards consigned them and to which, unfortunately, the democracies that were inaugurated after 1821 continued to consign them until very recently has, it is true, left its indelible mark. And for the Indian resurgence that is now clearly beginning, it might be well to point out that this must represent the continuation, not of the superstructure of the Inca ruling class and its European continuators, but of the principles inherent in the clan.

CHAPTER XIV

What Remains of the Ancient Glory
THE MODERN AYMARA[75]

OF FEW MATURE AND COMPLEX CIVILIZATIONS
has time, corruption, and exploitation taken so devastating a toll
as of that of the Aymara and Quechua. The ruins are still there,
the present people are overwhelmingly Indian in blood, the languages are still spoken with considerable purity, and custom
upon custom has persisted in one guise or another. Yet everything connected with the Indian was until recently simply part
of the Indian problem, to be treated with the proper rhetoric,
with a false romantic nostalgia, and to be then promptly discarded as something between an eternal nuisance and blessing.

Today this fortunately has changed. It is realized that the
ancient civilizations, Incaic and pre-Incaic, may have passed forever, but it is felt utterly erroneous to treat the present Indian-
speaking or Indian-feeling peoples as though they were simply
the debased descendants of the Incas. To a thinker like J. Uriel
Garcia, the Incaic is simply one period in the history of the
Peruvians and Bolivians just as was the pre-Incaic and the Spanish
colonial, but no more. "Do you wish to know wherein the difference between Incaic and Indian lies?" asks Señor Garcia. "Well,
it is the same difference that exists between what is static and
what is dynamic, what has attained its final expression and what
is unfolding itself for expression in a new future. Inca civiliza-

277

tion has perished for all times, but the Indian still exists and will exist as long as the Andes proudly lift their heads into the sky and as long as the Americans retain their creative energies and hold steadfast to their true feelings and ideals."[76]

Most of us north of the Rio Grande know lamentably little of this new Indian. For us he represents simply an impoverished and illiterate peon, carrying on a furtive existence in the midst of the cultural detritus of ancient Peru. We think of him as the representative of a people with no incentive to develop a new life and with so little feeling for continuity that he is not even aware that many of these ancient ways still persist.

Belonging to this class of Americans who had little appreciation for this new Indian but who knew an enormous amount about him was that strange and fascinating pioneer, the famous archaeologist, historian, and ethnologist, Adolph F. Bandelier. To this Swiss-American the archaeology of the two American continents owes more than it has ever properly acknowledged. He first came to South America in 1892 and stayed there till 1898, studying the ruins of the coast and highlands of the ancient country of the Aymara and Quechua and amassing facts about the customs and beliefs of their descendants. Particularly was he attracted to Lake Titicaca, lying 12,500 feet above the level of the sea. In the little village of Copavacana, on the Bolivian shore overlooking the large island of Titicaca, Bandelier was fortunate enough to obtain a detailed record of the life of a modern Aymara. It is this record that I shall recapitulate.

I will follow the life of an individual, from birth to death, as Bandelier has done in his manuscript. Let us begin, therefore, with the customs connected with childbirth.

When a woman feels the approach of the labor pangs, she is taken to a room and shut in it, together with a woman officiating as midwife and a helpmate, a near male relative of the woman. The midwife is always a medicine woman and belongs to the so-called *kolliri*, a division of doctors. She bears a particular title, *usuiri*, *usu* meaning disease.

The patient is kept in constant motion. Wherever possible, she is made to get on chairs or tables, jump down from them or

Wooden Cups from Cuzco

from any other elevated places in the room, anything to keep her moving. Delivery takes place in a sitting posture. The usuiri receives the baby and hands it quickly to her assistant. It must under no conditions be allowed to touch the floor, for if it does so it will forever remain unhappy. The child is then bathed, carefully bundled up, and given to the mother. While this is being done, the usuiri pretends to sew up the mouth corners of the child with a needle, for it is believed that this will keep the mouth of an individual permanently small. Only then are visitors admitted and presented with wine. The mother is not allowed to partake of any food or drink.

In some very special cases the usuiri is a man. But whether man or woman, this person is always a distant relative of one of the most important type of medicine men, called *chamakani*. It is the latter who examines the helpmate to determine his fitness and competence. When the moment of actual delivery has arrived, the usuiri, if a man, strokes the patient's back gently, three times, with the back of a knife, from the neck down. To hasten a difficult delivery the patient is shaken, and if this does not produce the desired effect, she is given a beverage made of the plumes of the ostrich mixed with sweet oil and sealing wax. If all else fails, she is given sliced soap and lemon juice.

If the birth takes place at night the usuiri goes outside to look at the stars; if in the daytime, she waits till night has set in and stars are at their brightest. From the appearance of the sky the future of the child is prognosticated, a bright red star overhead being regarded as the most favorable omen. For this the child is sometimes also taken out into the open. If a boy, the child at once receives the name of some famous medicine man or wealthy Indian; if a girl, it is named after a wealthy woman or some noted female medicine woman. The placenta, or afterbirth, is washed in water, changed a number of times, then tied and sewed up. The husband thereupon buries it in a corner of the room together with the water, coca, and a great variety of other substances. Only the husband, the usuiri, her assistant, and the mother are allowed to witness this operation.

Three days after delivery the remainder of the umbilical cord is cut and a piece given to the mother for keeping. It is only after all this is over that the formal baptism in church takes place. Until baptism the child is fed honey mixed with the urine of a small boy. The mother is not allowed to nurse it because it is not a Christian in their eyes until properly baptized. The baptismal rites used are the regular ones, and the names then given are those connected with the saint's day on which the child is born. There are thus two kinds of ceremonies, a private "pagan" one at the house and a public, Christian, one in church.

For eight days after delivery the mother remains abed and is never left alone. Day and night someone must attend her. A number of customs are observed during this seclusion that probably hark back to Incaïc times, if not earlier. Although people, for instance, may enter her room, nobody is permitted to stand in the door, lest the child get a cloud in the eye. In the daytime the mother is allowed no sleep. When this trying period is over, the woman rises, washes herself for the first time with *romero* in tepid water. She puts on a new dress, and her feet are wrapped up firmly above the toes to prevent disease.

In case of miscarriage, whether accidental or artificial, nobody is allowed to assist. To produce abortion, the Indians use a plant called *lehuenka*. The fetus is not buried but thrown into a stream, and the clothes must remain outdoors for one night. The lehuenka is also taken to prevent conception. Abortion, as well as miscarriage, is called *limbo*.

From the date of its birth on the child has to submit to a long series of ceremonials. Since the remote past, so Bandelier insists, it can be confidently stated that only the materials used have changed. Until the child is three or four years old it carries on its back, in a little bundle, the following articles: a small knife, camphor to be used against witchcraft, and sulphur and garlic to protect it against ill winds. The knife is always placed under the pillow during sleep. Until after its third year no child is left alone at night.

A number of customs and beliefs cluster around children. If a pregnant woman takes up a child, this is believed to cause its nose to be stopped up. Should this happen, the woman who caused the illness must cure it by dragging the child across her body on the bed. Children are not permitted to weep overnight, lest the evil spirit called *lari-lari* come and hurt them. During the first year no child is taken out into the field, for it would then fall sick, shrivel up, and die. If a baby has been set on the ground, it is compelled to swallow a mouthful of the soil, the belief being that the earth at that place was hungry and caused the illness. To make amends, coca, alcohol, chica, wine, and cigarettes are placed on the spot as offerings. No child, until it has reached its third or fourth year, is permitted to look at anything dead, whether a human being or an animal. If, however, this occurs, the child is wrapped in leaves of the nunumaya shrub that have been twice dried in the sun.

When a child has reached its third or fourth year, an important ceremony takes place. Up to that age no water has been allowed to touch its head, except, of course, the holy water at baptism, and even that must be rinsed off. The ceremony is celebrated regardless of the season, but always during a waxing moon, and the child's hair is then cut off for the first time. For this purpose the mother washes its head superficially and ties the hair in as many braids as possible, each braid being tied with a bright colored ribbon or tape. After this a godfather, if it is a boy, a godmother if a girl, are chosen, and the first braid is cut off. The mother has a tray or plate ready which she presents to the godparents, who place on it a present in money, sometimes as much as the equivalent of ten dollars. As many persons as possible are invited, and each one cuts off a braid, paying for this privilege in accordance with their means. This continues until every braid has been cut off. The money is kept by the mother for the child's benefit. Out of the hair a wig is made to be placed on the head of the particular saint's image in the possession of the family. The ceremony is always an occasion of great rejoicing and ends with a drinking bout of several days' duration. When several children have their hair cut at the same time, the hair is sometimes distributed among such relatives as have images of saints in their houses.

It is believed that if a child takes a particular fancy to anyone and that person moves away, it falls sick. The remedy employed to sever this attachment is peculiar, to say the least. The clothes of the favored person are washed, and the child has to imbibe the dirty water.

About the age of five years, children, male as well as female, are sent out to herd either sheep or llamas. The little girl carries on her back the bundle which every woman carries. In her case it is, of course, very light, and symbolical rather than real. If after a certain length of time the children show initiative and are trustworthy, they are presented with a pair of sheep or llamas, male and female, so that when of age they will be in possession of a little flock of their own. Herders change annually on the first of the year. The new herder comes in his best clothes and takes charge of the flock in presence of the owner, the previous incumbent, and the family. All congratulate him, and he marches off with his wards.

The marriage customs present a strange mixture of the old and the new, with the old clearly predominating. However, they vary somewhat from place to place. Some will be obsolete in one town and still function vigorously in another. Thus the custom of the bridegroom and bride jumping across a fire, while, for instance, still observed on the Puna and other places, has been abandoned by the Indians of the capital. It is certain, however, that a couple contemplating marriage live together for some time, usually a year, previous to the marriage ceremony. Such trial brides, as long as the religious marriage has not been performed, are called *prestadas*, that is, "borrowed."

A week before the church marriage the bridegroom goes at night to the house of the girl, accompanied by his people and with the customary music of flutes and drums. Singing and dancing, he then conducts her through various byways and paths lit up by lanterns as they pass. This nuptial dance is called *amay-katati*. The bride receives presents of bread, brown sugar, wine, alcohol, and the like. At the end, there is, of course, the customary carousal.

The church ceremony is without any special interest. Although the trial year for the pair is considered a perfectly legitimate procedure and respected as a time-hallowed custom, the church ceremony is always insisted upon as essential. If, after the expiration of the year, the parties continue to cohabit without ritual union, they are looked upon as immoral. Children born from such a union are called *hinchu-kanu* (dirty ears), and the couple itself, *kuchi-kencha*. When such a couple occupies the same house as a regularly married one, the hinchu-kanu, or illegitimate children, are not allowed to associate with the legitimate ones, for it is believed that such association would bring misfortune upon the latter.

Thus the Aymara have two types of marriage rites, just as they have two kinds of ceremonies for naming children, a primitive and a Christian, the former always preceding the latter and looked upon by the Indian as equally if, indeed, not more essential.

Burial customs are of the most varied kind, some European, some Indian in origin, and many of mixed origin. For instance, at La Paz it occasionally happens that an Indian is buried in a coat resembling the frock of a monk. A coffin is seldom used. The corpse is wrapped in a blanket, taken to the cemetery, placed on the ground, and covered with stones. Mourners as well as carriers sit upon it and eat and drink. After this the corpse is buried. A child is always interred with a knife inside of its shroud to protect it from evil spirits.

After the burial there is considerable drinking, and indeed every occasion and pretext is used by relatives and friends for repairing to the grave to offer their libations to the dead. Prayers are sometimes offered in the chapel of the cemetery, but in most cases exclusively at the grave. Burial rites have perhaps changed more fundamentally than the others mentioned before, because in the seventeenth century the church was very active in suppressing the old methods of interment and the beliefs clustering around them.

From this account of the life cycle let us now turn to the most important of all the professions that has survived from pre-Spanish days, that of the medicine man.

Throughout Bolivia the medicine men are found subdivided

into distinct groups, each group limited, on the whole, to specific types of curing and healing. There is first the class called kolliri, to whom curing and healing are incidental to other practices. They do, however, possess a very specific type of magic that has curative powers and with which wounds can be healed. The second class, found everywhere, is the *laika*. Besides curative powers the laika are rain makers and also know how to provide for successful hunting and fishing. A third class encountered by Bandelier and his wife are the *yatiri*, medicine men who discover lost property and the like, and who, it seems, are also in possession of powerful war medicines to be used to help their friends when hostilities break out between tribe and tribe or community and community. Today the relative position of these three classes appears to be about the same; none seems superior to the others, although the kolliri do appear the lowest in rank.

It is probable that the laika as well as the yatiri may perform cures in addition to their other functions. They are clearly acquainted with the properties of most of the herbs current among the Indians. The kolliri similarly, in spite of the fact that their functions are the least differentiated, seem to be those who perform the various surgical operations, more particularly trephining. Laika, it may be added, seems to be a term used not only at present but one that was current centuries ago for sorcerers. Black witchcraft is also designated by that name, and the wife of the laika is often supposed to be a witch charged with converting people into stones.

Apparently in precolumbian times there was, as might have been expected, a very definite grouping, and different individuals became medicine men in different ways. This is borne out by Arriaga, in his *Extirpacion de la Idolatria del Peru*, published in 1621, a work referring as much to the Quechua as to the Aymara, although the terminology is essentially Quechua. According to him, there are three ways in which men attained positions as priests of the *huacas*. The first was by succession from father to son. If the (oldest) son was incapacitated for some reason or other, then the next nearest relative succeeded, and so on. The second was by election. This was resorted to when the first method was out of the question. The electors were the priests of the first order, and they selected anyone that they felt was qualified, always, of course, with the approval of the curacas and caciques. Any person who was struck by lightning and remained alive was regarded as "divinely" selected for the post. The third class consisted of those who appointed and selected themselves. They occupied themselves primarily with the minor matters of the profession, devoting themselves exclusively to curing and divining, and they were generally old men and women who entered the profession to eke out a simple living.

Arriaga's account would thus indicate that all the medicine men functioning today belong to the last class. This might have been expected. Whatever classes exist today must therefore be regarded as secondary and as having developed after the conquest. There may, however, be one exception: the medicine men called *chamakani*. They conceivably represent a faint survival of the status and the function of the two more important classes mentioned by Arriaga. For that reason and because Bandelier's manuscript gives such an excellent description of the difficulties that once attended and still attend the investigation of such matters in Bolivia and Peru, I will quote from it verbatim:

Besides these three groups of medicine men, we everywhere heard of another more occult class of wizards to which the name chamakani (from *chamak*, dawn and the possessive *ni*) is given. While we [Bandelier and his wife] had succeeded in discovering the general attributions of the three former classes, the position and function of the chamakani remained a mystery to us. We noticed that they are not very numerous, much respected by the Indians and mestizos, feared, sometimes hated, but very influential. What the chamakani really is, no Indian consented to tell; we met a few of their number, but they avoided us as much as possible. We felt their occult power but never could make them subservient to the interests of our mission. As often as we were among Indians for months, one or more of these mysterious beings would turn up as if to observe us, suspiciously watching our doings without ever giving us any chance to ascertain their own. The Indians would sometimes laugh when we pronounced the name, but more commonly they would hear it with displeasure, as if the chamakani were outside of the common order of beings and to be avoided rather than approached, at least by us! We were assured that the chamakani was dreaded chiefly because he is a powerful evil sorcerer and because he sowed discord. More than one *hacendado* assured us he would never tolerate a chamakani on his premises, as he invariably caused trouble between him and his Indians. And yet, after some time, we would find out that there was one residing on the hacienda, unbeknown to the owner and shielded from persecution by the Indians. This showed that the wizards in question exercise remarkable power over the aborigine, much more than any other medicine man.

We were also told—and our own observations confirmed it—that the personal appearance of such wizards is usually unprepossessing. Those we met were not always old men, but their dress was humble, even tattered, indicating indigence and neglect. No token of distinction, still less of authority, was apparent, and we never saw on any of them a crucifix, which the yatiri and others frequently display and which is a favorite ornament of the *kallahuayas*.

While still keeping house at La Paz we had to employ a *tongo*, that necessary evil of Bolivian homes. The last one we had was a young man, married, of less filthy habits than the majority of these people. He often brought to the house his only child, a little boy called Martin, who soon took a great fancy to my wife. In the kitchen, father and son naturally associated with our orphan wards and there was, in Aymara, free chatting. In the course of such kitchen talk the Indian began to drop occasional hints at customs of his race, which the eldest girl never failed to report. My wife instructed her to lead the Indian on, recommending caution, lest he might suspect intentional questioning and either become mute or turn to lying. These instructions were followed, I must say, with much tact and shrewdness.

Our tongo once carelessly remarked that one of his relatives was a chamakani and that his little boy was destined to become one also. This statement was treasured at once, but the Indian would talk only to the oldest of the girls, claiming that such matters were not for the ears of children. He also insisted that she should not breathe a word of his talk to my wife, lest I might hear about it! . . .

The substance of the information thus secured, Bandelier states, was that a boy was destined to become a chamakani if there was a very bright red star overhead when he was born. The selection began with this preliminary presage. It was not, however, regarded as an absolute command from above, but rather as an indication, a divine preference. The ultimate decision rested with one of the older chamakani, the one who belonged to the family or stood closest to it, either because of long residence in the neighborhood or through other ties. Bandelier's Indian stated that his father had been a chamakani and that his brother was one likewise, and that, while he himself was not, his son would be turned over to the uncle for training as soon as he had reached the proper age; that is, fifteen or sixteen. Until then the neophyte, who must belong either to the family of the medicine man or that of his wife, knows nothing of the destiny that has been arranged for him. The actual training for the profession thus begins after the age of fifteen or sixteen. The first instruction deals exclusively with what might be called the lower forms of magical practice. It continues until the initiating chamakani feels that he is about to die. Only then does he communicate the last and most important secrets to his pupil and appoint him his successor.

Bandelier points out that this is exactly the course pursued by the caciques or chief-penitents of New Mexican pueblos. He claims that there too the latter hold in reserve the principal secrets of their office as long as possible, communicating them to their chosen successor only when they feel that their end is approaching.

There is a difference of opinion about the nature of the inheritance of the position according to Bandelier. Many Indians claim that the son succeeded his father. Others insisted this was by no means a fixed rule. The difficulty of determining this is further increased by the fact that the initiating chamakani calls the pupil his son by courtesy.

There is no guarantee that the person destined for the position of chamakani will necessarily be accepted. His adoption as "son" is for the period of apprenticeship only. The primary thing to be determined, in all cases, is whether he can keep a secret under all conditions and circumstances. The basic requisites for the position are characteristically discretion, reserve, and dissimulation. No one can become a chamakani without them, and a candidate is given almost a lifetime in which to develop them. If possible, no one becomes a chamakani until he is forty or fifty years of age, lest people might not pay him due respect. As is so frequent among oboriginal peoples, outsiders, and that included Bandelier, never were told the secrets. The medicine man tells these as well as everything connected with his profession only to his successor, and the successor in his turn always keeps inviolate what he has learned.

Although chamakani is the common and ordinary term applied to these medicine men, it is, significantly enough, considering their role and influence, only a nickname. Its etymology might have suggested that to us at once for, we have seen, it actually signifies he-who-owns- or he-who-has-darkness and is, naturally enough, indignantly rejected by these practitioners and regarded as an insult. His proper title is *hacha-tata*, or *great father*.

There are two possible interpretations of the term or nickname, chamakani. The most current one, quite naturally, is that the medicine man, working as he does, mostly at night and in a dark room, is the agent and representative of the powers of darkness, that the realm of darkness is his particular abode. Hence it follows he is chiefly an evil sorcerer. Such is the impression among the non-Indian part of the population. This is clearly of Christian origin and is the customary manner in which triumphant faiths depreciate the gods and practitioners of conquered peoples. It is quite an untrue characterization. Actually he is a beneficial rather than a dangerous personage for his people; that is, apart from his extortionate practices. Bandelier's surmise, for which he admitted he received no confirmation, was that since his office, like that of every other sorcerer and medicine man, dated from the times of remotest antiquity, called *chamak-tempu*, or the *dark times*, his nickname might possibly signify "he-who-keeps-the-secrets-of-the-creed-and-lore-of-the-dark-past."

There is always only one hacha-tata in any *estancia* or hacienda. He is usually, if not perhaps always, married, but separates himself from his family on every Tuesday, the official day on which he practices his profession. For that purpose he has a building set apart from his residence whither he goes as often as he has been called on to exercise his skill and power. This must always be on a Tuesday or Friday, unless he is called to aid somebody in imminent peril of life. Such cases are, of course, rare.

In contradistinction to the kolliri, the laika, the yatiri, and their various subdivisions, whose knowledge was not only of a limited kind but confined to certain fields, the hacha-tata is in possession of their collective information besides those particular secrets which he only transmits to his successor. His position is clearly superior to that of all other medicine men. Bandelier regarded him as the occult but real head of the tribe. It is he who examines the other shamans and, if he finds them competent to perform their special duties, authorizes them to do so. No action of any importance is undertaken by the tribe, no resolution of moment adopted, without his knowledge and consent. He is really the power behind the throne, the real leader of his people, be it a community or a hacienda. The hacha-tata—and there are as many as there are Aymara communities and haciendas with Indians of Aymara stock—are all equal in rank and independent of one another. Bandelier, however, claims to have found faint traces that on very important occasions they meet either in small sections or as one general group according to the nature of the occasion for which they have been called upon to deliberate. Such meetings are, of course, held with the utmost secrecy, and most Indians hardly hear about them.

It is not to be wondered at then that, under the circumstances, the belief is widely current that the hacha-tata is the one who, in the last analysis, by his quiet, unostentatious manner, designates the persons who fill such important civil posts as those of the *flacata* and *alcalde*. The hacendados and the Bolivian government, so Bandelier continues, may believe that they appoint these functionaries but, in reality, they but accept and confirm the choice of their Indians. So, at least, the Indians claimed. The Indians consult the hacha-tata, and he points out the individuals most agreeable to the superior world and best fitted to perform the duties of these offices.

The hacha-tata makes it a point to appear modest in personal appearance. Many of them even affect abject poverty in order to conceal their wealth. For they are, actually, by far the richest people in the tribe. Nowhere in the world do medical practitioners work for nothing. The hacha-tata form no exception. They can and do become extortioners and exploiters and thus, in their own fashion, act as a kind of introduction and foretaste to the larger and more virulent white extortioners and exploiters. Representing the highest instance in everything, whether it be sickness, witchcraft, or the giving of official advice, it is natural that they should feel that the compensation to be received for their services should be commensurate with the position they hold in the community and, of course, the superior knowledge they possess, which is all the stronger because more disguised. When a kolliri is at his wits' end he sends the patient to the hacha-tata. When a laika or yatiri is nonplused in his search for stolen things, or whoever be the sorcerer who is harming an individual, he turns to the hacha-tata as a last resort. Many individuals prefer to apply to him directly, and thus pass over the lower order of medicine men, but find the profession too well-organized and are frequently rebuffed. The hacha-tata listens to their case, and if he finds it easier than he expected, he refers it back to the inferior medicine men, possibly with the statement that the knowledge and power of such practitioners are ample for the occasion.

His field of work is enormous. He is, for instance, sometimes consulted by women in the first stage of pregnancy so that he can determine for them the probable date of delivery. When he is appealed to in case of disease, the patient, unless it be absolutely impracticable, is carried to his house. He is, of course, always rewarded with the proper presents. These consist mainly of coca, wine, alcohol, sweetmeats, and victuals such as potatoes, sheep, and the like. Money is seldom refused, but this practice is not indispensable where the clients are poor. His procedure with the coca leaves is quite interesting. He throws them on the floor in order to determine, for instance, the case and nature of a given ailment. He avoids making the sign of the cross and has no crucifix, as do the other medicine men, and this must be regarded as an indication that his duties have nothing in common with the Christian faith. After he has closely scrutinized the coca leaves, he informs his client of the conclusions at which he has arrived and gives the proper remedies, such as herbs, liquids etc.

We come now to one of the most interesting as well as the most fundamental functions of the hacha-tata, that of finding out how the soul of a recently deceased individual feels a week after his death.

Two distinct ideas may possibly be represented here: the Catholic one of a purgatory, and the ancient belief in a long journey which the soul must take ere it comes to its haven of rest. The Indian ideas certainly predominate.

Eight days after death the soul is expected to return, and a meal consisting of cooked meat and potatoes is spread for it. Then the hacha-tata is called to the house at night. He first goes into the field alone, wrapped in a black poncho and carrying wine, chica, and, of course, alcohol and coca. These ingredients he spatters and sprinkles around him, meanwhile calling out the name of the deceased and adding: "I bring thee alcohol, coca, etc.," enumerating the articles one by one. "Dost thou wish chica? Dost thou wish wine? I give thee everything and expect thee tomorrow?" Then he shakes his black poncho in the air and cries aloud: "Offspring of a dog, offspring of a guinea pig!" To this somewhat strange and enigmatic invitation the soul always complies, it is said, and he appears, on the following night, in the room formerly occupied by the deceased. The family is assembled in an adjoining room. After the medicine man has performed his incantations alone and in the dark, he returns to the family and tells them that the dead one is speaking. In fact, they are allowed to hear his voice. The shaman informs them of the wishes of the soul. They are often of the simplest kind, a demand for a new blanket, for instance, for a poncho or for food. At times the soul may inform them that there is some treasure hidden in a certain place for his children or give some similar information. Ventriloquism plays an essential part in this colloquy of the deceased with the hacha-tata. The table in the outer room must be covered with a black cloth and four candles are always kept burning on it. The hacha-tata remains at the home of the deceased until the next morning and goes home always well remunerated.

Notwithstanding his usually beneficial or at least harmless functions, the hacha-tata, as we might expect, is also appealed to for evil witchcraft. On such occasions an owl is always used. On the day preceding the night appointed for the rite an owl is captured and plied with liquor till he is drunk. A silver coin of five cents, half a real, or medio is then forced down the unfortunate animal's throat. The feet of the bird are now tied, and the incantations begun in a darkened room of the medicine man's outhouse. The medicine man is very careful not to pronounce the word *Dios*. After nightfall the owl is taken into an open space and left to die. The hacha-tata does not touch it again. However, at times it happens that some Indian will brave the unknown dangers involved, creep up in the dark, and steal the coin. The carcass of the owl is abandoned to dogs and buzzards.

It must never be buried.

The explanation offered for the ceremony is this. The coin represents the soul of the animal or, rather, it is placed inside of the bird to give it a soul, for the Indians of today have learned from the Christians that animals have no souls. By choking the bird to death, the same fate is prepared for the intended human victim.

To bring this discussion of the hacha-tata to a conclusion, let me quote verbatim Bandelier's summary:

In all these practices there is always a certain amount of jugglery. But for all that and although even the highest shamans play to a certain extent upon the ignorance and credulity of their public, it cannot be denied that they mostly believe in the reality of what they perform. Their ultimate secrets we cannot surmise. Hypnotism, suggestive influence over man might be their essence. These are accidental discoveries preserved through untold generations either as individual secrets or as the exclusive property of societies. That such exist among the Aymara is beyond all doubt, and they seem to be analogous to if not identical with those discovered among North American Indians.

The power and influence wielded by the hacha-tata has tempted other wizards or wily Indians to usurp the title. I believe, from what we know at present, that members of inferior orders—laika, yatiri, and kolliri—sometimes claim to be chamakani among Indian communities dwelling in isolated localities and exercise, for a time, certain authority under false pretenses. Such impostors are really dangerous. These probably are the chamakani which the Indian fears and hates. The notorious Yujra spoken of in connection with Yaricachi and Atauallani seems to belong to that class, for a genuine hacha-tata would not resort to robbery. It might be different in a case of insurrection against the whites. If there were a probability of a successful termination [of such a rebellion], the hacha-tata would be in favor of it, since restoration of the ancient faith and ancient society would be the result. Their role would be unquestionably limited to oracular utterances and to counsels. However, their experience, their supposed intercourse with higher powers . . . would guide the actions of others. But the hacha-tata are at the same time a safeguard against such a general outbreak, for they are well aware of its difficulties.

Should they ever consent to it then, woe unto the country! Remember that they are to be found in each community and that their combined influence on the Indians might become exceedingly dangerous for the whites and the mestizos. The latter are even so accustomed to apply to them for help and advice, they are so deeply impressed by many of the superstitions to which the great Indian wizards owe their power, that it is a question indeed if a number of them would not rather follow their lead instead of joining the whites.

Bandelier's somewhat grotesque fears of an Aymara revolt against the whites shows the lack of understanding all outsiders of his time possessed of the true situation. Fifty years ago it held equally for those Bolivians who regarded themselves as pure Castilians as well as for the mestizos. For them the Indian was a derelict, one who owed his debasement not simply to the greed, cruelty, and exploitation of the Spanish conquerors and their descendants but also to what they would have designated as the Indian in him; namely, his rejection of civilization, of the faith the Europeans had brought with them. They could think of nothing else except these facts. The Indians to them were irreconcilables, merely the debased descendants of that last of the Incas, Atahualpa, who had answered Fray Vicente with angry words when the priest had admonished him to "worship God, three and one, instead of his false gods" and had told him that he must become "the friend and tributary" of the King of Spain to whom the Pope, Christ's representative on earth, had bestowed the right to conquer and the duty of converting the inhabitants of the lands so conquered.

What was it the angry Inca had replied? According to the chronicler Francisco Lopez de Gomara, the answer was clear and distinct. "Being a free man," he said, "he would never pay tribute to anyone or recognize anyone as his superior, in spite of the fact that he would be delighted to become the friend of the emperor and know him, that he granted that he must be a great prince. Nor was he much inclined to obey the Pope, a person who took it upon himself to dispose of something which was not his and to give away a kingdom which he had never seen and which he, Atahualpa, had inherited from his father. In so far as concerned the matter of religion, his own was quite satisfactory and he felt quite happy with it. Nor did he care to enter into a discussion of matters so hallowed and approved by years. Christ, so he understood, had died. The sun and the moon had never died. And, finally, how could the friar be so certain that it was the God of the Christians who had created the world?"

That the good friar did not understand is intelligible. That fifty years ago most people still persisted in not understanding is equally understandable, even although the reasons for their ignorance are rooted in other than religious causes. The facts for a proper appreciation of the situation have always been present, just as they have existed in that whole area that stretches north from Bolivia and Peru to the Rio Grande. And they suggested clearly that in every aspect of life, from the purely economic to art and religion, the Spaniards had only partially conquered this new land. They had swept over it at first like a whirlwind, only to succumb subsequently to compromise after compromise. The newcomers could introduce Spanish loan-words into Aymara and Quechua only at the price of introducing Aymara and Quechua loan-words into Spanish. And so it was in everything else. Let us take an example.

The worship of the Indian for *El Señor de los Temblores* in Cuzco, a recent scholar has told us,[77] is merely one aspect of their traditional idolatry. What they adore and the figure before whom the Indians make their genuflections is not Christ on the Cross but a specific and material representation of a particular Christ figure, with all the imperfections, defects, and blemishes which distinguish it and set it off from other crucifixes and representations of Christ, the Lord of Earthquakes. When in 1834, so Señor Aguilar tells us, an attempt was made to clean the figure and deprive it of its imperfections, the clamor of the populace was tremendous. How could a properly washed *Señor de los Temblores* possibly work miracles? A white *Señor de los Temblores?* It was unthinkable. . . .

The role of the Spaniards in the Andes has quite correctly been characterized as belonging to those chapters belonging to the adventures of Don Quixote which the great Cervantes had forgotten to write. Here in Peru and Bolivia, like Don Quixote, they too were challenging windmills when they attempted, by direct assault, to wipe out civilizations like those of the Aymara and Quechua and Chibcha, all of which had a long and valid historical evolution, full of unusual significance in the long panorama of world history.

Yes, these Andean civilizations were more dangerous than even windmills to threaten and call out to battle. They accepted the challenge in their own way, and before he quite realized it the Spaniard was enveloped and completely enwrapped by them, and when he had extricated himself, he emerged with a new personality and physiognomy, one quite different and distinct from that which he had presumably brought with him from the mother country, Spain. As Garcia quite correctly observes, his somewhat chaotic individualism, his intense religiosity, his epic spirit of adventure, even his all consuming land hunger were trapped by the deep valleys and the high sierras of Cuntisuyu and the broad plains of Kollavinas. He could not but react sympathetically and increase his stature and develop a new historical conscience. In its turn this new conscience and awareness reacted positively and creatively upon the Andean historical scene. "The light, the perspective, the form, the emotions, they all took on a new value. It was the promise of a new world in which the spectacle that greeted our eyes yesterday appeared as something different in the light of the new dawn. . . . Three ethnical elements combine to form this new spiritual rhythm that controls and regulates the tumultuous ferment of our people, tumultuous and still in motion, because today it has not yet crystallized into a psychological unity: the Indian, the mestizo, and the Caucasian or creole, three types that in the process of their approach, the one to the other, have one unifying principle in common—the soil and the legend-saturated Cordillera. These are the types to which the tradition classification can be easily adapted: *El Chincha, El Anti, El Kolla,* and *El Cunti.*"[78]

Thus the descendants of the Aymara and Quechua have come into their own again, and because they are in the majority they act as the catalyzing agency that will create the new synthesis for which Ricardo Rojas, the well-known Argentine thinker, has coined the term *Eurindia.*

CHAPTER XV

Where the Two Streams Meet

FROM ECUADOR TO GUATEMALA

FROM BOLIVIA AND PERU NORTHWARD TO THE
Valley of Mexico, both in the mountains and along the coast,
there is no break in the general high level of culture that prevails. It is a strange fact, this, not at all simple or easy to
comprehend. Why should peoples select the almost unlivable
altitudes of Peru and Bolivia, the hot and by no means healthy
coasts of Peru, or the superlatively wet and almost impenetrable
forests of Central America and Yucatan as their homes? Why
should just these portions of the two continents have become
the great cultural centers of the New World? And to make
the problems still more difficult of solution, archaeology and
geography seem to have conspired against us. There is no indication that the foundations of these great civilizations are to be
sought for here. Nor is this the original home of the two great
food staples upon which they both rest—maize and the potato.
Small wonder then that many enthusiasts and some scholars
have cast their eyes lovingly across the Pacific to Indo-China,
and still farther, across the Indian Ocean to Egypt, to seek for
their origins. Yet this seems altogether improbable, from practically every point of view, although it is not completely outside
the range of possibility. Most of us, however, have preferred to
stay at home and ferret out its evolution here.

Until recently two theories as to the origins of the great civilization were generally held: one to the effect that big things result from the accumulation of little things; the other, that it was evolved in Mexico and subsequently spread, at a fairly high level, southward to Peru. This is an old difference of opinion, an old quarrel. The first represents what might be called the generous, the democratic, theory. Everyone, large and small, from far and near, has made his special contribution. There has, in short, been a pooling of achievements for a common purpose. This would then mean that the whole continent, north of the Valley of Mexico, formed the base of a pyramid of which southern Mexico and Central America was the apex and that all of South America east of the Cordillera formed the base of another pyramid of which Bolivia and Peru was the apex. The second theory is more aristocratic in taste and assigns to a gifted race the honor of having created its salient traits. Fortunately we do not have to decide these questions, so heavily weighted with social-ethical evaluations, here. Let us instead adopt what historians have called or what, at least, they should have called, the method of disingenuous objectivity and see where it leads. Starting from northern Peru, we shall accordingly push northward and see what happens.

In Ecuador, in the territory of the old kingdom of Quito, lying in the inter-Andean plateau, we come across a most interesting civilization. According to the traditions collected by Padre Juan de Velasco, it was brought to this region somewhere around the year 1000 A.D., a strangely ominous period, we have seen, for invasions and migrations in America. The ruler of this new state was a "monarch," and he was surrounded by "noblemen." Descent was in the mother's line; that is, these people had matrilineal clans. Among other things, they were great weavers of cotton and wool. Their religion was of a highly organized kind centering around the worship of the sun and the moon. Otherwise their habits were somewhat normal, according to Velasco. A commoner could have but one wife and no concubines; a noble, one wife and a few concubines; and the ruler, one wife and an unlimited number of concubines.

Although some doubt has been cast upon Velasco's veracity, there seems no reason for questioning most of what he says. That he had concocted his story out of the whole cloth is inconceivable. We must allow, of course, as always, for oversimplification and not pay very much attention to the ridiculous terminology he uses. But then we moderns have no right to throw stones in the matter of terminology.

What naturally interests us here in this Ecuadorian State are two things: the type of government, and the fact that it is supposed to have been brought in from without. There are only three other places in the New World where such a "theocratic-monarchical" system is to be found: among the Zapotec-Mixtec of Oaxaca in southern Mexico, among the Inca, and among the Chibcha of Colombia. The Chibcha are on the path of our journey north, so let us now turn to them.

Among the Chibcha[79] we encounter for the first time among the great civilizations a theme that recurs repeatedly among all the others; namely, the sudden appearance of a divine individual to whom all the best elements in their culture are due. His name was Bochica. According to the story, much of the value of his gifts to his people was almost neutralized by the evil machinations of his beautiful wife, and finally he had to drive her away. She became the moon. But Bochica, too, did not tarry long after his work was done. He disappeared almost as suddenly as he had appeared, to spend thousands of years, in a beautiful valley far away from mankind, in the practice of asceticism.

Is this merely the greatly distorted reworking of the culture-hero myth so common in many parts of South and North America, or can it not be dismissed so simply? Definitely not. That episodes and themes of a culture-hero cycle are present, and that in the form in which the Spanish chroniclers reported the legend the figure of Christ has also entered into its texture, admits of little doubt. But much more is really involved in this story than mythical fancy. Here in Colombia there is mounting evidence to indicate that a higher culture did rather suddenly succeed a lower one. The legend of Bochica may well then be the precipitate of such a cultural movement. That the culture of which the legend speaks came from Tiahuanaco, on Lake Titicaca, it is quite reasonable to assume. The social organization of the Kingdom of Quito and that of Colombia clearly belong together, and with them we must equate that of the Incas, always bearing in mind that the latter must have borrowed from the Aymara of Lake Titicaca and from the old Tiahuanaco civilization all of those "monarchical" and sacrosanct aspects surrounding the person of the ruler. To invest an earthly chief with such sanctity is not necessarily a sign of age at all. Rather is it the sign of a conqueror, one who needs many and new insignia to bolster up his position and to legitimatize his power.

This new state that Bochica is credited with having established in Colombia was as monarchical as was that which Velasco claimed for the rulers of Quito. Unlimited powers were supposed to have been concentrated in the ruler's hands. As in Peru, he made the appointments of the priests of the major temples. No one could come into his presence without a gift; no one dared look upon his countenance. He was surrounded with all the appurtenances of a divine king. He wore a headdress of gold, his brow was covered with a golden crescent, and he sat on a throne of gold studded with precious gems. The litter in which he traveled was hung with golden plates. Obsequious officials preceded it, spreading beautiful textiles before him and scattering flowers on the path along which he was to pass. This is truly the land of El Dorado we have at last come to, and this is its king.

Yet there was another side to this picture, strange and somewhat somber, although of unusually great interest for the light it seems to throw on the origin of El Dorado's sovereign. To attain to this glory he had to be ritually invested and this investiture entailed a long and painful ordeal. For five years he had to live in seclusion, completely cut off from the rest of the world. Only at night could he leave the temple in which he was confined. Frequent scourgings alternated with rigorous fasts. He was constrained by oath to confess to any breach of the numerous and onerous restrictions that hedged him about on all sides. And after confessions, penance followed penance. Thus did the mortification of the flesh go on from month to month and from year to year until the five years of probation were over. Then, to signalize the fact that his day of freedom had approached, his nose and ears were pierced and in them were inserted the gold ornaments to which his exalted rank now entitled him.

Scourging and mortification of the flesh had thus constituted his ordeal, an initiation into a new way of life. He was to receive his reward now. Even if we allow for imaginations fired by stories of El Dorado, the ceremonies at the ruler's installation have, for us, an atmosphere of fairyland and romantic wish-fulfillment. But we must be careful not to confuse our reactions with those of the Chibcha. For us it is a pageant, for them it was a ritual, a series of ceremonies in which every detail had a meaning. That it was, at the same time, a spectacle goes without saying.

The ruler's investiture with office was a ritual in which all participated, nobleman and commoner. All repaired to the sacred lake of Guatavita dressed in their finest garments. Everywhere there shone and sparkled beautifully fashioned ornaments of gold. Gorgeous feathers encircled the heads of spectators and actors alike. Innumerable sacrificial fires, freshly kindled, lit up the waters of the lake. The new ruler approached. Naked, he stood there, his body anointed with adhesive earth and then covered with powdered gold dust. A romantic journey still lay before him. With four chiefs he embarked upon a raft richly and lavishly ornamented with gold. At his feet lay heaped up, mound high, gold and emeralds. Slowly the raft flowed toward the middle of the lake. Arrived there, the new ruler plunged into the waters to wash off the powdered gold from his body. Then as he was again seated on the raft, the mound of gold and emeralds were hurled into the lake.

If we knew more about this amazing ceremony of investiture I feel certain it would turn out to be some ritual-drama that has been secondarily associated with the authentication of a chief's power. Some things stand out clearly; for instance, the resemblance of the ruler's long ordeal and probation to the initiation rites of youths and medicine men throughout South America and particularly the Amazon area. It will be well to remember this.

But there are other salient traits of Chibcha culture that call to mind far more specific regions. Human sacrifice was entrenched there in a fashion equaled elsewhere in America only among the Aztecs. The two methods, that of the cutting out of the heart and the killing of the victim by trussing him up and shooting arrows at him were both practiced. Of still more significance was the sacrifice of children to ensure rainfall. Some of them were carefully reared until they had reached the age of puberty. They spent their childhood in the temples as singers and novices. The most profound veneration was paid them until the time for their immolation on the altar of the Sun.God. Who does not think immediately of the well-known Aztec ritual in which a youth is worshiped as the living image of the God Tezcatlipoca, then sacrificed at the end of a year?

Taken in connection with the ritualistic cannibalism of the Tupinamba described on page 97, we cannot escape the conclusion that all these rituals are related. But where did they originate? Who borrowed from whom? Our answer will take us into the most controverted points of American ethnology: first, what is the precise relationship between the great Mexican and Central American civilizations, on the one hand, and the great Andean on the other; and, second, what influence did the former have on the South American tribes east of the Andes?

A generation ago the general feeling prevailed that the two great centers were largely independent of each other and that if there was any marked influence it was from the north to the south, from the Maya to the Nasca, Chimu, and Tiahuanaco. This attitude was largely based on the belief that maize had been domesticated in the North and that the wild species from which the domesticated variety had been developed was *teocintli*. Today we know this is quite wrong and that maize was probably domesticated in South America. Indeed the northern Chaco, a region quite close to Bolivia, has been suggested as its place of origin. That one fact, however, really completely

A Native Priest with His Wife
and Child, Colombia

A Young Boy Neophyte Training
for the Priesthood, Colombia

The House of a Native Priest's Wife, Colombia